(Re)searching Women

(RE)SEARCHING WOMEN

Feminist Research Methodologies
in the Social Sciences in Ireland

Edited by
Anne Byrne and Ronit Lentin

First published 2000
by the
Institute of Public Administration
57-61 Lansdowne Road
Dublin 4

ISBN 1 902448 46 4

British Library Cataloguing in Publication Data
A catalogue record of this book is available from the
British Library

This publication was grant-aided by the Publications Fund of
National University of Ireland, Galway.

Cover image: Margaret and Mary Sheehan
Cover design by Butler Claffey Design, Dún Laoghaire
Typeset in Garamond 10/11.5
by Wendy A. Commins, The Curragh
Printed by ColourBooks Ltd

Contents

Acknowledgements

We would like to thank the following people for helping to put the book together: Barbara Bradby, TCD; Sara Cantillon, UCD; Ann Cleary, UCD; Linda Connolly, UCC; Lawrence Cox, WIT; Celia Davies, Open University; Andrew Finlay, TCD; Breda Gray, UCC; Ellen Hazelkorn, DIT; Su-Ming Khoo, NUIG; Carmen Kuhling, UL; Madeleine Leonard, QUB; Susan Liddy, MIC; Ann Lyons, NUIG; Jo Murphy-Lawless, TCD; Barbara O'Connor, DCU; Pat O'Connor, UL; Orla O'Donovan, UCC; Martha Shaughnessy, NUIG; Ailbhe Smyth, UCD; Efrat Tseelon, UCD.

Thanks to the participants in the seminar held in Trinity College Dublin in April 1999 and to Sylvia Earley for her assistance on that day. Thanks to the Department of Sociology, TCD and to NUI Galway for their financial support. Finally, a big thank you to all our contributors, and to Tony McNamara and Kathleen Harte of the IPA who helped us to bring this work into the public domain.

Notes on Authors

Anne Byrne is a lecturer in the Department of Political Science and Sociology, National University of Ireland, Galway, where she teaches courses in Irish sociology, qualitative research methods, group work, feminist and women's studies. Her current research interests concern identity issues, feminist pedagogies, feminist research methodologies and social in/exclusion. She has been editor of the *UCG Women's Studies Centre Review* (2 volumes), the *Irish Journal of Sociology* (3 volumes) and, with Madeleine Leonard, *Women in Irish Society* (Belfast: Beyond the Pale, 1997). Her most recent publications include 'Familist Ideologies and Difficult Identities', in Marilyn Cohen and Nancy Curtin (eds), *Reclaiming Gender, Transgressive Identities in Modern Ireland* (St Martins Press, 1999) and 'Singular Identities: Managing Stigma, Resisting Voices', in *Women's Studies Review*, vol. 7, 2000.

Cynthia Cockburn is Professor in the School of Social and Human Sciences at The City University London. A feminist researcher and writer, her interests have included community activism and local governance; men, masculinity and technological change; women, work and trade unionism; and sex equality in organisations. Her published work in these fields includes *The Local State* (Pluto Press, 1977); *Brothers* (Pluto Press, 1983); *Machinery of Dominance* (Pluto Press, 1985); *In the Way of Women* (Macmillan, 1991) and, with Susan Ormrod, *Gender and Technology in the Making* (Sage, 1993). Since 1995 her research has been concerned with women's organisations in war situations and her most recent book is *The Space Between Us: Negotiating Gender and National Identities in Conflict* (Zed Books, 1998).

Mary Daly is Professor of Sociology at the Queen's University of Belfast. A native of the Republic of Ireland, she has previously worked there as well as in Germany and Italy. She has published widely on comparative social policy and on sociological topics relating to Ireland. Her main research interests currently lie in how welfare states affect gender relations, the sociology of the family and poverty and social inequality. Her latest book is *The Gender Division of Welfare* (Cambridge University Press, 2000).

Ricca Edmondson studied in Lancaster and Oxford, then worked as a translator in Berlin before carrying out research at the Max Planck Institute for Human Development. She now teaches in the Department of Political Science and Sociology in the National University of Ireland, Galway, and works on the theory of culture and argumentation, qualitative methods, the environment, health, ageing and time.

Ronit Lentin is course co-ordinator of the postgraduate programme in Ethnic and Racial Studies at the Department of Sociology, Trinity College Dublin. Her most recent book is *Israel and the Daughters of the Shoah: Re-occupying the Territories of Silence* (Berghahn Books, 2000). She is the editor of *Gender and Catastrophe* (Zed Books, 1997), *The Expanding Nation: Towards a Multi-ethnic Ireland* (Department of Sociology, TCD, 1999) and *Emerging Irish Identities* (Department of Soicology, TCD, 2000). She is European and Middle East editor of *Women's Studies International Forum* and member of the editorial board of *Sociological Research Online* and has published extensively on feminist research methodologies, Israel and the Shoah, gender and racism, and gender and genocide. She is an antiracism activist and founder-member of the Irish Association of Minority Ethnic Women.

Maria Lohan is a research fellow at the Employment Research Centre, Department of Sociology, Trinity College Dublin. Her main research interests lie in the sociology of science and technology, with special reference to information communication technologies (ICTs) and transport; and gender studies, with special reference to the construction of masculinities. She has published in feminist journals, such as *Women's Studies International Forum* and in science and technology studies journals, such as *Science Technology* and *Human Values*.

Kathleen Lynch is a founder member and co-ordinator of the Equality Studies Centre at UCD. She has a deep and long-standing commitment to the understanding and promotion of equality and social justice both locally and globally. She has published widely on issues of equality and is currently working on a book with her colleagues in UCD on *Equality: Theory and Practice*. Her most recent book *Equality in Education* (1999) is published by Gill and Macmillan.

Rosaleen McDonagh is a disabled Traveller and a former chairperson of the Irish Traveller Movement. She now works with the National Traveller Women's Forum. She has completed a BA in Theology in Trinity College Dublin and contributed an entry on the exclusion of disabled Travellers within the Travelling community in the 1995 Task Force Report on Travellers and articles on feminism and on the intersection of ethnicity and disability to various publications. She was also involved in the development stages of the Independent Living Movement in Ireland. She spends most of her time working on Traveller rights issues.

Marie Mulholland is a feminist and community activist from Belfast. She is co-founder of the Women's Support Network and was its co-ordinator until 1998 when she moved to Dublin. She is currently completing an MA in Women's Studies at UCD and has recently taken up a position with the new Equality Authority in the Republic of Ireland.

Cathleen O'Neill works as an educator in a Dublin North Inner City project for women stable drug users where she delivers a broad range of education and personal, political and social development modules accredited by University College Dublin, the Department of Education and Science, and the National Council for Vocational Awards. She is passionate about equality and believes strongly in supporting people to 'name their own world' and to be part of the problem-solving process. She carries these beliefs into any research process that she is involved in.

Romanie van Son's current interests include issues relating to development, health, education and exclusion. Romanie has experience with these from a number of vantage points, including that of arts worker, counsellor, social researcher and teacher/lecturer in first, second, third level, and special education. Educated in Holland and Ireland, she is currently working on a postgraduate research thesis in the University of Limerick, which has as its main focus social exclusion and visual research methods.

Introduction: Feminist Research Methodologies in the Social Sciences

Anne Byrne and Ronit Lentin

I am not a feminist, but ...

How often have we been told by our friends, students, mothers, sisters, daughters, that being a feminist is all very well, but that they, the speakers, are definitely not feminists? And how often is a 'but' tagged on to this statement? 'I am not a feminist, but I believe in equality for women ...' 'I am not a feminist, but I draw the line at violence against women ...', 'I am not a feminist, but it really annoys me that working women have to work a double shift ...' And so it goes on. Women, who according to all our (feminist) criteria, are definitely feminists in their outlook, their aspirations and their practice, often shy away from the 'f word', which in this 'post-feminist' era has acquired a bad reputation, something between *déjà vu* and backlash. Young women tell us again and again that in contemporary Ireland women can be whoever they want and do whatever they wish. That the old, unequal times are over. That feminists are harsh, shrill, bitchy. That men still prefer blondes, or rather, don't want to go out with feminists.

In an Israeli study aimed at understanding why so many women shun the label 'feminist', Ariella Friedman (1999) asked women to state their associations with the terms 'feminism', 'woman', and 'femininity'. Respondents associated 'feminism' with equality, but also with liberation, struggle and power; they associated 'woman' with motherhood and relationship, and 'femininity' with love, sexuality and sensitivity. Friedman concludes that the ambivalence many women feel towards the feminist label has to do with its perception in masculine terms such as struggle, power, politics: 'it's possible that part of the rejection of the term "feminism" stems

1

from the reluctance to damage women's femininity, and from the perception of femininity and feminism as contradictory identities' (Friedman, 1999: 32).[1]

Friedman's observations are relevant to the feminist researcher who occupies two contradictory identities: the identity of a 'feminist' committed to political change and the identity of a 'researcher' committed to producing social research that is ethical, credible and authentic. The feminist researcher is often criticised by the academy for being 'too political' and the research so produced is criticised for not being serious social research. Feminists are often also critical of other feminist researchers located in the academy, pointing out that transformative politics and liberatory research practices are not possible when the researcher is a privileged academic, confined by the rules and regulations which circumscribe academic knowledge and knowledge production.

Lentin has argued bluntly elsewhere, when justifying her choice for feminist research methodologies in the face of growing positivism in the social sciences and of a return to funded research which supports the 'institutions of ruling' (increasingly carrying the tag 'Europe'), that she will 'be a post-feminist only in post-patriarchy', and that 'we need to continually challenge not only patriarchal formulations of knowledge, but also the global patriarchal backlash which seems to claim we have entered the post-feminist era' (Lentin, 1994: 53). But was she, on the one hand, dismissive of the real concerns of women who – in the consumerist 1990s, where the ideals of the 1960s are a virtual blast from the past – are more concerned about careers and advancement than about ideologies? And on the other, did she choose to ignore the centrality of discourse over 'material reality' and the prevalence of post-modernism in feminist literary and cultural studies scholarship, where 'feminism,' like other 'isms' has been consigned to the dustbin of history?

Often, when claiming they are 'not feminists, but ...' women may protest too much. Feminism is practised everywhere in Ireland – in community groups, in universities, in the professions and in

---

[1] Friedman does not, however, link the fear of feminism to a fear of a lesbian tag. Indeed, in Ireland too, lesbianism is still a neglected area in feminist research which may explain why there is no specific chapter focusing on lesbianism in this volume (for a discussion of the relevance of the fear of the lesbian tag, see Byrne, 2000).

the service and business sectors. Despite our diversity, and despite the diversity of our practice, it is often academic, middle-class Irish feminists who have been too quick to claim the middle ground and declare feminism as 'theirs'. As Cathleen O'Neill argues:

> (In) the mid-1980s for the first time I became aware that I was a 'community woman'. A new term, usually used pejoratively, a different status for a new social grouping which was formed without consultation. Working-class women suddenly became the focus of a debate within the women's movement (O'Neill, 1999: 42).

So who are Irish feminists? And, conversely, who are those Irish women for whom the 'f word' is so threatening? Do 'we' accept as feminist any woman who wishes to describe herself thus? Is there a unified feminist position across class, age, sexual orientation, ethnicity, and, dare we bring it up, a/cross-gender? Should feminists, having protested male academic and political orthodoxies that have excluded women for centuries, establish a new (feminist) orthodoxy? In the face of the plurality of feminist work in Ireland, both research and practice, we would like to argue here against such orthodoxies and broaden the scope to allow for self-definition. After all, as feminist researchers, we often deal with dilemmas that have no absolute solutions. We therefore believe that we cannot talk about what feminist research *is*, only about what it *includes*, and therefore, any exclusive definitions of who is a feminist or what is feminist about a research project are out of place. Reinharz (1992: 7), for instance, considers as feminist, researchers who identify themselves in their research publications as feminists. Such a definition would, we hope, make room for women for whom the 'f word' is anathema, including those holding the 'I am not a feminist, but' point of view.

Yes, we hear you answer, but if anything goes, is there any point in naming our work as 'feminist' at all? And does the term 'feminist methodologies' imply a simplistic dichotomy between 'feminists' and 'non-feminists'? Should not any researcher who writes about women, be s/he a feminist or not, be included in the scope of feminist research and practice in contemporary Ireland? And what is the point of this collection at all, we hear you ask?

In this introduction, we look at what is feminist about our research and practice. We attempt to define feminist methodologies and position them historically and ideologically within the context of

Irish social science paradigm and practice. Feminist research methodologies stress gender as a basic theoretical concept, a deconstruction of the power relationship between researcher and researched, a political commitment to the emancipation of women, and models of research and practice which privilege participation, representation, interpretation and reflexivity. If this is the case, we need to ask why it is not taught and practised by all social scientists.

Since the 1970s, feminist researchers (e.g. Oakley, 1981; Bowles and Duelli-Klein, 1983; Stanley and Wise, 1983; 1993; Daly, 1987; Smith, 1987; Abbott and Wallace, 1990; Hill Collins, 1990; Fonow and Cook, 1991b; Lentin, 1993) have been critical of objective, value-free, neutral, scientific, 'male' models of inquiry and have argued for a reform of the discipline and profession of sociology. Rather than a sociology 'about' women, feminist researchers sought to create a sociology 'for and by women', a *feminist* sociology. As others have done before us, we position feminist research principles as an answer to the positivist turn in the social sciences. We address the limits of feminism as research and practice by posing questions about the intersectionality of gender with other categories such as class, 'race'/ethnicity, sexuality and (dis)ability, and about collaboration, consent, power relations, voice, authority and accountability. Contributors to this volume engage with the 'ethics, methods and politics' (Daly, 1987) of feminist research. We also look at writing feminist research texts and at the link between (re)searching women and (re)searching the self. The challenge now, as eloquently posed by the contributors to this volume, is to create a sociology 'with' women.

Towards a definition: feminist methodologies in the social sciences

Feminist research methodologies enjoy a greater visibility now and are a source of reference for practitioners in the human and social sciences, particularly in the discipline of sociology. But let us begin with a caveat: one of the good things about the growth of feminist scholarship is the massive proliferation of diverse and contested feminist epistemologies. In writing about feminist scholarship in Ireland, we have chosen to focus on research practices inspired by feminist epistemologies and methodologies. It is difficult to separate epistemology from methodology in any research enterprise. Fonow and Cook (1991a) describe epistemology as 'the study of assumptions about how to know the social and apprehend its meaning', and methodology as 'the study of actual techniques and practices used in the research process' (Fonow and Cook, 1991a: 1). Paying attention to feminist epistemology invites reflection about 'how we know what we know' and is part of the basis for developing principles guiding our research. Methodology is the medium through which we transform these principles into practice.

The variety of taught courses at under-graduate and post-graduate level in feminist methodologies particularly in the US, Europe, Australia and New Zealand indicate the increasing visibility of a feminist paradigm as part of a basic social science education. Research publications continue to detail feminist practice and this volume seeks to situate Ireland within these theoretical and practical developments. The research practices in any social science community have influenced and been influenced by, amongst other things, the methodological education of students and researchers. As Daly (1987), Jackson (1987), Lentin (1993) and Inglis (1997; 1998) (see also Lynch in this volume) have observed in their different ways, Irish social science has been primarily dominated by positivistic and post-positivistic paradigms with little that can be claimed to be a model for alternative, radical, emancipatory and feminist models of inquiry. Despite the strong tradition of ethnographic qualitative research in Ireland, positivism continues to hold sway in the allocation of funding resources for research, in informing policy and in the public perception of what is authentic social research.

In a review of taught programmes at Irish third level institutions conducted for this volume, we learned that Irish social science under-graduates are being exposed to feminist methodologies in their research education. Some under-graduate courses provide two to six hours of lectures on specifically named 'feminist research methodologies' in the context of a 24-session course on Qualitative Methodologies, for example. More commonly, however, under-graduate research methodology courses draw on methodological writing by feminist authors but without specifically naming the methodological approach as distinctively 'feminist'. The academics surveyed noted that research methodology courses 'would include a high feminist methodology content' or that 'at least half of the seminars involve some engagement with feminist methodological writing'. Students are introduced to debates about epistemological frameworks, feminist (and other) critiques of positivism, feminist approaches to qualitative interviewing, the politics of research, emancipatory and participatory methods, and the feminist emphasis on developing a reflexive sociology. Reflexivity was commonly identified as the most significant contribution of feminist methodologies to students' education. For example, one reply we received stated that a feminist methodology enables 'the students to reflect critically on their own experience, position and interests and how these connect to their professional practice ... and as a contribution to reflexive self-development which will enable the students to distinguish more clearly between the clients' needs and their own, and meet both in appropriate ways'.

In the replies we received it was evident that under-graduate students are required to read methodological writing by authors identified as 'feminist'. Examples given included Ann Oakley (1981), Donna Haraway (1987), Pamela Abbott and Claire Wallace (1990), Liz Stanley (1990a), Patti Lather (1991), Ann Game (1991), Diane Reay (1996), and Beth Humphries (1997). A number of academics wrote that a feminist point of view informs their teaching of research methodologies; others noted that feminist research methodologies are 'crucial' and 'essential' for adequate training in and appreciation of methodological practices, debates and the challenging of issues both at under-graduate and post-graduate level. Though students are exposed to feminist epistemologies and methodologies, the acceptance of these as named, distinctive paradigms is not widely evident. Subsuming feminist scholarship is one of the consequences of the integration of feminism within the traditional academic disciplines. The education of post-graduates in the complete repertoire of methodological knowledge and skills, encompassing positivist and interpretative paradigms, is crucial for the development and survival of sociology as a discipline in Ireland.

This volume is part of our attempt to argue that feminist research methodologies are being fruitfully utilised in student training and education, in action-based community settings, and in post-graduate, academic and some policy research in Ireland. We believe that exchanging, in a public setting, our various reflections on feminist research practice gives visibility to this scholarship and contributes to the further development of an Irish feminist research practice. An increasing number of Irish feminist social scientists in the 1990s are beginning to employ the term 'feminist' to describe their research methodologies – for example see contributors to Byrne and Leonard (1997). Post-graduates as well as under-graduates are also beginning to name their research methodologies 'feminist': see for example the lists of theses in the *Irish Journal of Feminist Studies* as well as volumes I, II and III of *In from the Shadows: The UL Women's Studies Collection* (Lentin, 1995; 1996; Aniagolu, 1997). Some contributors to the *Women's Studies Review* (UCG, 1992-9) and the *Irish Journal of Sociology* are also becoming less coy about using the term in their published work, and journals such as the *Irish Journal of Feminist Studies* and *F/M* have also acted as a spur. However, it must be said that while gender, social justice, the search for egalitarian research relationships and a commitment to producing research that contributes to undoing the oppression of women characterise Irish research on women's lives, many researchers are still largely reluctant to publicly name their research as 'feminist', even in the methodology section of their published work. While utilising a feminist methodology, naming oneself as a feminist researcher ought to be unproblematic. However, in a survey we conducted via e-mail in February 2000, scholars who do name themselves as feminists in their published research texts often find it difficult to sustain their academic feminism *vis-à-vis* universities, departments and colleagues, as we demonstrate below.

Feminist research methodologies, impelled by a concern with social justice, were initially focused on making women's experiences present and visible, revealing evidence of economic, legal and social gender-based inequalities. Feminist research methodologies are designed to reveal the gender problematic, through prioritising women's lived experience of the social, telling this experience 'in their own voice'. This is the claim of a distinctive feminist method-ological practice and from it follows a fundamental re-working of how we 'do' research.[2] In the first instance, the feminist researcher

[2] Although we are both sociologists, we are aware that our analysis of feminist research methodologies is applicable to other areas of feminist scholarship. In fact, in the seminar we organised in April 1999 at TCD, participants challenged us to broaden our remit beyond sociology.

accounts for herself and her motivation in carrying out a particular piece of research, placing herself reflexively within her research text. Our own investigative assumptions and procedures are made explicit as we seek to explain how we know what we know. A feminist research practice politicises the research act, not only in terms of producing research findings which can be used to lobby for change but also in re-working the connections between the researcher and her topic, as well as the traditional subject-object relationships of researcher and researched. Making decisions about who is author/knower in the research process and whose influences ought to be felt in data collection, in analyses and in the production of written research accounts, becomes part of developing a feminist research design. The practice and consequences of research are scrutinised in terms of their beneficial or harmful outcomes for women as an oppressed group.

The debates about feminist theory have undergone much exploration and transformation since the early 1970s. A causal explanation for the oppression of women – be it male control over women's fertility and bodies, a patriarchal system of inheritance, capitalism's need for docile workers – across all cultures, was sought. In contrast, contemporary feminist theorists understand there cannot be one causal explanation and seek instead localised, contextualised explanations of the construction of gender in different cultures and within specific societies. In response to the challenges by Black and majority world feminists, contemporary feminist theory and research have expanded the concept of gender, intersecting it with other societal divisions, particularly 'race'/ethnicity and class, but also sexuality and, to a lesser extent, dis/ability.

Although feminist research methodologies are more commonly associated with a qualitative, interpretative approach, there are many research projects making good use of quantitative methods (see for example Jayaratne and Stewart, 1991; Smith, 1997; Yeates, 1997; Cantillon, 1997; Drew, Emerek and Mahon, 1998; Drew, Humphreys and Murphy, 1999). It is not the method (for example, qualitative or quantitative) which makes research methodologies feminist, but rather the commitment to several feminist principles, as variably defined by feminists writing about research methodologies with prime attention given to the researcher-researched relationship and to the deconstruction of power relationships in the research process.

Sandra Harding (1987) stresses that it is not the method which makes feminist methodologies different to 'malestream' methodologies, but rather the alternative origin of the problems, which concern women rather than men; the alternative hypotheses and evidences used; the nature of the relationship between the researcher and the so-called 'subjects' of her inquiry. Shulamit Reinharz (1992) sees feminism not as a method in itself but a perspective on existing methods. Liz Stanley, on the other hand, sees feminism 'not merely as a perspective, a way of seeing, nor even this plus an epistemology, a way of knowing; it is also an ontology, or a way of being in the world' (Stanley, 1990b: 14).

According to Reinharz, using multiple research methods and disciplines, feminist research methodologies involve an ongoing criticism of non-feminist scholarship and is guided by feminist theory. As political research, feminist research strives to create social change while at the same time representing human diversity, including the researcher as a person, developing social relationships with the people studied and defining a special relationship with the reader (Reinharz, 1992: 240). Stanley and Wise (1990) locate five sites of the feminist researcher's behaviour and analysis: in the researcher-researched relationship; in emotion as a research experience; in the intellectual auto/biography of the researchers (see also Lentin, in this volume); therefore, in how to manage the different 'realities' and understandings of researchers and researched; and thus in the complex questions of power in research and writing (Stanley and Wise, 1990: 23). Dorothy Smith (1987) argues that feminist research methodologies must never lose sight of women as actively constructing as well as interpreting the social processes and realities that constitute their everyday lives. She examines the way the production of discourses and ideologies colonise women's lives. This approach is not radically different from more conventional sociological approaches that insist that 'what is going on out there is what the actors say is going on out there' and that actors are experts about their own worlds (see Schwartz and Jacobs, 1979).

While feminist research methodologies are no more a unitary category than is the category 'woman', it is possible to posit, as do Vickie Routledge Shields and Brenda Dervin (1993), feminist research methodologies as constituting four organising principles: women's experience of their social and personal worlds as primary 'scientific sources' (Harding, 1987); gender and gender relations as socially constructed and historically specific; reflexivity – defined as the analytic attention to the researcher's role and to the research process itself as researchable – and intersubjectivity, placing the feminist researcher on the same plane as the researched; and a political commitment to women, which, by providing them with the information they need, and by employing dialogical research strategies, seeks their emancipation (Lentin, 1993: 125-26).

As part of developing and maintaining a critical stance in our research practice, the elements of feminist research are constantly challenged by feminist and non-feminist researchers (see for example, Acker et al, 1991; Gluck and Patai, 1991; Hammersley, 1992; 1995; Ribbens and Edwards, 1998; and the debates in journals such as *Sociology, Sociological Research Online, Feminist Review, Gender and Society* and *Women's Studies International Forum*). The issues debated include the usefulness of the experiential account, the difficulties of representing voice and prioritising the subject, the difficulties in maintaining an emphasis on process in research, the feasibility of empowering research participants, and striving for an ethical feminist research practice. This interrogation can only be beneficial as we seek to present for public debate the many dilemmas raised by a feminist research practice and struggle to make research decisions that at the very least 'do no harm' and which may even 'do some good'. These dilemmas are shared with many other radical research methodologies: a feminist research methodology gives us permission to be explicit about the problems we encounter as we seek to reduce the possibility of further exploitation in our research relationships with other human beings.

Beginning the debate about feminist research in Ireland

In July 1987, Mary Daly presented a paper titled 'Feminist research methodology: the case of Ireland' at the Third International Inter-disciplinary Congress on Women, held in Trinity College Dublin. In that paper (included in this volume unchanged as a historical statement illustrating the position of feminist research methodologies in Irish sociology), still relevant today, Daly examines the defining characteristics of a feminist research practice and assesses the extent of such a practice in the Irish context. For Daly feminist research is linked to women's 'struggle for political, economic and intellectual recognition and power, and therefore has a political agenda' (Daly, 1987: 16). Combined with a critique of dominant research methodologies, feminist research methodologies are committed to producing 'information about women's lives that is meaningful (and valid) and can lead to their empowerment' (Daly, 1987: 16).

Arguing that 'women in Ireland cannot lay claim to a body of feminist scholarship', Daly addresses the ethics, methods and politics of her own research practice and that of other social scientists in Ireland. She expresses her unease with the exploitative relationship between researcher and researched, questions the efficacy and utility of research methodologies and interrogates the connections between the outcomes and consequences of social research, the researcher's own political ideology and the larger social order. While commenting on poor dissemination practice in relation to research results, Daly points out that research participants in Ireland have no control over the use to which research is put and that Irish researchers are unwilling to 'take their research further'. Little or no attention had been paid to the role of researchers in perpetuating relations of power and inequality and there had been no appraisal of the power imbalance between researcher and researched. Significantly, she argues that the lack of debate on research practice in Ireland meant that positivism continued to prevail, that survey-type research was being funded and that 'the bulk of research activity in sociology in this country continues to be undertaken for two reasons: to provide information for policy making and to increase the store of academic knowledge' (Daly, 1987: 14). Daly concludes that (in 1987) 'feminist research methodology has not influenced research practice in sociology in Ireland to any significant degree' (Daly, 1987: 16).

Daly identifies three factors which might account for the lack of impact of feminist research methodologies on social research practice: the lack of collaboration among feminists; the existence of gate-keeping practices concerning control over the legitimacy of scholarly work, appointments to academic positions, provision of funding and access to scholarly publications; and the fact that the content and orientation of work by feminist scholars has been limited to 'adding women on' or 'rediscovering women's lost history'. Each of these limitations arises because of academic regulation of knowledge and knowledge producers, and Daly advises that 'we must undertake a fundamental re-appraisal of the capacity of existing methodologies and structures of knowledge to comprehend the experience of women' (Daly, 1987: 17).

Six years later, Ronit Lentin (1993) argued that feminist research methodologies form a separate research paradigm. On reviewing a sample of published research by Irish feminist social scientists and Women's Studies scholars, she draws similar conclusions concerning the extent of feminist scholarship in Ireland to those arrived at by Daly. Lentin observes that feminist research methodologies are neither reflected in published research nor debated in the Irish context. Specifically she notes that 'there have been too few published feminist studies which have made visible the lived experience of Irish women or which have included the researcher's lived experience and reflexivity as part of the research process and findings' (Lentin 1993: 120). Lentin argues that 'a more rigorous adherence to feminist methodologies' can bring the interests of researcher and researched, academic and non-academic women closer, and is an important strategy for bringing attention to the material reality of Irish women's lives. Lentin's analysis points to the difficulties for 'academic feminists' negotiating their own ideological commitment to feminism, developing strategies for survival within the academy and responding (or not) to the necessities of the women's movement beyond the academy. However, left to academic feminists, the debate on feminist methodology, she concludes, is (in 1993) 'still in its infancy in Ireland'. Like Daly, she had hoped that by placing feminist research methodologies on the Irish sociological agenda, debate about the development and focus of Irish sociology would ensue.

In a lively response, Mahon (1994) disagreed with Lentin's assessment concerning the extent of feminist scholarship in Ireland. While Lentin emphasises reflexivity and making the lives of women studied visible, Mahon argues that research which arises from feminist theory and a feminist politics *is* feminist research. For her, an explicit reference to a feminist practice is not required. Drawing on this expansive definition, arguably a substantial body of feminist scholarship, meaningful to women's lives and informing public and social policy could be said to exist in the Republic of Ireland. This exchange of ideas and debate about feminist research and feminist methodologies is welcome and necessary for the further development and enhancement of teaching, research and scholarship and for revealing the varieties of feminist activism.

These three accounts concerning feminist research methodologies were part of a wider invitation to interrogate Irish social scientists' general research practices and to enter into dialogue about naming the structures, relations and consequences of research practice in Ireland. A similar invitation was also made in the 1970s and 1980s, when John Jackson provided a history of the development of social science in Ireland (Jackson, 1972) and described the formative role of government funding in shaping policy and state-oriented research (Jackson, 1987). Contributors to Liam O'Dowd (1988) also commented on the state of social science research in Ireland, drawing attention to the dominance of the positivist theoretical and methodological paradigm in the development and funding of social science research. Tom Inglis (1997) whose work is concerned with the formative influence of the Catholic Church on Irish society, asks whether the Church's control extends into research agendas and whether 'the mechanisms of censorship and repression reach so deep that sexuality [for example] was not conceived as being an issue of sociological concern? What other issues have been written out of Irish sociology?' (Inglis, 1997: 23). While Catholicism has impacted on who the Irish were and who we have become, we can only assume that its influence has also extended to how Irish sociology has developed.

Research institutes such as the Economic and Social Research Institute (ESRI), the National Economic and Social Council (NESC) and the Institute of Public Administration (IPA) were representative of a more positivistic approach to research, while some practitioners in Irish universities, as well as visiting scholars, favoured a more interpretative approach to sociological research, according to Jackson. But the lack of a public context or of publication outlets meant that the structures, rewards and motivation for dialogue, reflection and exchange were non-existent. Any critique of, or exchange between, either position remained firmly in the background. Advocates of either paradigm chose to develop scholarship and expertise within their own tradition, with no attempt to reform or engage with the other. This was an entirely reasonable and pragmatic response aimed at utilising intellectual resources to expand and develop methodological expertise within one research paradigm. Importantly, however, most government funding favoured the positivistic quantitative approach.

In 1994, a group of sociology post-graduates in Trinity College Dublin organised a conference on research methodologies in the Social Sciences in order to 'break through the intellectual and social isolation experienced by so many post-graduate researchers' (Tormey et al, 1994). As Bonner (1994) observed in his introduction to the conference proceedings, the problems of community sought resolution in debating the problems of research methodologies. The diversity within the interpretative tradition is reflected in the contributors' articles as is the relevance of methodological debates in knowing the social. Again the debate about the scientific status of positivism versus interpretativism was left to one side, as was positivism's favoured position in the allocation of funding resources for research.

Revealingly, a report to the Minister for Education and Science (Bric, 1999) on the case for an Irish Research Council for the Humanities and Social Sciences, commented that within the Humanities and Social Sciences 'the methodology of research is becoming more "scientific"' (Bric, 1999: 16). The argument is presented in these positivistic terms in order to convince the reader that the Humanities and Social Sciences can generate knowledge that is reliable, valid, worthwhile and of 'economic benefit': in the report 'scientific' research is represented as being of 'economic benefit'. At the same time, Bric argues, Humanities and Social Sciences research 'can inform a public policy that must not be driven solely by the demands of economic development' and have a role 'in explaining, interpreting and evaluating the implications of the powerful forces which impact on our society' (Bric, 1999: 18). While the report was written with a specific brief and context in mind (i.e. making a case to the government for a joint council to fund and develop research in Ireland), the representation of Humanities and Social Sciences methodology as 'scientific' and therefore worthy of funding, is highly problematic and should not go uncontested.

Similarly, in its consultation document on the role of research for health, the Health Research Board defines research as an activity in which 'results are generalisable', using a methodology which 'is designed so that the results will be of value to those facing similar problems or can be reproduced in similar circumstances' (HRB, 2000: 14). While much bio-medical and technological research may be adequately represented by this scientific, positivist definition, interpretative research methodologies which could be utilised in the sociology of health are ignored. In the late 1980s Hannan (1988) observed that state funding agencies had little confidence in qualitative research methodologies and were impatient with 'methodological squabbles' within the discipline of sociology. However, the fact remains that the positivist tradition has received state funding, while the interpretative tradition has not. In the current bid for control of research funding, this pattern is about to repeat itself. In the context of funding policy-relevant research, Hannan states that a lot of emphasis is placed on 'shared concepts of reliability, validity and bias objectivity' and that 'the relevant audience or customer paying for one's work generally shares the "objectivist" views of falsifiability' (Hannan, 1988: 28). State and public perception of legitimate social research is firmly based on the positivist, empirical paradigm: those doing such research will receive public funding; others will not. Hannan argues that:

> there clearly has not been enough good qualitative work done in most areas of policy relevant research – but then there has been very little good qualitative sociological work of any kind done in Ireland – to persuade state funding agencies that they need work of that kind (Hannan, 1988: 28).

Twelve years on, we see a growth in feminist and other emancipatory, reflexive sociological research, which draws on both qualitative and quantitative approaches. The challenge now is to meet funders' doubts as to the validation and 'falsifiability' of non-positivistic research projects. More recently, state agencies are beginning to be interested in funding research which has a qualitative dimension (e.g. O'Neill, 1922; and Fahey, 1999).

It is perhaps time to move out of our methodological 'bunkers' in Irish sociology (cf. O'Connor, 2000). It is evident that within the paradigm of feminist, emancipatory and interpretative research methodologies a public debate has begun to take place (albeit intermittently, over a period of time), reflexively questioning the methods, ethics and politics of our research practices. We hope that this volume contributes to that debate, as we believe there is an urgent need to consider the future organisation, development and funding of Irish sociological research to include a multiplicity of methodologies.

The feminist researcher and the academy

In the early days of the development of Women's Studies courses within academic institutions in the US, a debate ensued about the de-radicalisation of feminism which would come as a result of institutionalisation (see Bowles and Duelli-Klein, 1983). Some feminists employed by and working for the academy argued that feminist teaching, research and activism would result in institutional awareness of injustice, would challenge women's oppression and would provoke change. Others argued against such possibilities, pointing to the power of the academy to regulate and validate academic knowledge, appointments and resources, positing a future for academic feminism as marginal both to the academy and to the women's movement. Academics (and community activists) in Ireland have engaged in this debate (see for example, Byrne, 1992; Byrne and Keher, 1995; Byrne et al, 1996; Byrne, P. and Lyons, 1999; Connolly and Ryan, 1999; Connolly, 1999; Daly, 1987; Davies, 1993; Kelly, 1995; Smyth, 1992, 1996; Smyth and McCann, 1999; Special Issue *IJFS*, 1997), in addition to their concern about the legitimisation of Women's Studies as an academic discipline and the strenuous, time-consuming, voluntary activities involved in building Women's Studies courses, programmes and centres.

Given that both of us are feminists, researchers and academics, we asked colleagues in Sociology and Women's Studies working for universities and research organisations whether it was important to name oneself as a 'feminist researcher' in published work and what issues are involved in identifying oneself as a feminist *vis-à-vis* one's institution/organisation. We received twelve replies to our questions, mostly from women academics within the social sciences. Of these one academic said it was not important to name oneself as a feminist in her published work:

> In my experience being a woman is difficult for academia to handle.
> Being in sociology is a further turn off; being in Women's Studies
> is an even further step. To me writing is about influencing people
> through one's own ideas. That means that they first have to hear/

read what you say. Hence it is not important to identify myself as a feminist researcher in my texts.

Another academic woman wrote that there is no need to name herself as a feminist in journals with 'obviously feminist titles' as it would 'convey a "holier than thou" message'. However, if publishing in other journals, she 'might be a bit more explicit about spelling out that this is a feminist point of view'. Importantly, she focused on the difference between naming oneself as a feminist and utilising a feminist perspective in her work:

> As for naming myself as a feminist, I've no problem about doing so, and frequently do in certain contexts where one can assume a fairly clear and simple meaning of the term. I think the problem in academic writing is that there has been such a heterogeneity of meanings attached to the term that to call oneself a feminist immediately begs a lot of questions as to what kind of feminist, etc. So it's not something I'd do at the beginning of an article, rather towards the end, and more to characterise the arguments I've put forward rather than myself.

Another academic's reply indicated that she was critical of attempts to reify distinctions between feminist and non-feminist methodologies:

> As someone who works within a feminist, critical, reflexive frame-work, I am very uneasy with the term and practice 'feminist methodology': it implies a rather simplistic and erroneous dichotomy between feminist/non-feminist and usually qualitative and quantitative dimensions. While feminist insights have no doubt informed much awareness of reflexivity, relativity, subjectivity and agency on the part of practitioners and respondents, the very binary (feminist/non-feminist or positivist or traditional or whatever term is used) is paradoxically alien to feminist thinking, at least in its post-modern variant.

Ten women stated that it was important to publicly identify oneself as a feminist, though at least five mentioned that their identification depended on the audience and context. The reasons given by those who said it was important to name themselves as 'feminist' in their texts were epistemological, methodological, personal and political: the necessity of being a defender for feminism, preventing the demonisation of feminism in the academy and maintaining a feminist presence in intellectual life. For example, one woman wrote: 'It is

personally of great importance to me to identify myself as a feminist sociologist because I am committed to the position that women's voices and perceptions of their circumstances form the core of any piece of research, whatever the complexity.'
Another wrote that she feels:

> ... a sense of responsibility to make feminist discourses visible in the university and to contribute to making feminist studies/Women's Studies accepted as a genuine academic discipline and a genuine form of intellectual work.

Another wrote that it was important for feminists in the academy to represent the diversity of feminisms which include radical critiques and struggles for equality:

> ... it is important that we as feminists actively and deliberately take on this label and illustrate the diversity of perspectives or 'feminisms' that the term feminism has come to encompass, although to do so inevitably involves defending this perspective to individuals both within and without the university.

Women academics also said that:

> ... feminism informs my way of being and living in the world ... the production of feminist knowledge, all knowledge is a political activity and I want to clearly identify the politics to which I subscribe in my research activities.

> ... in most of my published texts I have explicitly located my analysis within the context of a feminist perspective or an engagement with debates within feminism.

Those who said that naming oneself as a feminist researcher was important but that it depends on the audience and context, explained that they were more likely to do so in publications that deal with methodology and gender issues. One academic observed:

> Yes, it is important to name 'myself' as a feminist researcher in published texts, but not always necessary. Many young academics in particular are reluctant to name themselves 'feminist' in the current academic climate. In this sense 'naming' is important, if feminism is to maintain a presence in intellectual life. Regardless of this, in each publication that I do, as a sociologist I would usually state explicitly the methodological and theoretical perspective adopted. Feminist theory informs most of my work, to different degrees.

And in any case, whether it is named in a publication or not – I 'am' a feminist.

Another academic observed:

> Sometimes I do and sometimes I don't. But whether I do or don't it is always a deliberate act, a conscious positioning, taking account of an audience.

Forming a community of support was seen as a personal benefit of naming oneself as a feminist. One respondent noted that 'it is a useful identity in the context of those who are supportive of feminism' and 'mutual interest in feminist issues can lead to fruitful sharing, solidarity and very enjoyable mutual co-operation.' Negative consequences also ensue, leading to 'friction and competition with both feminist and non-feminist colleagues', according to one of our respondents. Another felt that 'because there are so few self-declared feminists in the university, it can be lonely being a feminist, and known as such in the university.'

Women said that while there was institutional support and encouragement for feminist and Women's Studies courses and research, clearly there was no tolerance for a feminist analysis of institutional structures, organisational practices or ideologies. This was eloquently put by a respondent who wrote:

> I have received encouragement and support for teaching and conducting research concerning feminism. ... However, when I and others bring a feminist analysis to issues relating to how our department, faculty and university function, we meet with blatant hostility and ridicule. In other words, feminism is fine in the seminar room, but there it must stay. I find the university environment deeply inhospitable to women and even more so to feminists. ... It's quite acceptable to name myself as a feminist in the university, so long as my feminist gaze is not directed at the university and so long as it remains divorced from activism.

Another respondent also wrote about the paradoxical consequences of naming oneself as a feminist in the academy. Depending on the ethos in the academic department, in some instances being a feminist could be problematic – 'particular members on an interview panel might not view it favourably'– but in her experience in another academic department, 'naming oneself as a feminist could confer positive advantages since methodology and feminist research emerged as a strategic research thrust.'

Another said that she actively associated herself with the term 'feminism' and that:

> Feminism is still perceived as having purely negative connotations, both inside and outside the university, a tendency which undermines the willingness of female students and staff to explicitly call themselves feminist.

Another woman researcher wrote:

> In relation to the academy, there is no positive value whatsoever in my being identified and in identifying myself as a feminist sociologist. If anything, it is a form of negative currency. The kinds of research agenda being pursued by the academic enterprise rarely interface with the kind of work I do, as a researcher who raises all her own grants. Moreover, there is no serious intent on the part of the academy that I have seen in a period of over ten years to adequately resource either the work of Women's Studies or the work of building feminist research initiatives.

From the replies we received there seems to be little structural encouragement for women working together across the disciplines. While there is encouragement for feminist teaching and research within academic departments, the structure and demands of loyalty and of making a time commitment to academic departments in the first instance is inimical to the development of a feminist community or feminist activism on campus. This in effect is a form of control, restricting feminism in the academy to research and teaching, and as observed by another respondent: 'naming oneself as feminist was politically correct in the university system provided you don't ask for more payment or time off in lieu of your "extra-curricular" feminist teaching and activities'. Indeed, one feminist academic believed that her lack of promotion was because of her radical feminist activism:

> I have named myself as a feminist researcher for such a long time now that it's not something I think about in a conscious way. I suspect, since I have not been promoted to the level my qualifications/publications would lead me to expect, that doing feminist research, which names itself as such, is not highly valued by the university – rather the contrary. However, I would add that not only of course do I define myself as 'feminist' but also as a 'radical' and as a lesbian. A further factor is that most of my writing and research is explicitly political with strong activist dimensions.

Likewise, a respondent observed that in identifying herself as a feminist researcher she ran the risk that her intellectual work would not be considered as legitimate scholarship.

The replies we received indicated that while for some there may be academic rewards in naming oneself as a feminist, the academy holds a repertoire of deterrents regulating and ensuring the presentation of an acceptable face to feminism within its walls:

> I think there is a tendency to separate 'deserving' from 'undeserving' feminists, and academic women have to tread a tightrope between being praised for being good girls and keeping the university abreast of important new developments like Women's Studies, and on the other hand, 'going too far', or going on a 'feminist rant', which indicates male disapproval.

Our third level educational institutions remain hostile to and attempt to repel initiatives by women academics to apply their feminism in transforming not only organisational structures and behaviours but also our relationships with knowledge and knowledge production. In presenting knowledge production as a political activity, feminist academics are questioning the very business of the university. This can be reflected by some students, as one respondent wrote:

> Disapproval comes also from students, many of whom are frightened of being deprived of their femininity if they become associated with feminist ideas. They can also feel doubly cheated if they find then that feminism itself is heterogeneous, and not easy to define. I greatly enjoy negotiating these debates with students, and feel that I win some, just as I lose some every year, and that students overtake me in their capacity to relate all this to contemporary reality and popular culture.

While academia may be hostile to feminist analyses and activism, and feminists are vulnerable to institutional power and the personal and career risks associated with integration or marginalisation, the perception is that if one removes oneself from the arena transformation will not ensue. In a recent paper on 'Resistance in academia', Pat O'Connor writes that 'the abandonment of the academy to hegemonic masculinity in the third Millennium is not an attractive option' (O'Connor 2000: 9). However, one of our respondents did wonder whether:

the time has not come for Women's Studies to part company with
the academy, whether the work that is there to do should not be
carried out in a different frame of reference, in order to build and
maintain credibility.

Another respondent suggests an alternative strategy:

> I have actually made a decision when I started my publishing career
> that I don't want to ride on the 'minority status ticket', that I want
> to 'speak prose', I don't want to speak in tongues. Not that I have
> any problem with being labelled feminist (although I have a problem
> with being 'labelled' anything, such interdisciplinary that I am),
> but because I wanted to add my voice to the mainstream discourse.
> It is one thing to be marginalised within the mainstream, quite
> another to be outside. In some sense it is like deciding that I want
> the message (and method is also a message) to get through without
> the possibly distorting screen of labels, because labels can put
> people off, can put them in a stereotyping frame of mind, and can
> also be suspected of merit (if it is seen as being allowed entry on
> a quota-like basis). If, however, you insert feminist messages within
> a mainstream conversation, people address the substance, not the
> tags. I know it sounds like 'minority politics', but to the extent that
> it is possible, I believe that it is more effective.

Feminist researchers, situated in the academy, are both constrained
and enabled by that position: in being 'outsiders within', the challenge is to exercise our 'academic freedoms' for emancipatory and
transformative work (see Lynch, in this volume).

Moving from theory to practice: (re)searching women, (re)searching the self

What do we mean when we say we use a feminist research
methodology? What are the implications for practice? What are the
implications for our own selves? In the next section we talk
individually about the meaning for us of doing feminist research.

Anne Byrne

In January 2000, at the age of forty-three, I completed a PhD in
Sociology (Byrne, 2000), and only recently learned for myself why
I embarked on such a difficult and time-consuming project. In

November 1999 I accepted an invitation to attend a twenty-five year school reunion of the Leaving Certificate class of 1974. I met my school friends and with difficulty I tried to adjust the images of eighteen year old faces held for so long in my mind's eye with the forty-something women standing before me as familiar strangers. Perhaps it was because of this initial, disturbing, merging of realities that the remainder of the evening took on a surreal quality where voices seemed louder, and silences more intense, as we looked at each other wondering what to say, how much to tell, why we had come to such a gathering in the first place. In that initial meeting, I noticed that some stayed only a short while, perhaps feeling uncomfortable, unwelcome.

While I may have known at some level why I decided to revisit this past, I now can express why I went. In attending that reunion I met myself as others saw me, a person I no longer was. I too searched for my familiars of long ago but they were no longer there. The evening brought many emotions, including strong feelings of joy, pain and anger. I expected the first two, but not anger. The joy was felt in the thrill and excitement of meeting the others, the pain and anger were my own as I heard women speak with bitterness about the effects of class difference in our school and the limited educational opportunities offered to us. As a classmate pointed out on the night, though we were taught by women who themselves had been to university, little effort was made to encourage us to advance on to university education. Another woman told the story of our career guidance, an event I had completely forgotten. The day before the Leaving Certificate, a woman who ran a 'beauty and deportment' school instructed us how to sit on a chair like a lady, legs elegantly sloped to one side, hands clasped on our laps. As an extra tip she taught us how to sit in and step out of a car.

The school was streamed into four classes and some girls in the top stream were encouraged to enter primary school teaching or nursing. Some in the other streams were sent down the road for secretarial training. Of the four classes, comprising about 160 girls, only six of us attended at least the first year of university and only two finally graduated. My school was not a middle-class school: though a few girls were from middle-class backgrounds, most were working-class. The reality of material and class inequality came rushing back as I was reminded of what I had always known, of what I had witnessed. One woman told me that though she was in the top stream, one day without warning she was plucked from the classroom and deposited in a lower stream, opportunity being swept away by a decision in which she had no say. In other women's stories I heard the regret for themselves, passionately wishing that they had had the opportunity to study for a specific, chosen career. Though provided with a basic education, opportunities to move on were denied to most of my classmates. I heard women speak with anger about their ill treatment as their intellectual lives were taken hostage. That night women said out loud that they felt they were regarded as 'no good' because of their class background, and that they would therefore never amount to anything. And I remembered being witness to this injustice in my classroom. The power of the powerful and the vulnerability of the powerless was one of the most lasting lessons I learned at school. Later, as educational opportunities expanded, from what we learned from each other that night, some women took adult education and degree courses, part-time or as mature students. One or two others did post-graduate work in later life. I did too.

What has this story got to do with feminist research? At the school reunion I understood at last why I had decided to do a PhD. Given the opportunity, I took it. I needed to find out what I could do even though I was no longer eighteen years old. The effects of utilising a feminist research methodology in my PhD have spilled over into the rest of my life: an intended consequence perhaps of a research methodology in which the 'personal is political'?[3] For me, a feminist research methodology is value-laden, is ideologically driven and is committed to exposing questions of gender injustice and gender oppression. As a researcher, in choosing a feminist research paradigm I am committed to producing 'unalienated', emancipatory knowledges and devising challenging research practices which invite a continual re-working and re-formulating of researcher-researched relationships. These practices push the boundaries of participation, representation and interpretation as

---

[3] For a discussion of the effect of feminist qualitative research on researchers' personal lives see Cotterill and Letherby (1993).

much as possible, and crucially involve the researcher in a debate with herself and others about the theoretical, political, practical and personal consequences of her work.[4]

The movement in feminist research processes is primarily from the private to the public, though it does not exclude movement in the opposite direction. Both public and private, though social constructs, are evident and consequential in individual bodies, and are felt and realised in personal experience.[5] In a research project, part of which I detail in this volume, I worked at the individual, personal level revealing private, intimate knowledges of lives marked by stigma and 'Otherness', introducing this transformed knowledge into a public, academic setting. A feminist research design helped me to confront the ethical problems that this approach raises, particularly as I am not a member of the researched group.

The challenge is always to work between 'manipulative distance' and 'spurious identification' (Patai, 1991: 145). However, I believe that in retreating from the difficulties posed by feminist research methodologies, refuge has often been sought in researching the self. Much feminist research is also about discovering the researcher's/author's/my own self-identity, and I believe that my chosen research topic is connected to the researcher's/my own

---

[4] Anne Byrne first came across the term 'alienated knowledge' in the context of feminist research practices in Stanley's (1990a) Marxist dissection of academic knowledge production. Stanley demonstrates that the social context in which knowledge is produced is not demonstrably written into research accounts while the relations and forces of production remain implicit only and therefore invisible to the process of knowledge-making. She writes that '(t)he result is alienated knowledge, a product apparently complete, bearing no apparent trace of the conditions of its production and the social relations that gave rise to this. It is, no more and no less, as much an alienated commodity produced within patriarchal capitalism as any other alienated capitalist commodity' (Stanley 1990: 11). The feminist antidote in social science is of course to publicly produce 'unalienated knowledge' or close, familiar, private knowledges which are potentially transformative.

[5] See Ribbens and Edwards (1998) for a discussion and diagrammatic representation of the relation of the personal to the public and the private in the context of a research setting. While concepts of public and private are much debated, overlap and vary, the public sphere is usually regarded as those settings in which goal-oriented, individualistic, formal, large-scale organisations are emphasised while the private sphere is more associated with informal relationships and intimate, familial type, domestic settings.

biography. In using a feminist research framework, I am made aware that I am in the act of researching myself. I observe myself researching others, I pay attention to the decisions and mistakes made and the conditions of their making, I watch myself before and after meetings, speaking and saying good-bye to research participants, and I make connections between this topic and my life as it is lived now. Finally, the feminist researcher/I must be willing to take risks in design, interpretation and representation and will reveal, and make visible and accountable, the research process from before inception to the story so far.

I observe that feminist research methodologies are in continuous composition and creation. I draw and learn from the accounts of others. Resources are continually generated as more researchers adopt and adapt feminist research practices in response to the research context and participants' needs. There now exists a growing documentation and publication of feminist research practices, of failed and successful projects (e.g. Wilkinson and Kitzinger, 1995; 1996; Shakespeare et al, 1996; Ribbens and Edwards, 1998). This is reassuring as I discover that others have struggled with similar issues, problems and decisions. At some level, I can access this struggle through reading about feminist research processes and the conditions which produce 'familiar' feminist knowledges.

Ronit Lentin

I must begin with a confession: I am a (very) late entrant to academic life. I managed not to finish my first degree (it seems years ago, in the 1960s, in Israel, when, for various reasons I dropped out of a series of courses). On my arrival in Ireland in 1969, I worked in a variety of occupations, mostly involved with writing. I spent several years with RTÉ and the rest of the time as a freelance journalist covering mostly women's issues and health issues. When the Centre for Women's Studies at Trinity College Dublin set up a post-graduate programme in Women's Studies in 1990, I was fortunate enough to be accepted, despite not having completed my first degree. As soon as I began the course, I knew I was coming home. The academic mode of production in general, and feminist studies in particular, suited me perfectly and I continued to work on a doctorate in the Department of Sociology at TCD.

Living in Ireland as a 'foreigner' (albeit with an Irish passport) positions me variably as an 'outsider' and an 'outsider within', never part of the collective Irish 'we'. At the same time, as a Jewish Israeli, I am also part of the majority in my native Israel, which has occupied Palestinian lands and people since 1948. For me feminism, stemming from the awareness of power differentials, was an avenue of articulating my differing positionalities – that of a daughter of a family of Romanian Jews who had experienced persecution, deportations and refugeeship; that of an Israeli, aware of the unequal relationship between occupying Israeli Jews and occupied Palestinians; and that of a Jew in Irish society, where antisemitism is too close to the surface for comfort.

In 1980 I published a collection of interviews with Palestinian women writers and political activists in Israel and in the West Bank and Gaza Strip (Lentin, 1980). The interviews focused on the then burning feminist issue of the link between 'the personal' and 'the political'. It was the first collection of its kind to be published in Hebrew. Looking back, I shudder at my naïvety. I attempted to conduct dialogues with the women, whom I admired for their intellectual and political achievements, but who were part of the occupied while I was part of the occupiers. Including myself in the published verbatim transcripts, I spoke about my political commitment to 'their' liberation and attempted to reflexively position myself in relation to 'their' oppression. The text opened a window into the lives of Palestinian women, our significant (yet exoticised) 'other'. However, being a journalistic project, it did not undertake an analysis of the process – I was particularly unaware of the ethical consequences of publishing, in Hebrew, texts of interviews conducted in English, and therefore inaccessible to some of my interviewees.

I was reminded of all this in February 2000 when I presented a paper at the annual conference of the Israeli Association for Feminist Studies and Gender Research in Bet Berl College, Israel, together with Professor Nahla Abdo, a Palestinian born in Nazareth (Israel) who now resides in Canada. Our topic was the collection of auto/biographical narratives of dis-location of Palestinian and Israeli women that we are editing jointly (Abdo and Lentin, forthcoming). Preparing for the conference, our differences surfaced, particularly in relation to nationalism and its relation to feminism. More importantly, our encounter forced me to re-focus on the power differentials between us. Regardless of our academic and political differences and similarities, while in Israel-Palestine our dialogue must be informed by these power differentials, with me being part of the occupiers and Abdo part of the occupied. In dialoguing with Abdo I felt compelled to assume responsibility for my nation-state, even if I do not share the blame for the excesses of the occupation.

Power in feminist research is not a zero-sum game, and as a feminist researcher I am positioned and implicated differently on a matrix of dominations. Feminism provides a link between my positioning as an 'outsider within' – both as a woman in a patriarchal academy and as a Jewish-Israeli other – and my political and academic commitment to the 'cartographies of intersectionality' (Brah, 1996) as the account of my research trajectory reveals.

In 1992, as a doctoral student, I gave my first departmental seminar about feminist research methodologies, which I intended to use in researching the personal narratives of Israeli daughters of Shoah survivors in relation to the masculinisation of Israeli society. The previous year, taking a course in qualitative research methodology as a post-graduate student, I 'discovered' feminist methodologies. Specifically, I discovered the notion that the experience of oppression can create a unique type of insight and an ability to penetrate 'official' explanations and grasp gender relations and their mechanisms (see Fonow and Cook, 1991a: 1). I understood that my position, as a feminist researcher in a patriarchal academic institution, but also as a member of an ethnic minority in Ireland, was that of an perpetual 'outsider within'. The African American sociologist Patricia Hill Collins argues that bringing groups of marginal intellectuals such as Black feminist sociologists, as well as others who share this 'outsider within' status *vis-à-vis* sociology, into the centre of the analysis, may reveal views of reality obscured by more orthodox approaches (Hill Collins, 1990). Having dis-covered *experience* as a site from which to conduct feminist research, and having situated myself reflexively within my research project, I went on to propose feminist research as constituting a separate methodological paradigm (see Oakley, 1981).

The seminar, and subsequent seminars on other occasions and the ensuing publications (Lentin, 1993; 1994; 1995), were sobering experiences. On one occasion, a professor of sociology in one of Ireland's universities admitted that his objection to my presentation stemmed from my declared feminism: 'the word "feminist"', he later explained, 'is like a red rag to a bull.' On the one hand, colleagues argued, like Martyn Hammersley (1992), that while feminism has made and continues to make a major contribution to the social sciences, feminist sociology cannot be considered a separate methodological paradigm based on distinct political and philosophical assumptions. Research, my colleagues argued, as does Hammersley, is a more pragmatic process. Moreover, if feminist research was indeed a separate paradigm, there would have been no need for non-feminists to take it seriously. Hammersley, and my colleagues, seem to say 'don't call it "feminist", and sociology will take you seriously.' On the other hand, colleagues, and among them feminist colleagues, argued that doing good sociology (or adhering to your disciplinary strictures, depending on your position within the academy) is more important than calling your research 'feminist': 'I do not think that researchers can by interviewing women, even reflexively, call themselves feminist sociologists or indeed that what they produce should automatically be called sociology' (Mahon, 1994: 166). In other words, the argument against opening the can of worms called 'feminist methodologies' is on the one hand that feminism has brought nothing new to social research, and on the other (or perhaps it is another way of saying the same thing), that feminism is secondary to 'scientific' modes of producing knowledge.

Revisiting the debate, I took myself to task (Lentin, 1999) for homogenising 'Irish women' when I called for their greater visibility in published social research without problematising Irish womanhood in relation to class, 'race'/ethnicity, sexuality, (dis)ability, all constituting 'an intersection of subordinations' (Yuval-Davis, 1997) with the co-factor 'gender'.

Making women visible is only one outcome of the insistence by feminists within the academy of calling their research 'feminist'. Another is the increasing acceptance, by students, but also by fellow academics, of reflexively situating themselves within their research processes. As course co-ordinator of a post-graduate course in Ethnic and Racial Studies at Trinity College Dublin, the question of situating ourselves *ethnically* within our research projects is as crucial as it is in relation to gender. Gender has certainly come of age as an acceptable 'variable' – compared with former years when students, who had to take mandatory sociology lectures in first year, used to sneer when the first year sociology gender lecture came up. Yet other differences, such as 'race'/ethnicity, class, sexuality or dis/ability, make it clear that more work needs to be done beyond scientist positioning of variables to serve as comparative measures to examine society. And the more we make these differences visible, the more we ourselves, as women, positioned differently from each other, become visible, to ourselves, and to society.

Women, and increasingly marginalised women – from ethnic minorities, from varying levels of dis/ability, from differing sexualities – are saying they want to name their own worlds, in their own words, and to initiate their own projects. In 1999-2000 I was one of the supervisors of a research project on the expectations and needs of young women from ethnic minorities in Europe conducted by five young women from Portugal, Sweden, Italy and Ireland, titled *Attitudes and Expectations of Minority Women in Europe*. Each young researcher interviewed 25 young women from ethnic minorities. In a meeting held in Torino in October 1999, they spoke about the research process as relating not only to the greater visibility of their research narrators, but also to their own emancipation. The following quotes from the researchers demonstrate the double consciousness of oppression and privilege and the link between passion and emancipation. The quotes show that when a research project is conducted reflexively – when researcher and researched share the same platform by being both knower and known – researchers are both empowered and dis-empowered by knowing, first hand, about the experiences of the women they research. It also attests to the *necessity* of feminist research projects (see Stanley, 1996, on research as 'necessity') to excavate not only the concerns of the researched, but also those of the researcher (italics mine):

> (Sonia:) I wanted to discover the real reality of black women in Italy. … To hear their own experiences in their own words made me reflect and get angry … during the interviews I also suffered, because these women sharing their experiences as immigrants were frustrated, unlucky, because most are here to help their families back home. … *It made me feel angry because I knew what it felt like to be approached sexually.* … In Torino there are lots of projects for

immigrants, but none of them are *with* immigrants, only *for* them, without involving them.

(Nella:) I wanted to work with women. Being a black woman, working as a youth leader with an anti-racism movement, *I felt my voice was not being heard.* I was always the last one to be heard. As a woman I have a different perspective to a Black man. *So I had to do something about it.* This research project helped me. I wanted to make sure there were other people who felt like me. My biggest frustration is that this project is coming to an end and I still don't have an answer.

(Nadia:) I became more frustrated by the girls' need to talk. All said they felt they needed the interview to help them articulate their experiences of discrimination – this made me angry and frustrated *because of their lack of opportunity to discuss these issues elsewhere.*

If there is one thing which unites us as reflexive feminist researchers it is the knowledge that we can take nothing for granted, that knowledge is always situated, and, more importantly, implicated in complex power relations, and that excavating women's testimonies is always a painful, but fruitful process.

Creating a sociology with women

The issue of collaboration is key to developing a sociology 'with' women. Patai (1991: 147) argues that only in those research projects that are in the control of the community can ethical research be conducted to any extent without exploiting research participants. Our current thinking about undertaking feminist research is characterised, above all else, by our commitment to processes of collaboration with research participants. While the academy exhorts us to be 'objective' in order to produce 'scientific' knowledge, many feminist scholars have shrugged off this requirement for objectivity, dismissing it as impossible. Stanley, for instance, sees 'objectivity' and 'subjectivity' as false dichotomies, 'artefacts within the sexual political system', which need deconstructing by 'looking closely and analytically at the constitutive social and institutional practices concerned, in the setting by which these are generated' (Stanley, 1990b: 120). Barbara Du Bois (1983), positing 'passionate research', argues that while traditional western science separates observer and observed, knower and known, in feminist scholarship the knower and the known are of the same universe and, as women, we inhabit our world with 'double consciousness'. We are in, and of, our society, but in important ways also not 'of' it. Far from being mushy or navel gazing, 'passionate research' demands rigour, precision and responsibility, precisely because of its passion. Nancy Miller argues that the flowering of personal criticism in the 1980s is a consequence of a (post-modern, post-colonial) disillusionment with meta-narratives and theories (Miller, 1991). We would like to add that the increasing use of the personal and the passionate in conducting social research is also the reflexive response by certain social scientists, some of them feminists, to tendencies in academic social sciences to return to scientism and positivism.

If there is one thing this volume is committed to, it is a rejection of scientist 'objectivity', in favour of a situated researching subject, seeking to make women's experiences, the social construction of gender (in the case of Lohan, this volume, the construction of masculinities), and the research process itself explicit and visible. We aim to renounce an academic élitism which implicitly tells research subjects, 'I know something which you don't,' calling upon them to provide us with their experiences and life stories so that we, the researchers, can use *their* experience to produce *our* analysis. The chapters in this volume evince a commitment to a new kind of collaboration with our research subjects, without whom, we are fully aware, our research projects would not have been possible in the first place.

However, collaboration is neither easy nor simple as the chapters in this volume demonstrate. Just as working-class Irish women (see O'Neill, 1999, and in this volume) have been challenging what they see as a monolithic 'Irish feminism' for its failure not only to recognise class differences between women, but also to move and make room for working-class feminists to name their own worlds, so now women from ethnic minorities (see for example, McDonagh, in this volume) are beginning to sound similar criticism (belatedly, but in line with critiques by majority world feminists such as Chandra Mohanty, 1991, and Kum Kum Bhavnani, 1993, to give but two examples).

Lest we delude ourselves that collaboration in the research process is a smooth path, let us remember that collaboratory and emancipatory research methodologies must be viewed through the lens of two contradictory discourses. The first is an argument against emancipatory research methodologies as representing the abandonment of the obligations of the researcher (see Hammersley, 1995). Martyn Hammersley, perhaps the loudest critic of feminist research (in 'On feminist methodology,' Hammersley, 1992), suggests that if feminists did not use the 'f word' to describe their work, it would be very akin to other forms of research and therefore far more acceptable. He argues against the politicisation of feminist and other emancipatory approaches to research, and positions 'personal experience' versus 'the scientific method' as a problematic binary, since it assumes that research is not political before it is politicised (Humphries, 1997) and that 'experience' can be unproblematically contrasted with 'science'. Hammersley's argument against feminist research methodologies tends to homogenise both 'feminism' and 'research methodologies', and his discussion of feminist research as rejecting 'the hierarchy in the research relationship' ignores the critique by majority world feminists (e.g. Mohanty, 1991) of the imperialism and racism of (Western) feminist research itself.

The other discourse, no less alarming, is the discourse of 'good intentions', on behalf of liberal left-leaning researchers, who claim to use research projects as a means of empowering weakened, disadvantaged populations. Emancipatory research methodologies identify traditional research as deeply implicated in power, and set as their goal 'the equalising of power between researcher and researched and the changing of oppressive relations of power'. However, both approaches are implicated in power (Humphries, 1997: 3.5-3.6). The very act of engaging in an attempt to emancipate others perpetuates the relations of dominance. The contradiction between the commitment to empower and the impossibility to confer power is crucial: 'in her attempt to share power as a researcher, she is inevitably implicated in power in the process' (Humphries, 1997: 3.6). Liberty and emancipation cannot be conferred, despite the commitment of contributors to this volume to complex processes of collaboration, and of feeding back research contents at all stages of data collection, data analysis and writing up. Nor is liberty something which can be gained once and for all. And even careful processes of self reflexivity, while fundamental in feminist research methodologies in privileging consultation, participation and feedback, can deteriorate 'into a self indulgence which places the researcher as the norm' (Humphries, 1997: 4.10).

Mindful of this pitfall but impelled towards a sociology 'with' women, we want now to reflect on three collaborative principles: participation, interpretation/representation and reflexivity.

•Participation

It is assumed that research is always about other people. But a feminist reworking of the research process focuses on participation as a central issue and shows that participation touches every aspect of the work from inception to the public presentation of people's lives. Thinking about participation invites clarity about the consequences of the work for self and others and engages all of us in a debate about ownership of experiences, privacy and what constitutes permissible research topics.

Debates around participation include debates about both the possibility and the desirability of collaboration, already mentioned above. Shields and Dervin (1993) argue that because collaborative methods of research rely so heavily on human relationships, engagement and attachment, the researched are actually at greater risk from the researcher, particularly (see Riessman, 1987) when factors other than gender (notably 'race', ethnicity and class) are not taken into consideration. Patai (1991: 147) disputes that ethical research is ever possible, and argues that neither purity nor safety resides in calling one's research 'feminist'.

According to Kristina Minister (1991), it is the very performative nature of qualitative feminist data collection processes (such as in-depth interviewing, life story, oral history and other narrative methods) – involving topic selection determined by interviewer questions, one person talking at a time, the narrator 'taking the floor' with referential language, and keeping within the boundaries of selected topics – which may deny women the collaborative, participatory and inclusive communication forms that women value. 'If examined in contexts similar to its natural context, women's constructions of self and gender can be recorded, analysed, and interpreted so that it will reconstruct human history' (Minister, 1991: 39). Therefore, in order to offer women the forum to communicate in ways that support them, Minister proposes non-hierarchical feminist data collection processes. These include: equalising the power relations inherent in the (age, class, ethnic affiliation and education) differences between researched and researcher as much as possible; adjusting to the temporal and spatial expectations of the researched (allow them to fix interview times and venues); taking time to get to know the researched; asking for their comments and suggestions throughout the research process; allowing for mutual self-disclosure and questioning; revealing the purpose of the researcher's project and avoiding having a topic list or controlling the interview topics; offering verbal and non-verbal communication signals to assist the researched (such as attentive body postures, utterances such as 'uh huh', completing or repeating sentences, acknowledging previous utterances).

Reinharz, framing feminist research methodologies within what she terms 'experiential methodologies', suggests that researchers can facilitate the process of collaboration by:

> providing clear opportunities to be interviewed, scrutinised and questioned by the subjects ... meaningful research builds on finding out what is meaningful to oneself and one's research collaborators. Having subject input also minimises researcher bias since it includes diverse points of view (Reinharz, 1983: 177).

Another central issue in the collaborative process is that of preserving the anonymity of our research subjects, often presented as a central ethical issue. However, this may be problematic, particularly when we attempt to give voice to hitherto unvoiced discourses of women. Although often vital, particularly in quantitative research that generates abstract principles about aggregates of people, masking the identities of the researched in a project designed to explore lived experiences and life worlds ought to be questioned. The wish of researchers and researched for anonymity often reflects cultural constructions of privacy and power. Instead of the conventional view of confidentiality and anonymity as 'rights' and 'principles' of 'ethical research', Ruth Linden suggests that:

> ... we can explore the meanings and consequences of revealing or masking their identities. To strive to honour our respondents' wishes by negotiating the terms of inscription with them would introduce an unprecedented level of accountability into ethnographic writing (Linden, 1993: 111).

• *Interpretation/Representation*

Ideally, feminist research builds interpretation together with the researched. This fundamentally alters the dynamic of interactions in the research process (for instance during interviews; see Byrne's and Lohan's chapters in this volume), contributes vitally to questionnaire/interview design and broadens the concept of consent to participate in a research process. Interpretation and representation are bound up with each other. Representation involves the researcher in a consideration of how to represent people's accounts of their lives as told to the researcher accurately and meaningfully. In reporting the account, we seek to develop an interpretation which is ours, but only because we are willing to give it away and receive it back with other interpretations, other voices attached. We must stress that a researcher's representation of the words of the researched, avowedly feminist as it might be, may not be recognised or agreed to by the researched and a balance between the versions must somehow be struck, since the interpretations are always the result of the interaction and reflections negotiated between researcher and researched through the research process. Indeed, issues of consent, collaboration, voice, authority and representation are never easily resolved, despite all the care feminist researchers might take during the data collection stage. For example, Stanley, reporting on a project mutually agreed with her mother (Stanley, 1985), admits that 'what started as a collaborative project became entirely one-sided'. This happened not only because her mother had a stroke before the project ended, but also because her mother had little comprehension of what the public revelations about her life might mean (Stanley, 1996: 50). Chapters in this volume attest to differing issues arising from processes of interpretation and representation.

• *Reflexivity*

This involves a transparent research process as well as attention to the researcher's own experience and involvement with the research. A feminist research practice involves a commitment to ourselves and others to show how we know what we know. Stanley (1996) posits 'research as necessity' in relation to the nature of representation within accounts of the social world. Feminist researchers often carry out particular research because of the resonance between the topic or approach and the personal context of the research. In some ways, even if our research topic lies outside our own lives and experiences, as feminist researchers we always research our own lives, being implicated both as members of the oppressed group – women in patriarchal society – and of the élite – feminist researchers, academics or otherwise.

The consequences for researchers of employing feminist research methodologies

While engaging in feminist research, we have both felt on occasion (like many others, as the survey above attests) the lack of a community of feminist and non-feminist scholars on hand, with whom we could speak about the issues thrown up by the research process, from the very mundane to the philosophical, and share problems concerning analysis of data. We have mostly had to depend on written, textual or internet sources which, though valuable, are one-way. We learned from these sources often without the benefit of comment from others on our thinking processes. This is a separate matter from sharing written research interpretations with participants and peers or offering accounts for judgement to academic supervisors or referees. It is more about creating an immediate, collaborative community, supporting the processes which allow the generation of good research practices and products.[6]

This isolation and general lack of support for feminist research was echoed by the participants of a seminar we organised on 29 April 1999 at Trinity College Dublin, at which contributors to this volume spoke about their research projects. Many participants said that this was the first opportunity for them to discuss feminist research and their evaluations were mostly complimentary (e.g. 'inspiring, honest, energising and motivating'; 'very insightful variety of practices and approaches'). However, all participants commented on the shortage of time to discuss the many issues raised. According

---

[6] However, Ronit Lentin would like to acknowledge the support of a TCD-UCD feminist post-graduate discussion group focusing on the auto/biographical in feminist research. The group, which met several times in 1994-5, demonstrates the benefits to a feminist researcher, particularly at a post-graduate stage, of the intellectual and personal support a community of like-minded feminist academics can offer.

to one participant, 'given that we are marginalised and feel lonely, a network of feminist researchers/activists would be really useful.' The same participant suggested that 'more positive angles on feminist research would have been helpful, especially for younger/new researchers.'

Being reflexive takes its toll, not only on work relationships with colleagues in the academy and with students, but also on the researcher's personal relationships. While it is mandatory that feminist researchers should take care, first and foremost, not to damage their informants, they must also guard their own integrity: being publicly reflexive in conferences and in our research texts can be both emancipatory and dangerous.

Writing feminist research

Writing and reading feminist texts is often different from writing and reading other social science texts. Adrienne Rich (1993) has spoken about writing and reading poetry 'as if your life depended on it', but says that we are often encouraged to write as if only our livelihood, or 'the next step, the next job, grant, scholarship, professional advancement, fame' depended on it. Writing as if your life depended on it means, according to Rich:

> to write across the blackboard, putting up there in public words you have dredged, sieved up from dreams, from behind screen memories, out of silence – words you have dreaded and needed in order to know you exist. No, it's not too much; you could be laughed out of school, set upon in the schoolyard, they would wait for you after school, they could expel you. The politics of the schoolyard, the power of the gang. Or, they could ignore you (Rich, 1993: 33).

If we return to Stanley's (1996) notion of feminist research as 'necessity', writing feminist research texts can, arguably, have a similar degree of urgency. This may explain why feminists often use the 'auto/biographical I' (Stanley, 1992), frowned upon by supervisors, departments and universities, but often admired by non-academic audiences of women, eager to have their experiences admitted into the public domain, and by students, who take heart at the 'permission' feminism gives them to be reflexive. There is a serious dichotomy, we would suggest, between the 'objective' language of scientism and positivism and the language of reflexivity and creativity often, but not always, used by feminist researchers in their research texts. Stanley (1998a) cites Adrienne Rich as insisting that 'objectivity is what men call their subjectivity'.

According to Stanley (1992), feminist auto/biographical writing, as opposed to more conventional auto/biographical writing, often fractures linearity and chronology, and rejects the essential role of the self as waiting to be articulated and of notions of authorship as the unique mind of an individual writer. Feminist auto/biographies often insist on a multiplicity of voices and genres, not merely as a post-modernist reaction to 'the death of the author'. This fragmentation of voices and writing styles owes more to feminists recognising, at last, differences not only between women and men, but also between women.

However, reflexive modes of writing academic texts are not universally supported, even by social scientists favouring qualitative research methods. In a review of the narrative organisation and craft of writing social science texts, Silverman (1997), for example, expresses irritation with textual representations of research which move outside both the expected form and content of social science accounts, particularly as published in mainstream academic journals. His specific criticism was in reference to an ethnographic work on the family, represented as a series of nine poems by Laurel Richardson (1994), published in the *Journal of Ethnography*. This, he implies, is an example of reflexivity gone too far:

> In part, my worries relate to the image that we present to the world. A focus on the narrative construction of our texts may be an emancipatory activity. However, when carried on too much or too far, it is difficult to resist outside critics who accuse sociology of navel-gazing ... when it comes to certain rhetorical moves – for instance the construction of social science texts not just as dialogues, but as say poetry (e.g. Richardson, 1994) – am I alone in experiencing distaste and even despair? (Silverman, 1997: 240)

It is understandable that in relation to the nine poems in question, in the context of their location in an academic journal, a reader would be more satisfied with them as a representative form if they had been accompanied by the author's interpretative text. But this is exactly Richardson's point in contesting dominant representational practices in sociological writing:

> ... poetry is arguably closer to lived experiences and more likely to affect its readers and listeners ... it engages readers in frankly interpretative labours. A sociopoetics draws lay readers to social theorising, and sociologists to a critical confrontation with their value-constituting practices (Richardson 1991: 177).

Richardson's interest in various representational forms for sociological writing challenges the idea that dominant sociological discourse and interpretation has a privileged place or indeed form.

There are several contradictory reactions to feminist creative modes of writings, both academic and community-based. One reaction by the academy to feminists writing differently – using first person narratives, using a multiplicity of genres, deviating from the tried and tested structure of academic texts – has been to dismiss us as 'not really'. Not really social scientists, not really able to 'cut it' in the academic rat race, often publishing in feminist (albeit fully peer reviewed) journals only, and working outside and across our respective disciplines. This has been used time and again to stymie our promotion. Stanley (1998b) likens feminists in the academy to other 'aliens' and 'refugees':

> Being 'in and out' may be a state of mind deeply embedded in some of us, the in-betweenies, but for many more it is an actual interstitial state lying on the boundaries of academia, a transit camp, a shanty town brought into existence through the issuing of passports, the patrolling of borders, the careful regulation of movement of peoples, the forceful distinction between true citizens and migrant workers and aliens. These issuings and patrollings and regulations are structures which regulate the relations between states, but they are also social and political processes carried out by actual people, the 'citizens' and 'officials' and 'guards' of academic life (Stanley, 1998b: 183).

Stanley's *Knowing Feminisms* is a collection of works by feminists in the academy, writing in non-linear styles about new ways of knowledge and new ways of communicating these knowledges. In this collection, Ailbhe Smyth writes a poem about the meanings of borders for an Irish feminist (Smyth, 1998): poetry as theory is one contribution feminists have made to writing 'research' texts. Lentin

(2000) has introduced short pieces of fiction into her book on the gendered relations between Israel and the Shoah (see also Lentin, this volume) because, she argues, her book,

> a feminist auto/biographical process, is a sociological undertaking, which also aims to deconstruct the separating lines between 'doing sociology', 'doing personal narratives', and 'doing literature'. As a fiction writer, who is also a sociologist, who works with fiction and poetry writers and film-makers who are also expert commentators on Israeli society and its relationship with the Shoah, I have moved between the sociological, the literary and the personal, and between a literary prologue, auto/biographical personal chapters, 'sociology' chapters, and a literary epilogue. I am all these voices (Lentin, 2000, 214).

Another reaction, no less paralysing, to feminist writings, has been to argue that men, or the academy, have already 'been there, done that'. Thus, Ruth Behar (1995) writes about the explanation by post-modernist anthropologist James Clifford as to why women were not included in the ground-breaking collection *Writing Culture* (Clifford and Marcus, 1986): 'women anthropologists were excluded because their writings failed to fit the requirements of being feminist and textually innovative.' Since 'experimental' ethnographic authority – like positivistic social science – is grounded in a masculine subjectivity, women's writing can be excluded both as deviating from conventional norms of good practice and as irrelevant to unconventional norms of innovative practice.

However, despite the tendency of some academic feminists to adopt the 'master's tools' in order to construct new feminist orthodoxies, often in a language not accessible to our research participants, to our students and, ultimately, to ourselves, there is a growing number of feminists whose writing combines genres, experiments with form and contents and situates both researcher and researched as living, experiencing subjects at the heart, not only of our research, but also of our writing.

This volume

The contributors to this volume show a commitment to processes of collaboration and participation in all their complexities. While individual contributions provide detailed observations concerning specific but varied projects and examine the disparate consequences for researchers and researched in utilising feminist research methodologies, there are several shared commonalities. The chapters in this volume represent research work that contributors consider to be part of an emancipatory, feminist research paradigm, work that is going on in contemporary Ireland. Contributors bear witness to the idea that research is a political act involving research choices which have political consequences. This pertains not only to the researcher's choice of methodological paradigm, but also to how she chooses to design, implement and work through the research process in collaboration with research participants (see Cynthia Cockburn and Marie Mulholland, Kathleen Lynch and Cathleen O'Neill). Contributors also provide evidence that research is a personal act, with personal consequences that spill over into researchers' own lives (Cathleen O'Neill, Maria Lohan, Ronit Lentin) and into the lives of the researched (Cynthia Cockburn and Marie Mulholland, Rosaleen McDonagh, Cathleen O'Neill).

Contributors are engaged with debates within feminist epistemology, interrogating categories, working the artificiality of the tension between objectivity and subjectivity and with the material reality and inequalities of researcher-researched relationships (Ricca Edmondson). Specifically, contributors are concerned with how consensus about the outcomes of research is reached and with following through to inform social policy decisions. In a number of chapters the concern with how consensus is reached is marked (Anne Byrne, Kathleen Lynch, Cathleen O'Neill, Rosaleen McDonagh), although devising ways of working with research participants is a key element of contributors' research practices. Kathleen Lynch reminds us that the onus for democratising the research process lies with researchers. Contributors to this volume offer compelling arguments for collaborating with research participants (see also chapters by Cathleen O'Neill and Rosaleen McDonagh). All the contributors are aware of the limitations of positivist methodologies and are concerned about the paucity of debate and evaluation of dominant and alternative paradigms. The explicit concern with questioning the status of knowledge and how we know what we know makes feminist methodologies attractive for researchers. Contributors observe the need for an 'extended epistemology' providing more than the partial view offered either by researchers or by the researched. This volume represents yet another strand in the debate concerning the 'ethics, method and politics' of research practice in Ireland (Daly, 1987): we look forward to your response.

Kathleen Lynch's chapter, 'The role of emanciptaory research in the academy', discusses the paradoxical position of feminist researchers in academic institutions which are implicated in the 'cultural reproduction of élites'. Lynch revisits the debate about the potential of feminist researchers in the academy to achieve emancipatory change, inviting us to reflexively consider our own research practices and the ideological context in which Irish social research takes place. Lynch provides an informative account of the historical development of Irish social research, characterised by the dominance of the positivist paradigm. As argued earlier, although the ethnographic tradition has been developed to a limited extent in Ireland, it is over-shadowed by the preference for policy-oriented research funded by government or voluntary or statutory agencies, which have favoured large-scale surveys and the use of empirical, quantitative, so-called 'scientific' methods. In only funding positivist-oriented research, the knowledge generated is further legitimated and the continuous proliferation of such research is guaranteed. While Lynch acknowledges the usefulness of the positivist paradigm, for example in measuring the effectiveness of social policies and in holding the state accountable for the persistence of inequalities, this is not what is of concern to her. Lynch points to the consistent acceptance by public and practitioners of what counts as valid research, acceptance of 'experts' as the only authentic knowers, combined with the unquestioning acceptance of 'objectivity' as reassurance that research is scientific, authentic and reliable. She argues that a 'culture of objectivism prevails which precludes a debate about the politics of research production'. Critics of positivism argue that interpreting the world from the viewpoint of the 'objective' researcher, using 'objective' research instruments, provides only a partial view of what is going on. Writing about models of participatory enquiry in social research, Reason has noted:

> If the propositions are generated exclusively by a researcher who is not involved in the experience being researched and are imposed without consultation on the practical and experiential knowledge of the subjects, we have findings that directly reflect neither the

experience of the researcher nor that of the subjects (Reason, 1994: 326).

Lynch observes that the positivist tradition in characteristically researching the powerless has no mechanism of entering into dialogue with research subjects concerning either research process or outcomes which may have consequences for their lives. For Lynch this is a 'human rights issue' and she proposes an emancipatory methodology for democratising the research process, outlining possibilities for creating knowledge in a partnership between researcher and researched. She concludes by presenting a challenge to feminist researchers committed to social transformation and invites us to exercise our academic freedoms and resist the academic culture of careerism and conformity, exposing 'the procedures and practices of those who control academic knowledge and discourse'. Lynch provides models of how we can democratise research structures and relations within the academy and engage in deeply transformative work.

Positioning herself as a 'working-class activist and researcher', Cathleen O'Neill's chapter, 'Naming our own world', is based on collaborative research in two projects in which she has worked. O'Neill evaluates the power of emancipatory research from the perspective of the 'researcher as insider'. Her prime concern is that research should benefit those who are researched, while challenging and extending the minimal research ethic of 'doing no harm'. The first project, researching women's experiences of poverty in Kilbarrack, north Dublin, was spurred by O'Neill's dissatisfaction with the ways so-called 'experts' had understood and written about poverty 'from the outside'. As a local working-class activist who shared conditions of poverty with the researched, and working with focus and support groups of local women, O'Neill constructed a collaborative project which not only highlighted the experiences of poverty (published by Combat Poverty Agency, O'Neill, 1992), but also resulted in a series of initiatives towards improving living conditions, including achieving the status of Designated Area of Disadvantage for the area researched. The second project was aimed at identifying education and development opportunities for stable women drug users in the SAOL project in north inner city Dublin and analysing the process and achievements of rehabilitation. The methodological principles of participatory research guided both projects, with participants becoming involved in every stage of data collection and production. In the SAOL project, this collaborative approach was chosen because it was in keeping with the educational and organisational ethos and processes used on a daily basis within the project where consultation with participants is a key tenet. Participants validated the findings at every stage. Through regular reviews of the study with the SAOL group, the researcher provided the opportunity to ensure a full understanding of the analysis, and for participants to maintain editorial control over the research findings and analysis.

O'Neill reflects on this process, sharing her own and the participants' evaluations of feminist emancipatory methodologies, emphasising the importance for women of 'naming their own worlds'. One of the now familiar claims of feminist research is that in devising participative or collaborative, non-oppressive research designs, the research process is more open and produces more accurate accounts of reality, an argument O'Neill herself makes. In devising a research design which allows research participants to name their own worlds and to collaboratively develop an interpretation and representation of their lives in an agreed formal report, O'Neill argues that the research becomes 'better' and 'more meaningful'. A number of questions arise: Can only 'insiders' engage in such a process? How do we know that the research produced is more accurate and for whom is it more meaningful? Holden (1996), and Reay (1996) for example, are among those who cite distinct disadvantage to being an 'insider researcher'. Perhaps the answer lies not so much in the differences between insider and outsider perspectives, but in the necessity of being politically and ideologically committed to collaboration, which can empower participants and produce meaningful research.

Describing themselves as 'feminists, researchers and activists', Cynthia Cockburn and Marie Mulholland provide us with revealing insights into the consequences for an activist organisation in becoming involved in a research project and the consequences for the researcher in doing research with an activist organisation. In their chapter 'Analytical action, committed research: What does a feminist action research partnership mean in practice?', the researcher (Cockburn) and the researched (Mulholland) write about the partnership and the interactions between an academic researcher and a feminist activist. Their chapter concerns the contradictions and difficulties of a methodology in which the researcher joins in the action of an activist organisation and in which the activist organisation takes on the extra responsibilities of meeting the demands of participatory research practices. The 'Women in Bridge-Building Project' has three aims: research, intervention and networking, based on the understanding that action research would make a practical contribution to the work of the three organisations involved: the Women's Support Network (Belfast, Northern Ireland), Medica Women's Association (Bosnia) and Bat Shalom (Northern Israel). Mulholland writes about the burden of the research on the organisation's resources and activities, and more specifically, about the effect of the research on internal organisational processes of negotiation and decision-making. She observes that the Women's Support Network bore much of the workload of editing, commenting and providing feed-back on materials produced by the research. Mulholland writes that 'this and other research activities was an enormous drain on our collective and individual capacities', pointing to the consequences for the researched of being involved in participatory research. Cockburn is also concerned about the different agendas, demands and pace between activism and research. She observes that it is difficult to separate action and research in a participatory model in which activists become involved in the research process and the researcher becomes involved in activism.

Revealingly, Cockburn could not stop being 'the researcher' despite the wishes of the women that she leaves her notebook behind 'and just hang out'. Despite the difficulties, challenges and mistakes, Cockburn describes her involvement in this research partnership as 'the single most rewarding research experience of my life'. Mulholland also notes the distinct personal and political benefits accrued to the organisations involved in the project, not the least being that the Women's Support Network has become an international commentator on the role of women in situations of conflict. In 'producing knowledge out of action together', Cockburn and Mulholland describe their research as 'committed research'. But they note that with the best collaborative intentions, in practice collaborative feminist research can place further pressures on the researched, as argued by Shields and Dervan (1993), a burden not to be glossed over in models of emancipatory research.

The construction of woman as Other has long been a critical concern of feminist sociological theorising which variously seeks to bring women from the margins into the centre of academic discourse or recognises the radical strength of being an Other in disrupting, destabilising, changing and challenging the discipline. More critically, attention to Otherness is based on theories of power and domination, of exploring the relationship between oppressor and oppressed, of undoing the construction of 'woman' as inferior and silent and revaluing women's experiences, voices and knowledges of the world. Othering is ultimately about relationship, and in her chapter, 'Researching one an-other', Anne Byrne argues that a focus on Othering generates sharp awareness of processes of exclusion and is a location from which much can be seen, sensed and said. The representation of Others' lives usually cannot be avoided in social science research, even if the researcher shares experience, connection or history with research participants. More commonly, we are not members of the group we are researching. The challenge is getting to know the world of the Other. Feminist research methodologies offer various strategies for 'interrupting Othering' (see for example hooks, 1981; Fine, 1994; Wilkinson and Kitzinger, 1996).

Some strategies are premised on the rule that we do not research what we cannot experience. Many of the demands exacted in using a feminist research framework are brought together in facing the challenges presented by the issue of Othering. Byrne describes a collaborative, feminist research project in which the researcher is not a member of the group being researched – single Irish women. She details the personal, professional and ethical challenges posed by drawing on and developing feminist research practices as the researcher and the participants attempt to build a shared interpretation of single women's identities in contemporary Ireland. The chapter describes a number of collaborative research practices which move towards 'a sociology *with* women', bringing what is privately experienced by the Other into a form of public knowledge that is change-oriented.

In her chapter, 'Writing between worlds', Ricca Edmondson raises new questions about writing sociological texts. According to her, writing is a form of mediation between worlds in which there are constant tensions of judgement about the liberties needed in order to represent the world one is describing, and what is needed so that readers appreciate what is going on in that world. Moreover, in qualitative research the investigator is her own main instrument. Feminist research traditions emphasise strongly the notion of reflexivity in order to stress the urgency of examining the researcher's integrity and accuracy. Edmondson argues that reflexivity does not entail merely importing the author's personality into her text but rather examining which of her claims are likely to be valid, and what justifies her audience in taking her seriously. While other chapters focus on the relationship between researcher and researched, Edmondson focuses on the writer-reader relationship, drawing our attention to the rhetorical devices researchers use in writing their texts. While a lot of attention is given to writing up research accounts, perhaps we need to develop alternatives to *written* texts as modes of interpreting, representing and communicating research results, as, for example, Romanie van Son's chapter suggests.

Maria Lohan reminds us that feminist methodologies are distinctive not only because they challenge us to think differently about knowledge in relation to women. They also challenge our taken-for-granted understanding of all 'scientific' knowledges. Lohan's chapter, 'Extending feminist methodologies: researching masculinities and technologies', extends a concern with feminist epistemologies to researching men's lives in the context of their relations with technology. Her research is among the few Irish feminist projects which research Irish men. Science and technology studies and feminist methodologies share a reflexive epistemology: both are concerned with how we know what we know. However, Lohan argues that the 'responsible reflexivity' of feminist epistemologies is more intellectually rigorous than the reflexivity practised in Science and Technology Studies. Lohan advances her argument by drawing on her experience of interviewing men, illustrating how a feminist methodology makes sense of knowledge concerning gender and technology.

Romanie van Son positions herself as a 'middle-class researcher' working in a development project with women living in a socio-economically disadvantaged community. As an outsider researcher she is committed to finding the most fitting and suitable ways of knowing both for herself and for the women with whom she is working. Aware of the potential of spoken language for miscommunication, misunderstanding and misinterpretation, van Son turns her practice of working with art and visual language into an alternative research method/medium. In 'Painting women into the picture', she writes that 'art was to be used as a vehicle, as a means – not as a receptacle or an end – for expression and for the telling of stories about the self, about women and about relationships.' Van Son argues that art can be used as a medium from which women can begin to construct and tell their own stories of their lives to themselves and to others. Van Son describes her work as making time and space for women as they familiarise themselves with the art materials, mixing paint colours, moulding and shaping clay. Her chapter documents the challenges for the researcher and the benefits for participants of working with art. Like other contributors, van Son is determined that participants be able to control and shape the content and direction of research and that research is beneficial to all involved.

In her chapter, 'Talking back', Rosaleen McDonagh identifies herself as a 'Traveller feminist' who has been 'used' and 'exploited' by researchers and who has witnessed the objectification of Traveller culture, the devaluing of Traveller identity and the representation of Traveller women as subordinated within a patriarchal culture in research carried out on Travellers. As a member of the researched, McDonagh argues that researchers' responsibility for the research process does not end with the production of findings or recommendations in a written report and urges the researcher to 'follow through' with the outcomes of research which can have real consequences for real people's lives (see Daly, 1987). Focusing on her experience of racism within the research process, McDonagh addresses power inequalities in researcher-researched relationships and questions the context, use and value of social research which benefits the researcher (through conferring of academic qualifications for example) but which is harmful to the researched. In 'Talking back' McDonagh outlines the basis of a charter for the researched as she places limits on research concerning Travellers, distinguishing between appropriate and inappropriate practices. Of fundamental importance is the inclusion of Travellers as active participants in the research process, with both researcher and researched moving towards a more collaborative, equitable relationship. McDonagh proposes that researchers negotiate with the researched about permissible areas of research, suggesting that only certain topics be researched, particularly those which actively advance the material improvement in Travellers' health and education, for example. She suggests that researchers become familiar with Traveller culture and scrutinise their own practice for racist and unethical behaviour. Finally she suggests that Travellers too must take responsibility for the research process.

Ronit Lentin extends other contributors' concern with the researched 'naming their own worlds' to the researcher herself becoming auto/biographically implicated in the research process as the researcher constructs, rather than re-constructs, her life and her self through working with her narrators' lived experiences. In her chapter, 'Constructing the self in narrative: feminist research as auto/biography', Lentin explores auto/biography as a feminist research strategy, placing the researcher's 'intellectual auto/biography' at the centre of her analysis, fully aware of the methodological dilemmas this raises. These dilemmas include the (im)possibility of 'doing' objectivity, the imposition on narrators by the demands of collaborative research, the blurring of the boundaries between researcher, friend and therapist, confidentiality and anonymity, and the ultimate impossibility of 'doing' impartiality. Other dilemmas raised by auto/biographical feminist research are the use of women's personal narratives as research and writing strategies. Describing her 'split subjectivity' as a member of a Shoah surviving family and of the first Israeli-born generation, Lentin argues that using personal narratives and the 'auto/biographical I' may help feminist researchers, writing in a multiplicity of voices, to 'name' themselves in the course of the research process, reminding us that reflexive feminist research may have serious implications, but also transformatory possibilities, not only for the researched, but also for the researcher.

Conclusion

Are we being too idealistic? While we continuously strive to follow principles of reflexivity, collaboration and emancipatory commitment to political change, anyone who has ever engaged in research knows it is a far messier process. As one of our survey respondents wrote:

> Of course there are huge difficulties and problems in honestly facing up to the ethical demands that stem from this (feminist) position. And in truth, the work is neither ever done nor ever done to one's best. There are always problems of overriding voices, of exploitation, of unacknowledged work. I very much accept that in my work as a feminist sociologist, I am always getting there; I have certainly never arrived at a satisfactory point where all the dilemmas that confront us in the field, as we write up, and as we publish results, have been adequately tended to at all. But it is a central part of my critical practice to realise that I am constantly being tested and challenged, and failing.

Another question we have to ask, but cannot answer fully, is whether truly emancipatory research is ever possible, given the power differentials in the existing structures. Power differentials between researcher and researched; power differentials within a patriarchal academy; class, ethnic, sexuality and (dis)ability power differentials; and power differentials in relation to funding and what is deemed as legitimate scholarship. This is a crucial consideration, but it must not stop us from striving and from holding on to the values that guide us in producing meaningful research.

The term 'feminist' is no longer a coherent, unitary, universal category. Like 'gender' and 'woman', there are many meanings for and many ways of being a 'feminist'. In interrogating these categories, the post-modern project has challenged the very basis of the political significance and transformative capacity of the women's movement. The relevance of feminist theorising, then, becomes inarticulate in trying to accommodate differences among women and questions the future viability of a feminist scholarship which marginalises itself and is marginalised by the academy. Another position is that the term 'feminist' is an umbilical cord tying scholarship and practice to the realities of injustice, oppression and inequalities, features of our existence as women which we witness in our everyday lives. In this sense to be a feminist is to be committed to researching, revealing and challenging injustice in women's lives in all their diversity, from a perspective which is grounded in feminist theory, ethics and politics.

In our survey inquiring about the politics and practice of naming oneself as a feminist researcher, respondents pointed to a range of possibilities in which they move and from which they can choose. Researchers utilise feminist epistemologies and methodologies as critical perspectives to position themselves and to provide a context for their intellectual work. In drawing on a feminist perspective, the feminist researcher also aligns herself with a broad community of scholars with whom she can share an identity. In utilising a feminist perspective, however, researchers do not always feel impelled to explicitly and publicly name *themselves* as feminist researchers in all contexts, with all audiences. Indeed such a naming can be perceived as being exclusive, 'holier than thou', and carrying the added disincentive that labelling oneself with the 'f word' is a barrier for others in listening to and reading what the feminist researcher has to say. Researchers who do put public labels aside believe that more attention is paid to the substance of their work, which nonetheless remains feminist in orientation and consequence and which challenges injustice in women's lives.

Not naming oneself as a feminist is one strategy of maintaining open dialogue and mainstreaming feminism with an audience potentially hostile to feminist ideas. Interestingly, our respondents did not perceive any inconsistency between resisting or mediating a public naming of oneself as a feminist and holding a private sense of themselves as feminist sociologists or researchers. We wonder is this not another way of saying 'I am not a feminist, but' ...? Indeed perceiving oneself as a feminist researcher is of great significance, providing coherence and meaning to the politics and ethics of one's life as a researcher. In this sense, to name oneself as a feminist researcher has deep ontological significance.

Working with each other it has become obvious to both of us that naming ourselves as feminists is a resistance strategy to being 'othered' and disempowered and to be rendered invisible. It also enables us to 'name our own world': a feminist perspective not only makes sense of the world which we inhabit (epistemology); it is also a way of being in the world (ontology) and of guiding our research practices (methodology).

There are many ways of being a feminist researcher, as contributors to this volume attest. Each contributor brings her own provocative insight and distinctive understanding and practice of feminist research methodologies. This volume represents a slice of what is going on in sociological inquiry from a feminist perspective in Ireland at this moment in time. Avoiding the pitfalls of establishing a feminist cannon of how to engage in research is difficult but necessary, as we learn that in using feminist principles to guide our research practice, we are free to make it our own.

References

Abdo, Nahla and Ronit Lentin (eds) (forthcoming), *Dissemi-nation: Narrating Palestinian and Israeli Gendered Auto/biographies of Dislocation,* Oxford and New York: Berghahn Books.

Abbott, Pamela and Claire Wallace (1990), *An Introduction to Sociology: Feminist Perspectives,* London: Routledge.

Acker, Joan, Kate Barry and Joanna Esseveld (1991), 'Objectivity and truth: problems in doing feminist research', in Mary M. Fonow and Judith A. Cook (eds), *Beyond Methodology: Feminist Scholarship as Lived Research,* Bloomington, Indiana: Indiana University Press.

Aniagolu, Chi Chi (ed.) (1997), *In from the Shadows: The UL Women's Studies Collection, vol.III,* Limerick: Department of Government and Society, University of Limerick.

Behar, Ruth (1995), 'Introduction: out of exile', in Ruth Behar and Deborah Gordon (eds), *Women Writing Culture,* Berkeley: University of California Press.

Bhavnani, Kum Kum (1993), 'Tracing the contours: feminist research and feminist objectivity,' *Women's Studies International Forum,* vol. 16, no. 2: 95-104.

Bonner, Kieran M. (1994), 'Post-methodology and social inquiry: an introduction,' in Roland Tormey, Anne Good and Carol MacKeogh (eds), *Post-Methodology? New Directions in Research Methodologies in the Social Sciences,* Dublin: Department of Sociology, Trinity College Dublin.

Bowles, Gloria and Renate Duelli-Klein (eds) (1983), *Theories of Women's Studies,* London: Routledge.

Brah, Avtar (1996), *Cartographies of Diaspora: Contesting Identities,* London: Routledge.

Bric, Maurice (1999), *The Humanities and Social Sciences: A Case for a Research Council. A Report to the Minister for Education and Science,* Dublin: Government Publications.

Byrne, Anne (1992), 'Academic Women's Studies in the Republic of Ireland', *Women's Studies Quarterly,* vol. 3 & 4: 15-27.

Byrne, Anne and Nuala Keher (1995), *Academics Don't Have Babies! Maternity Leave Amongst Female Academics.* Report for the Irish Federation of University Teachers, Dublin: IFUT.

Byrne, Anne, Pat Byrne and Ann Lyons (1996), 'Inventing and teaching Women's Studies: considering feminist pedagogy', *Irish Journal of Feminist Studies*, vol. 1, no. 1: 78-99.

Byrne, Anne and Madeleine Leonard (eds) (1997), *Women and Irish Society: A Sociological Reader,* Belfast: Beyond the Pale Publications.

Byrne, Anne (2000), *Single Women's Identities in Contemporary Irish Society,* PhD dissertation, Department of Government and Society, University of Limerick.

Byrne, Pat and Ann Lyons (1999), 'Approaches to feminist pedagogy: teaching Women's Studies', in Bríd Connolly and Anne B. Ryan (eds), *Women and Education in Ireland, 1999,* Dublin: Mace (Centre for Adult and Community Education), vol. 2.

Cantillon, Sara (1997), 'Women and poverty: differences in living standards within households', in Anne Byrne and Madeleine Leonard (eds), *Women and Irish Society,* Belfast: Beyond the Pale.

Connolly, Bríd and Anne B. Ryan (eds) (1999), *Women and Education in Ireland, 1999,* Dublin: Mace (Centre for Adult and Community Education), vol. 1-2.

Connolly, Linda (1999), '"Don't blame women": an exploration of current challenges facing feminist academics', in Bríd Connolly and Anne B. Ryan (eds), *Women and Education in Ireland, 1999,* Dublin: Mace (Centre for Adult and Community Education), vol. 1-2.

Cotterill, Pam and Gayle Letherby (1993), 'Weaving stories: personal autobiography in feminist research', *Sociology,* vol. 27, no. 1: 67-79.

Clifford, James and George Marcus (eds) (1986), *Writing Culture: The Poetics and Politics of Ethnography,* Berkeley: University of California Press.

Daly, Mary (1987), 'Feminist Research Methodology: The Case of Ireland', paper presented at the Third International Interdisciplinary Congress on Women, July 6-10 1987, Trinity College Dublin.

Davies, Celia (1993), 'The equality mystique: the difference dilemma and the case of women academics', *UCG Women's Studies Centre Review,* vol. 2: 53-72.

Drew, Eileen, Ruth Emerek and Evelyn Mahon (eds) (1998), *Women, Work and the Family in Europe,* London: Routledge.

Drew, Eileen, Peter Humphreys and Candy Murphy (1999), *Gender Imbalance in the Civil Service,* Dublin: Institute of Public Administration.

Du Bois, Barbara (1983), 'Passionate scholarship: notes on values, knowing and method in feminist social science', in Gloria Bowles and Renata Duelli-Klein (eds) (1983), *Theories of Women's Studies,* London: Routledge.

Fahey, Tony (ed.) (1999), *Social Housing in Ireland: A Study of Success,*

Failure and Lessons Learned, Dublin: Oaktree Press.

Fine, Michelle (1994), 'Working the hyphens: reinventing self and other in qualitative research', in Norman K. Denzin and Yvonna S. Lincoln (eds) (1994), *Handbook of Qualitative Research,* Sage: USA.

Fonow, Mary M. and Judith A. Cook (1991a) 'Back to the future: a look at the second wave of feminist epistemology and methodology', in Mary M. Fonow and Judith A. Cook (eds) (1991b), *Beyond Methodology: Feminist Scholarship as Lived Research,* Bloomington, Indiana: Indiana University Press.

Fonow, Mary M. and Judith A. Cook (eds) (1991b), *Beyond Methodology: Feminist Scholarship as Lived Research,* Bloomington, Indiana: Indiana University Press.

Friedman, Ariella (1999), 'On Israeli women's feminism, femininity and power', in Dafna Izraeli, Ariella Friedman, Henriette Dahan Kalev, Sylvie Fogiel-Bijaoui, Hanna Herzog, Manar Hasan and Hannah Naveh, *Sex Gender Politics,* Tel Aviv: Hakibbutz Hameuchad.

Game, Ann (1991), *Undoing the Social: Towards a Deconstructive Sociology,* Milton Keynes: Open University Press.

Gluck, Sherna B. and Daphne Patai (eds) (1991), *Women's Words: The Feminist Practice of Oral History,* New York: Routledge.

Hammersley, Martyn (1992), 'On feminist methodology', *Sociology,* vol. 26, no. 1: 187-206.

Hammersley, Martyn (1995), *The Politics of Social Research,* London: Sage.

Hannan, Damien F. (1988), 'Sociological research in Ireland: a response', in Liam O'Dowd (ed.), *The State of Social Science Research in Ireland,* Dublin: Royal Irish Academy.

Haraway, Donna (1987), 'Situated knowledge: the science question in feminism and the privilege of partial perspective', *Feminist Studies,* vol. 14: 575-99.

Harding, Sandra (1987), *Feminism and Methodology: Social Science Issues,* Bloomington, Indiana: Indiana University Press.

Health Research Board (2000), *Making Knowledge Work for Health: Towards Strategy for Research and Innovation for Health, A Consultation Document,* Dublin: Health Research Board.

Hill Collins, Patricia (1990), *Black Feminist Thought,* New York: Unwin Hyman.

Holden, Katherine (1997), 'The shadow of marriage: single women in England 1919-1939', PhD thesis, Department of Sociology, University of Essex, UK.

hooks, bell (1981), *Ain't I a Woman: Black Women and Feminism,* South End: USA.

Humphries, Beth (1997), 'From critical thought to emancipatory action: contradictory research goals', *Sociological Research Online,* vol. 2, no. 1 <www.socresonline.org.uk/socresonline/2/1/3.html>

Inglis, Tom (1997), 'Irish sexuality', *Irish Journal of Sociology*, vol. 7: 5-28.

Inglis, Tom (1998), Review of *Women and Irish Society: A Sociological Reader*, eds Anne Byrne and Madeleine Leonard, *fm*, Issue 2: 59.

Irish Journal of Feminist Studies (1997), Special Issue: Aspects of Irish Feminism, vol. 2, no. 1.

Jackson, John A. (1972), 'Some pitfalls in sociological practice', *Social Studies: Irish Journal of Sociology*: 8-23.

Jackson, John A. (1987), 'Social science in Ireland', *International Journal of Social Science*, no. CXII: 273-81.

Jayaratne, Tobi Epstein and Abigail Stewart (1991), 'Quantitative and qualitative methods in the social sciences: current feminist issues and practical strategies', in Mary M. Fonow and Judith A. Cook (1991), *Beyond Methodology: Feminist Scholarship as Lived Research*, Bloomington, Indiana: Indiana University Press.

Kelly, Mary Bridget (1995), 'Exploring feminist teaching: teaching feminism', *UCG Women's Studies Review*, vol. 3: 29-42.

Lather, Patti (1991), *Getting Smart: Feminist Research and Pedagogy With/In the Postmodern*, New York: Routledge.

Lentin, Ronit (1980), *Conversations with Palestinian Women*, Jerusalem: Mifras.

Lentin, Ronit (1993), 'Feminist research methodologies – a separate paradigm? Notes for a debate', *Irish Journal of Sociology*, vol. 3: 119-138.

Lentin, Ronit (1994), '"I'll be a post-feminist in post-patriarchy": reflexivity is a feminist issue', in Roland Tormey, Anne Good and Carol MacKeogh (eds), *Post-Methodology? New Directions in Research Methodologies in the Social Sciences*, Dublin: Department of Sociology, Trinity College Dublin.

Lentin, Ronit (1995), 'Explicitly feminist? Feminist research methodologies revisited', *UCG Women's Studies Centre Review*, vol. 3: 1-18.

Lentin, Ronit (ed.) (1995), *In from the Shadows: The UL Women's Studies Collection Vol I*, Limerick: Department of Government and Society, University of Limerick.

Lentin, Ronit (ed.) (1996), *In from the Shadows: The UL Women's Studies Collection Vol II*, Limerick: Department of Government and Society, University of Limerick.

Lentin, Ronit (1999), 'Racializing (our) Dark Rosaleen: feminism, citizenship, racism, antisemitism', *Women's Studies Review*, vol. 6: 1-18.

Lentin, Ronit (2000), *Israel and the Daughters of the Shoah: Re-occupying the Territories of Silence*, Oxford: Berghahn Books.

Linden, Ruth (1993), *Making Stories, Making Selves: Feminist Reflections on the Holocaust*, Columbus: Ohio State University Press.

Mahon, Evelyn (1994), 'Feminist research: a reply to Lentin', *Irish Journal of Sociology,* vol. 4: 165-9.

Miller, Nancy K. (1991), *Getting Personal: Feminist Occasions and Other Autobiographical Acts,* New York: Routledge.

Minister, Kristina (1991), 'A feminist frame for oral history interview', in Sherna B. Gluck and Daphne Patai (eds) (1991), *Women's Words: The Feminist Practice of Oral History,* New York: Routledge.

Mohanty, Chandra T. (1991), 'Under Western eyes: feminist scholarship and colonial discourses', in Chandra T. Mohanty, Ann Russo and Lourdes Torres (eds), *Third World Women and the Politics of Feminism,* Bloomington, Indiana: Indiana University Press.

Oakley, Ann (1981), 'Interviewing women: a contradiction in terms', in Helen Roberts (ed.), *Doing Feminist Research,* London: Routledge and Kegan Paul.

Oakley, Ann (1992), *Social Support and Motherhood,* Cambridge: Blackwell.

O'Connor, Pat (2000), 'Resistance in academia', paper presented to the International Conference on Women in Higher Education, New Orleans, January 2000.

O'Dowd, Liam (ed.) (1988), *The State of Social Science Research in Ireland,* Dublin: Royal Irish Academy.

O'Neill, Cathleen (1992), *Telling It Like It Is,* Dublin: Combat Poverty Agency.

O'Neill, Cathleen (1999), 'Reclaiming and transforming the (Irish) women's movement', *fm,* no. 3: 41-3.

Patai, Daphne (1991), 'US academics and third world women: is ethical research possible?', in Sherna Berger Gluck and Daphne Patai (eds), *Women's Words: The Feminist Practice of Oral History,* New York: Routledge.

Reason, Peter (1994), 'Three approaches to participative inquiry in qualitative research', in Norman K. Denzin and Yvonna S. Lincoln (eds) (1994), *Handbook of Qualitative Research,* Newbury Park: Sage.

Reay, Diane (1996), 'Insider perspectives or stealing the words out of women's mouths: interpretation in the research process', *Feminist Review,* no. 53: 57-73.

Reinharz, Shulamit (1983), 'Experiential analysis: a contribution to feminist research', in Gloria Bowles and Renate Duelli-Klein (eds) (1983), *Theories of Women's Studies,* London: Routledge.

Reinharz, Shulamit (1992), *Feminist Methods in Social Research,* New York: Oxford University Press.

Ribbens, Jane and Rosalind Edwards (eds) (1998), *Feminist Dilemmas in Qualitative Research. Public Knowledge and Private Lives,* Sage: UK.

Richardson, Laurel (1991), 'Postmodern social theory: representational practices', *Sociological Theory,* Fall 1991, vol. 9, no. 2, pp 173-179.

Richardson, Laurel (1994), 'Nine poems: marriage and the family', *Journal of Contemporary Ethnography,* vol. 23, no. 1, pp 3-13.

Riessman, Catherine K. (1987), 'When gender is not enough: women interviewing women', *Gender and Society,* vol. 1, no. 2: 172-207.

Rich, Adrienne (1993), 'As if your life depended on it', in Adrienne Rich, *What is Found There: Notebooks on Poetry and Politics,* New York: W.W. Norton.

Schwartz, Harry and Jerry Jacobs (1979), *Qualitative Sociology: Method to the Madness,* New York: Free Press.

Shakespeare, Pam, Dorothy Atkinson and Sally French (eds) (1996), *Reflecting on Research Practice: Issues in Health and Social Welfare,* Milton Keynes: Open University Press.

Shields, Vickie Routledge and Brenda Dervin (1993), 'Sense-making in feminist social science research: a call to enlarge the methodological options for feminist studies', *Women's Studies International Forum,* vol. 16, no. 1: 65-84.

Silverman, David (1997), 'Towards an aesthetics of research', in David Silverman (ed.), *Qualitative Research: Theory, Method and Practice,* London: Sage.

Smith, Dorothy (1987), *The Everyday as Problematic: Exploring the Relations of Ruling,* London: Routledge.

Smith, Emer (1997), 'Labour market structures and women's employment in the Republic of Ireland', in Anne Byrne and Madeleine Leonard (eds), *Women and Irish Society,* Belfast: Beyond the Pale.

Smyth, Ailbhe (1992), 'Women's Studies and "the disciplines"', *Women's Studies International Forum,* vol. 15, no. 5-6: 615-7.

Smyth, Ailbhe (1996), 'Reviewing Breaking the Circle: a pilot project', in Orla Egan (ed.), *Women Staff in Irish Universities, Proceedings of Conference in University College Cork,* Cork: Higher Education Equality Unit.

Smyth, Ailbhe (1998), 'Borderline crosstalk', in Liz Stanley (ed.), *Knowing Feminisms,* London: Sage.

Smyth, Ailbhe and Celesta McCann (1999), *A Study of Feminist Education as an Empowerment Strategy for Community-Based Women's Groups in Ireland,* Dublin: WERRC.

Stanley, Liz (1987), 'Our mothers' voices', Paper presented at the Third International Interdisciplinary Congress on Women, July 6-10 1987, Trinity College Dublin.

Stanley, Liz (1990a), *Feminist Praxis: Research, Theory and Epistemology in Feminist Sociology,* London: Routledge.

Stanley, Liz (ed.) (1990b), 'Feminist praxis and the academic mode of production: an editorial introduction', in Liz Stanley (ed.), *Feminist Praxis: Research, Theory and Epistemology in Feminist Sociology,* London: Routledge.

Stanley, Liz (1990c), '"A referral was made": behind the scenes during the creation of a Social Services Department "elderly" statistic', in Liz Stanley (ed.), *Feminist Praxis: Research, Theory and Epistemology in Feminist Sociology,* London: Routledge.

Stanley, Liz (1992), *The Auto/biographical I: Theory and Practice of Feminist Auto/Biography,* Manchester: Manchester University Press.

Stanley, Liz (1996), 'The mother of invention: necessity, writing and representation', *Feminism and Psychology,* vol. 6, no. 1: 45-51.

Stanley, Liz (1998a), 'Introduction: on academic borders, territories, tribes and knowledges', in Liz Stanley (ed.), *Knowing Feminisms,* London: Sage.

Stanley, Liz (1998b), 'Knowing feminisms and passing women: a conclusion', in Liz Stanley (ed.), *Knowing Feminisms,* London: Sage.

Stanley, Liz and Sue Wise (1983), *Breaking Out: Feminist Ontology and Epistemology,* London: Routledge and Kegan Paul.

Stanley, Liz and Sue Wise (1990), 'Method, methodology and epistemology in feminist research processes', in Liz Stanley (ed.), *Feminist Praxis: Research, Theory and Epistemology in Feminist Sociology,* London: Routledge.

Stanley, Liz and Sue Wise (1993), *Breaking Out Again: Feminist Ontology and Epistemology,* London: Routledge.

Tormey, Roland, Anne Good and Carol MacKeogh (eds) (1994), *Post-Methodology? New Directions in Research Methodologies in the Social Sciences,* Department of Sociology, TCD and TCD Sociology Postgraduates Group: Dublin.

Wilkinson, Sue and Celia Kitzinger (eds) (1995), *Feminism and Discourse: Psychological Perspectives,* London: Sage.

Wilkinson, Sue and Celia Kitzinger (1996), 'Theorising representing the Other', in Sue Wilkinson and Celia Kitzinger (eds), *Representing the Other: A Feminism and Psychology Reader,* London: Sage.

Yeates, Nicola (1997), 'Gender and the development of the Irish social welfare system', in Anne Byrne and Madeleine Leonard (eds), *Women and Irish Society,* Belfast: Beyond the Pale.

Yuval-Davis, Nira (1997), *Gender and Nation,* London: Sage.

Feminist Research Methodology: The Case of Ireland

Mary Daly[1]

This paper is part of a personal engagement. Schooled in the tradition of positivist sociology (still widely dominant in the education of social scientists in Ireland) I have for some time felt a disquiet about my own research practice. Three particular areas concern me. The first is a matter of ethics: the conventional relationship between the researcher and the researched I perceive as exploitative, denying the respondent fundamental rights in the research process and removing her/his control over the interpretations placed on the information generated by the research or the uses to which it is subsequently put. The second area of concern is the efficacy of the available methodologies. Over the course of a career that spans ten years in full-time employment as a researcher, I have come to seriously question the utility of conventional research methods, having experienced for myself the way that they can distort data and the fallacy of many of the assumptions that underlie the scientific method. My third area of concern is the relationship between my research practice and my own political agenda. Questions such as the following are central here: What happens as a result of the research that I carry out, and how does it relate to my own ideology? What kind of social order and relations of power am I through my research practice helping to perpetuate and reproduce?

It would be fallacious to regard these three concerns as solely personal problems. They are not. Each has a parallel for sociology as a discipline, questioning in turn the ethical basis of much of the research that is produced within the discipline, the efficacy of many

---

[1] Paper presented to the Third International Interdisciplinary Congress on Women, 6-10 July, 1987, Dublin, and reproduced here unchanged.

of the research methods available, and the relationship between scholarship within sociology and the larger social order. This paper looks at the potential of feminist research as a way of addressing these and other issues.

Feminist research methodology is explored therefore as part of a genuine quest for better practice. My aspiration is similar to that of Farganis:

> It is a sociology which offers understanding to subjects, which provides them access to the world they experience, starts with concrete, not abstract, notions, and unearths the ties of that everyday world to the structures of social organisations which surround it (Farganis, 1986: 60).

Focus is placed here on the possibilities which feminist research offers to produce research that is ethical and meaningful for all participants of the process. From within the discipline of sociology, the paper attempts to answer two questions:

– What are the defining characteristics of feminist research methodology?
– To what extent is it represented within existing research practice and scholarship in Ireland?

At the outset three clarifications are in order. First, the paper assumes general familiarity with and acceptance of the feminist critique of the androcentric nature of almost all existing scholarship. The evidence is presented too convincingly elsewhere to require restatement here (Smith, 1974; Bernard, 1975; Morgan, 1981; Oakley, 1986). Second, it must be said that a rather narrow view is taken of conventional methodology. It is used mainly to refer to empiricist positivist methodology within which scientific rationality and objectivity are key elements. Third, feminism is not a unitary phenomenon. However, it is in my view far less homogeneous at a theoretical level than it is as methodology, although it is characterised by the use of a diversity of research methods. It is these methods which this paper hopes to explore.

Feminist research methodology: its nature and form

The nature of feminist research is best understood by placing it within the context of its development – women's struggle for political, economic and intellectual recognition and power. Feminist research is linked to that struggle, its quest is to generate knowledge for and with women for the purpose of reclaiming women's experience and breaking down male-dominated structures. It has therefore a political agenda: to produce information about women's lives that is meaningful and can lead to their empowerment. Feminist research is characterised by three central insights:

– rejection of a limited definition of the kind of activity that produces knowledge and a critique of dominant research methodologies
– recognition that all research is political or based on interests
– commitment to utilise the knowledge generated by research for the empowerment of women.

Feminist research can lay claim to having invented few if any 'new' methods. Nor could it be said to involve a unique logic of enquiry or methodology. What makes feminist research different is:

• its focus on women
• the emphasis it places on understanding and redefining the social relations of the research process
• the linking of research to a particular ideology or political purpose.

Feminism shares some of its fundamental criticisms of conventional scholarship with other 'movements' within sociology. For instance, its recognition of the 'interest based' nature of all knowledge is mirrored in the work of Critical Theory and members of the Frankfurt School. However, feminism diverges from the Frankfurt School in its characterisation of the androcentric nature of existing scholarship, in the lesser importance it attributes to rationality and in that its political agenda is the empowerment of women rather than the liberation and communalisation of society (Farganis, 1986: 60).

To outline the distinctive features of feminist research methodology, it is helpful to compare it to conventional research methodology. A sense of caution is apposite here since this involves compartmentalising the research process into stages, an exercise that is especially artificial in the case of feminism. Nor should it be interpreted from what follows that feminist research methodology is in any sense a complete entity. Not at all. Feminist methodology is in the process of *becoming;* by its very nature it is developmental and cannot be a closed approach. There is therefore no absolute 'correct' feminist methodology, no one true way of carrying out feminist research, but the general principles can be outlined.

The following sections work through some of the defining characteristics of feminist research by comparing its method and practice to that of conventional research on a number of dimensions.

The nature of research as an activity

Conventional sociology views research as a distinct activity, a specific exercise engaged in to produce knowledge through the application of a set of techniques and procedures. Feminist research, in contrast, takes a broad view of the types of activity that constitute research: technically, any situation can be construed as research if it produces knowledge. The methods or techniques are not allowed to determine the research situation but are adapted to the ongoing activity. Research in the feminist mode is therefore not an activity that is unique or remote from ongoing activities or interaction. Indeed, certain scholars exhort feminist researchers to focus on the situation at hand, i.e. to use existing activities and routine interactions as a focus for research (Stanley and Wise, 1983; Cooke and Fonow, 1986). This is arguably especially important given the hidden or private worlds that many women occupy.

Epistemological assumptions underlying research

Positivism holds that in any occurrence there is one true set of events – 'the facts' – and that this 'truth' can be established only if the researcher follows particular procedures (Stanley and Wise, 1983: 193). Feminism, along with other emergent schools of thought (phenomonology, hermaneutics), disagrees. For these, truth is meaning which is established or constructed through the research process in consultation with all the participants. The search for a 'grand theory' is rejected: the goal for feminism is not to produce one theory which explains the position of all women, but to provide a framework which is capable of accommodating the diversity of women's lives (Reinharz, 1983; Rutenberg, 1983).

A further source of problems with the positivist method is its claim to be value-free or objective. First, one must question whether value-free research is possible. In that it is accomplished by the researcher suspending her/his judgement and values, it is virtually impossible to achieve. Problematic in this regard also is the tendency to assume that quantification is equivalent to objectivity. In addition, because knowledge is regarded as value-free, it is seen as neutral. Positivism therefore fails to recognise that its own research is an instrument of control and that its produce can be used to control the lives of others.

In summary, there exists a flourishing critique of the normative structure of positivism to which feminists like Dorothy Smith and Jessie Bernard have made a major contribution (Smith, 1974; Bernard, 1975). Two central failings of positivism from a feminist perspective are: its uncritical nature, especially in relation to its own presumed objectivity, and the fact that it ignores participants' construction of meaning and gives them little or no opportunity to contribute at this level.

The contrast between the epistemological assumptions that underlie positivism and those of 'alternative methodologies', feminism included, is perhaps best illustrated by adapting a diagram used by Reinharz (1983: 168-9). The following diagram contrasts some claims of positivism with those of alternative methodologies.

Positivist Sociology aims to be	'Alternative Methodologies' aim to be
Rational	Intuitive and rational
Scientific	Artistic and accurate
Objective	Objective and subjective
Impersonal	Personal
Oriented to structure	Oriented to process
Capable of producing general principles	Capable of producing specific explanations
Statistically valid	Meaningful
In search of a grand theory or one truth	In search of a common framework to accommodate the experience of all
Oriented to predicting and controlling events	Oriented to understanding phenomena

Motivations for undertaking research

Because feminist research has its roots in connecting political and intellectual practice, its ultimate goal is to effect some form of change. Within the feminist research tradition then, it is legitimate to undertake research for the express purpose of bringing about change, either in the researcher herself, in other participants of the research process, in the research circumstance or situation, or in all three. Here, the notion of research *for* women rather than *on* women becomes central (Smith, 1979). The empowerment of women is the ultimate goal and research is a vital tool in achieving it. Growth and change through the exchange and construction of meaningful information and knowledge is the key motivation for undertaking feminist research.

The practice of research

Arguably, one of the greatest strengths of feminist research is the emphasis it places on understanding and re-appraising the social relations of the research process. An important challenge that feminism has set itself is to create egalitarian relationships between the researcher and the researched. There are a number of aspects to this.

First, in its execution, feminist research actively tries to break down the customary hierarchical relationship between the researcher and the researched. In conventional research, the researcher/ respondent relationship is vertical, defined by the authority of the researcher. The researcher is the expert – the one who 'knows' – and is accorded almost total power over the research situation. Feminism challenges this, with enormous implications for the role of the researcher and the practice of research. For the researcher it requires that she shed the conventional role of authority and become part of the research dynamic – just one participant among many. Within the tradition of feminist research, the information produced by research is truly an outcome of the *research process* – in the sense that it is knowledge that has been validated by all those involved in the research – rather than a 'scientific' conclusion that has been reached by the researcher in isolation.

Thus the relationship between the researcher and the researched is redefined. A key element of this is that the respondent is given rights in the research situation; in the ideal situation she/he is allowed the freedom to structure the research exercise, the autonomy to draw up the issues which she/he feels are important, and some control over how the information is interpreted and how it is subsequently used. Thus, the researcher becomes a partner in the research exercise with the other participants and the old power balance of the relationship is overturned in favour of the respondent. Their emerging relationship is characterised by power sharing, co-operativeness, interaction, trust and honesty.

In this way, the rigid subject/object dichotomy which positivism regards as sacrosanct is outlawed. Instead of trying to suspend her own values and attitudes, the researcher adopts an attitude of conscious subjectivity (not to be interpreted as uncritical acceptance) whereby she contributes and shares her own experience as it becomes relevant (Duelli-Klein, 1983: 94-5).

What is defined and acceptable as data

In mainstream or positivist sociology, data is predominantly quantitative – it is either collected in a quantitative form or subsequently translated into a numerical format. The 'alternative methodologies', feminism included, have broadened the definition of what is acceptable as data. Qualitative information such as experience, emotions, feelings or actions, as described by the self or others, have become data. What is happening is that the personal or the everyday have become important foci of study in their own right. It has become legitimate to focus in detail on situations which involve just one or a small number of actors. Relatedly, the private, emotional dimensions of experience have become valid subject areas for research. Data has also been redefined to the extent that the researcher's own experience, either her/his substantive contributions on the topic of enquiry or her/his experience of the research itself, has become acceptable as data.

Methods of study

There is no distinctive feminist research technique, although a number of particular methods are associated with, and have been further developed or refined by, feminist researchers. It is argued that there is no one method that is universally suitable for research on women. Rather, a flexible approach is recommended, so as to allow the nature of the research situation to determine which method(s) are the most appropriate. The principles underlying feminist research indicate that whatever research technique is used it should:

- be applied in an interactional rather than a linear way
- yield information on the research process.

The latter point bears emphasis because it has become the norm in research to under-report the conditions under which data was derived, in the same way that is not unusual for a senior researcher on a research study never to have encountered the data-gathering situation or the respondents. For feminist research, in contrast, it is all important that the researcher outline the sources of her knowledge as well as the conditions under which it was constructed.

Feminist research has become associated with the qualitative methodologies, i.e. those that are person-centred and experiential. In an extremely useful article, Cook and Fonow (1986) outline some innovative applications that have been used in feminist methodology. They include visual techniques, linguistic techniques, textual analysis, collaborative strategies, triangulation of methods (the use of more than one research technique simultaneously) and refined quantitative approaches (the examples given relate to refining measures of female labour force participation in Third World countries, investigation of the effects of the context on survey responses to questions about abortion, the use of an 'attitudes towards feminism scale').

Outcomes of research

As has been emphasised throughout, feminist research is not just the pursuit of knowledge *per se*; it is ultimately oriented to bringing about change – its goal being to produce information for women which can be used in transforming their situation. A relationship exists between research and social action at three levels:

- producing information to back up claims for reform
- lobbying on the basis of research findings
- the research exercise itself being a means of bringing about

> change through consciousness raising, similar to Paulo Freire's
> concept of 'conscientization' which has been adapted to feminist
> analysis by Mies (1983).

This political agenda imposes certain responsibilities on the researcher. First, it suggests that the research does not end once the information has been written up or otherwise reported. Given that research may be a step in the process of change, the researcher (and the other participants of the research process in some cases) must continue to see through the dissemination of the research findings to the stage where some action is taken on them. This means that the researcher should ensure that the findings are accessible, both in the sense of being widely disseminated but also in that they are written or presented in a way that can be understood.

Having outlined the outstanding characteristics of feminist research methodology, to what extent have they informed research practice in this country?

The state of feminist research in Ireland

Women in Ireland cannot lay claim to a body of feminist scholarship. While a number of studies of women have been carried out, and while there is a general move underway to redress women's exclusion from existing scholarship, little of the work that has been done could be said to be distinctively feminist if the above criteria are applied. Among disciplines, history stands out as the academic discipline which has generated most work that is feminist in nature. Other academic disciplines have been less fruitful. It is insightful to consider the extent to which feminist research methodology as outlined, as distinct from studies of women, has informed sociological research practice in this country by taking each of the stages outlined above.

As regards what is considered to be legitimate research activity, the definitions of what is acceptable remain very narrow. Research is generally seen as survey-type activity which is specifically undertaken to answer the questions posed by the researcher, usually determined by the needs of the funder.

Relatedly, positivistic assumptions typically underlie most research practice in Ireland at the present time. Because the funders or sponsors of research, usually state institutions, consider only survey-type research as 'real' research, the positivist logic of enquiry is widespread here. It is interesting to note, however, that the constrained financial situation is effecting some change in the nature of the studies being undertaken. Surveys, because they are so expensive, are being engaged in more discerningly and there is some evidence of greater use, and greater sharing, of the results. There now appears to be a greater acceptance of process-oriented research, again due in part to the financial situation. A significant influence here has been the increasing popularity of evaluation research which, if undertaken by sociologists, tends to accord 'process' factors a central place.

There has been little or no change in the motivations for undertaking research. While individuals may undertake research for reasons that may be feminist (i.e. to bring about change in the position of women by generating new knowledge), the bulk of research activity in sociology in this country continues to be undertaken for one of two reasons: to provide information for policy-making; to increase the store of academic knowledge.

Like many other countries, some sectors of the Irish population are rapidly becoming 'over-surveyed'. Working-class communities in urban areas, suburban, market research-type (i.e. middle-class) respondents, and certain rural communities are amongst the most common populations for research in Ireland today. The possibility of a greater public familiarity with the research exercise has effected some change in the practice of research. It has become more difficult to conceal the purpose of the research from people and the fact that one is less assured of a positive response has forced researchers to consider the needs of the respondents and the potential benefits of the research to them. All of this has acted to increase, in however minimal a way, researchers' receptivity to the researched. It has not, however, led to any fundamental re-appraisal of the power imbalance between the researcher and the researched.

Data also continues to be viewed largely as quantitative in nature although there is some evidence that emotions, feelings and subjects which are of a private nature are becoming more acceptable as data. Postgraduate research is particularly important in this regard.

Some movement towards the diversification of research methods is discernible due again largely to financial constraints. There is also evidence of more flexibility in the choice and application of methods – a greater receptivity on the part of researchers to the limitations and strengths of particular methods.

Finally, with regard to the outcomes of research, little progress is being made. The application of the knowledge generated by research has generally been disappointing – little change has resulted from the research that has been carried out. To some extent this is a reflection of the fact that research has not been widely disseminated and that it is not presented in an accessible form. Researchers also have been slow to assume the responsibility to 'take their research further'.

Overall, then, it must be concluded that feminist research methodology has not influenced research practice in sociology in Ireland to any significant degree.

Although it is an exercise that is fraught with risk, it is important to try and isolate some factors that account for this. I suggest that there are three.

First, there has been little or no *collaboration* among feminists. In academic circles, women work largely in isolation from scholars within their own discipline or those from different disciplines. The ethos that prevails within the academy or university – competitive, product-oriented, overtly non-political – has been a key influence in that it has impeded the capacity of women to work together. Neither has there been any real collaboration in the sense of sharing and exchange between women in the academy and those in the wider community. It is noticeable also that even when they do contribute to education activities in the community, many women academics make little effort to develop egalitarian relationships with these women. This is especially disappointing given the exciting developments that have been taking place among women in urban communities in recent years. Linked in with adult education activities, many local women's groups have been formed, leading in some cases to a process of politicisation among groups of women in the community. Undoubtedly class or status factors are instrumental in maintaining the divide between academic women and women in the community.

A second contributory factor is the *gate-keeping practices* that have been engaged in by both male and female scholars. Located mainly within academic circles, they have done their work well in denying legitimacy to work that does not conform to a conventional positivist mode. Gatekeeping can take many forms. One of the most serious is the exclusion from jobs or positions. Important also is denying access to large-scale funding and to channels or activities which help to legitimate the findings of research, e.g. journal publications, conference presentations, etc.

A third factor that must be taken into account is the *content* and *orientation* of the work that has been undertaken by feminist scholars in this country. We have for the most part been content to 'add women on' and to rediscover women's lost history. While this is a legitimate goal in its own right, especially in the early stages of a feminist movement, it is unlikely to lead to a body of scholarship that is distinctively feminist along the lines outlined above. For this to take place, we must undertake a fundamental re-appraisal of the capacity of existing methodologies and structures of knowledge, to comprehend the experience of women.

So what are we to do?

I feel that it is imperative that Irish feminist scholars/activists begin to work together. Our task is clear: to develop concepts and frameworks that are capable of understanding the experiences of Irish women. In the words of Renate Duelli-Klein, to work towards our own paradigms, to develop ways to:

> Go about researching the process; the interaction, the mutual and inseparable dependency of facts and feelings, figures and intuition, the obvious and the hidden, doing and talking, behaviours and attitudes (Duelli-Klein, 1983: 98).

It is only when we begin to exchange our information, experience and feelings in an open and trusting way that we can build up a body of Irish feminist research.

References

Bernard, Jessie (1975), *Women, Wives, Mothers: Values and Options*, Chicago: Adlinc.

Cooke, Judith and Mary Margaret Fonow (1986), 'Knowledge and women's interests: issues of epistemology and methodology in feminist sociological research', *Sociological Inquiry*, 56, 1: 2-29.

Duelli-Klein, Renate (1983), 'How to do what we want to do: thoughts about feminist methodology', in Gloria Bowles and Renate Duelli-

Klein (eds), *Theories of Women's Studies*, London: Routledge and Kegan Paul.

Farganis, Sondra (1986), 'Social theory and feminist theory: the need for dialogue', *Sociological Inquiry*, 56, 1.

Mies, Maria (1983), 'Towards a methodology for feminist research', in Gloria Bowles and Renate Duelli-Klein, *Theories of Women's Studies*, London: Routledge and Kegan Paul.

Morgan, David (1981), 'Men, masculinity and the process of sociological enquiry', in Helen Roberts (ed.), *Doing Feminist Research*, London: Routledge and Kegan Paul.

Oakley, Ann (1986), 'Feminist sociology – is it possible?' in Ann Oakley, *Telling the Truth about Jerusalem*, London: Basil Blackwell.

Reinharz, Shulamith (1983), 'Experiential analysis: a contribution to feminist research', in Gloria Bowles and Renate Duelli-Klein (eds), *Theories of Women's Studies*, London: Routledge and Kegan Paul.

Rutenberg, T. (1983), 'Learning women's studies', in Gloria Bowles and Renate Duelli-Klein (eds), *Theories of Women's Studies*, London: Routledge and Kegan Paul.

Smith, Dorothy (1974), 'Women's perspective as a radical critique of sociology', *Sociological Inquiry*, 44, 1: 7-13.

Smith, Dorothy (1979) 'A sociology for women', in J. Sherman and E. Beck (eds), *The Prism of Sex: Essays in the Sociology of Knowledge*, Madison: University of Wisconsin Press.

Stanley, Liz and Sue Wise (1983), '"Back into the personal" or: our attempt to construct "feminist research"', in Gloria Bowles and Renate Duelli-Klein (eds), *Theories of Women's Studies*, London: Routledge and Kegan Paul.

2

The Role of Emancipatory Research in the Academy

Kathleen Lynch

Introduction

This chapter is written in the context of debates within feminist theory and cognate disciplines regarding the role of research in the academy.[1] It explores the limitations of positivist methodologies and examines the implications of adopting an emancipatory research perspective for equality issues. The epistemological framework for the chapter is one which supposes that the purpose of academic discourse is not only to describe and explain the world, but also to change it. It shares its intellectual and epistemological origins with critical theory (as developed by Habermas, 1971, particularly), Marxism, and other inter-disciplinary fields of investigation focused on transformative action including Equality Studies and Disability Studies. The basic questions it asks, therefore, are not only descriptive or explanatory; they are also visionary and utopian. The chapter tries to focus on potentiality as well as on actuality, on what is *possible* as much as on what *is*; it attempts to develop a concept of the alternative rather than simply accepting the given.

Research is inevitably politically engaged, be it by default, by design, or by recognition. No matter how deep the epistemological commitment to value neutrality, decisions regarding choice of subject, paradigmatic frameworks, and even methodological tools, inevitably involve political choices, not only within the terms of the discipline, but in terms of wider political purposes and goals.

---

[1] This chapter is a revised and edited version of a paper previously published in the *Economic and Social Review* (Lynch, 1999).

The academy and academic knowledge in particular are deeply implicated in the operations of power. To explore the business of power, this chapter examines the structural conditions under which feminist research (and research in cognate disciplines focused on the study of inequality or injustice) is undertaken. These are conditions of work that feminist research shares with many other researchers in the human rights and social scientific fields, conditions that impinge directly on the outcomes of research. For it is the case that many of those who study issues such as equality, human rights, race, gender, social class, poverty or disability are not simply detached scholars with no interest in policy or change. Most people who work on such issues do so because of the apparently unjust and evil outcomes which blatant racism, sexism, homophobia, classism, and/or disablism visit upon society (Siraj-Blatchford, 1995: 209). Their work has its origin in the Enlightenment vision of education and research as tools for the development and improvement of society, even though such a vision may not always be explicitly articulated.

The question which has to be addressed first, however, is whether the academy, which is so deeply implicated in the cultural reproduction of élites, can facilitate emancipatory change *via* research and education. Given the embeddedness of the academic world in the business of cultural production and reproduction, it is not at all self-evident how a given discipline or academic discourse can contribute to radical social change. Universities *qua* institutions are engaged in élite forms of cultural production. Moreover, they are heavily engaged in the practice of cultural monopoly, not only through their selection procedures for students and staff, but also through their rigorous boundary maintenance procedures within and between disciplines, and between what is defined as academic knowledge and what is not (Bourdieu, 1978; 1984). Yet, within all institutions there is scope for resistance; there are contradictions which can be exploited and utilised at all levels of education, including higher education (Giroux, 1983).

Research on equality and the limitations of traditional positivist[2] methodologies

There has been very little independent research funding available to the social sciences in Ireland since the foundation of the state. Although state aid for social scientific research was substantially increased in 1998, the research fund of the Irish Social Science Research Council (SSRC) was only in the region of £100,000 per annum as recently as the mid-1990s. While some of the international research foundations did offer grants to Irish researchers, there was no major foundation within Ireland sponsoring social scientific research. Up to the end of 1999 the bulk of the money available for such research was available for commissioned studies for state-sponsored projects. Such funding provided the core funding for the work of the Economic and Social Research Institute (ESRI) and the Educational Research Centre (ERC). The lack of funding for the Social Science Research Council, and the dearth of well-established research foundations, has meant that Irish researchers have had only two options in relation to research funding: they either undertook government-funded research (if and when they were invited to tender for it), or they sought out some of the minor funding offered by a host of voluntary, statutory and other agencies.

The lack of funding for basic research meant that much of the work undertaken was of an applied nature, frequently designed to answer a specific policy query for the funder. Such a system was, and is, heavily biased in favour of empirical (especially quantitative) research in the positivist tradition. The published work of the ESRI and the ERC exemplifies the stronghold which positivism has had in the social sciences in Ireland. Although there have been moves away from this tradition in recent years (as is evident from the nature of the material published increasingly in the *Irish Journal of Sociology* or in *Irish Educational Studies*), positivism still maintains a stronghold on social scientific practice. In view of its dominant position, it is important to identify its strengths and limitations, especially in relation to such a morally-loaded subject as equality.

---

[2] While positivist here refers primarily to quantitative studies, much of qualitative research operates out of similar principles in its research design (Oliver, 1992; Jayaratne and Stewart, 1995).

Much of the policy debate about poverty and inequality in society generally (especially in terms of social class/ socio-economic groups) has been framed within the language of analysis of positivism. Work within the positivist tradition has played an important role in the policy arena, particularly in matters related to education. The work of what are sometimes called the 'equality empiricists' has been especially effective in holding the state to public account regarding the implementation of its stated policies on equality. In Ireland, for example, the work of Breen et al (1990), Clancy (1988, 1995), Callan et al (1996), Cormack and Osborne (1995), Dowling (1991), and Hannan et al (1996) has played an important role in challenging the state on the effectiveness of various policies for the promotion of social justice in education and society generally. In the gender area, work by Barry (1996), Drew (1999), Mahon et al (1998), and Ruane and Sutherland (1999) has performed a similar function. In certain respects, this type of 'political arithmetic' is crucially important for holding the state publicly accountable. It is a vital tool of democracy in a world where inegalitarian ideologies are gaining hold:

> At a time of increasing social inequalities and injustice, when the 'self-regulating' market threatens to undermine the foundations of social solidarity ... and when the dominant ideology of meritocracy in liberal democratic societies has been seriously weakened at the same time that right-wing politicians proclaim the 'classless society', a new political arithmetic must be asserted as a vital tool of democracy as well as of sociology (Brown et al, 1997: 37).

When positivist research is sufficiently critical and independent, it also has the potential to facilitate social and individual reflexivity; it informs the general body politic, giving it access to knowledge which is detached from the powerful interests of government and media (Halsey, 1994).

In the international arena the merits of traditional positivist methodologies for the understanding of social phenomena generally, and inequality in particular, have been debated intensely in recent years. Positivism has not been without its defendants; Hammersley (1992; 1995), although not subscribing to a crudely positivist view, has been among the more vocal of these. Post-modernists, critical theorists and feminist scholars have been, however, among the most ardent critics of positivist epistemologies and methodologies (Bernstein, 1976; 1983; Harding, 1987; 1991; Humphries, 1997; Lentin, 1993; Reay, 1996; Smith, 1987; Stanley and Wise, 1983). Their work demonstrates how, despite its visible benefit as a tool of political arithmetic, mainstream positivism has severe limitations from both a philosophical and a moral standpoint (Reason and Rowan, 1981; Reason, 1988).

The model of the person employed by positivist models is one which regards people as 'units of analysis'; it treats them as 'variables' whose attributes can be neatly reified into dependent and independent types. People are not defined therefore in a holistic way; understanding of their subjectivity and their relational conditions of structured inequality often become invisible. What Bourdieu (1973) once referred to as 'the substantialist atomism of the social sciences' conceals the structural and relational conditions which generate inequality, injustice and marginalisation. The person is treated as a detached atom (undoubtedly with attributes of gender, class, race, ethnicity, etc); the language of analysis does not identify the sets of relations through which particular attributes are translated into particular inequalities. The research focuses on how particular characteristics, such as colour, class or religion, are associated or correlated with particular outcomes, such as occupational status, education or legal provision. There is a tendency to locate the causative factors contributing to particular inequalities therefore in the attributes of those experiencing inequality, in their gender, poverty, or race, rather than in structured relations, planned and unplanned exclusionary systems, which transform individual attributes into generative forces for inequality.

Moreover, once the research has identified correlations and associations between individual attributes and inequality outcomes, this is generally regarded as sufficient for promoting an understanding of the underlying causes of inequality. Such methodological individualism creates a silence around the social, economic, political, legal and cultural relations of inequality. There is no space in which to debate or frame radical structural critiques or alternative visions based on relational understanding.

While it could be argued that the failure to examine the relational character of inequality is a universal problem within the social sciences, rather than one which is tied to positivist methods, the fact that the issue has received so little attention is undoubtedly related to the culture of assumed objectivity which dominates positivist discourse. The role of the researcher is defined as that of 'disinterested' observer and analyst; one is expected to discover 'truths' via the use of reliable research instruments and rational discussion; the goal is to represent reality accurately, no matter how limited that particular reality may be. The researchers are defined as beyond politics; their knowledge is 'innocent' and untainted by political agendas. Thus, a culture of objectivism prevails which precludes a debate about the politics of research production. It allows methodological individualism to persist as long as it operates according to the scientific canon of objectivity. There is no framework for analysing the epistemological and ethical limitations of one's own position; questions regarding the purposes and outcomes of research are defined as being the work of policy-makers rather than researchers.

The methodological individualism underpinning positivism also focuses attention on the powerless rather than the powerful, while failing to explore relations between the two. While there are studies of inequality which focus on the impact and influence of the powerful and wealthy in society (studies on white collar crime by McCullagh [1995] and Tomlinson et al [1988] being cases in point), there are proportionately many more studies on the vulnerable and subordinate (Chambers, 1983). The lack of a substantial body of empirical data in Ireland on the egalitarian/social justice impli-cations of the operation of the money markets or the ownership structures of equities and other forms of corporate and productive wealth[3] indicates how biased the focus of analysis has been. We are often presented with a detailed analysis of the lifestyle of those who are subordinate or poor, while little attention is devoted to the analysis of the generative forces and processes which maintain others in positions of dominance and/or affluence. Feminists are not immune from this problem either, as oppressions of class, colour or ethnicity have often been either ignored in feminist debates or

---

[3] In his analysis of *The Wealth of Irish Households,* Nolan (1991) noted that one of the biggest problems in examining wealth distribution was the lack of accurate and comprehensive data.

analysed in a way which is far from emancipatory (Davis, 1982; Lugones and Spelman, 1985; Hill Collins, 1990; Byrne, 1992; O'Neill, 1992).

The relative social scientific silence which exists around the relational systems governing the interface between the powerful and the powerless is no doubt related to the ability (including legal protections) of particular groups to hide from the research gaze. The rich and powerful are in a position to refuse access to sensitive data about themselves; the poor – and women, who are increasingly represented among the poor (Nolan and Watson, 1999) – are rarely in this position. The focus of research attention on the attributes of those experiencing inequality means that the causes of injustice are often sought in the lifestyle of the marginalised themselves, the most visible and measurable group. Poor people or ethnic minorities thus become associated with, or even 'blamed' for, crime, not the poverty-inducing and degrading structures which induced and facilitated crime in the first place. Similarly, women are held individually and personally accountable for their marginalisation rather than the patriarchal structures which oppress them in the first instance (see Connell, 1987).

The dichotomy that is drawn between fact and value in the positivist tradition also discourages analysis of the impact of funding bodies on the nature of the questions asked. When research on equality is funded by the state, for example, it is frequently undertaken for the purposes of controlling or containing the 'problem of inequality'. Big research studies based on national data sets are big business. The research is designed to answer the questions of those who pay for it: it is undertaken in a managerial context.

Furthermore, large-scale studies of poverty, such as those currently being undertaken across several countries in the EU, are prime examples of state-funded, top-down surveys.[4] They are designed and planned by 'experts' generally without systematic dialogue and collaboration with the subjects of the research. Such research often 'studies those at the bottom while holding up its hands for money to those at the top' (Reason and Rowan,

---

[4] The European Community Household Panel Survey and the Irish Household Budget Survey are examples of this type of research. National data bases on poverty and related issues are collected through these.

1981: xv). The methodologies and interpretations employed are based on models and paradigms which have been derived from a conception of poverty developed by academics, and approved by senior policy analysts and policy-makers, without the consent of those who are the subject of the research.

Without intent, this type of research can and does operate as a form of colonisation. It creates public images about groups and contexts of inequality (in both the academic and the policy world) over which most people participating in the pain and marginalis-ation of injustice and inequality have little or no control. Poor people, Travellers, asylum seekers, disabled people, and increasingly, women, become the subjects of books and papers in which their lives are recorded by professional middle-class experts who are frequently removed from their culture and lifestyle. This creates a context in which professional researchers know and own (as do the policy institutions and state departments which pay them) part of people's worlds about which people themselves know very little. By owning data about oppressed peoples, the 'experts' own part of them. The very owning and controlling of the stories of oppression adds further to the oppression as it means that there are now people who can claim to know and understand you better than you under-stand yourself; there are experts there to interpret your world and to speak on your behalf. They take away your voice by speaking about you and for you. This is sometimes referred to as the 'hit and run model of research' wherein the career advancement of the researchers is built on their use of alienating and exploitative methods of inquiry.

Colonisation by experts is especially acute for low-income working-class communities and for ethnic minorities and other groups, such as Travellers, whose cultural traditions are strongly oral (Lynch and O'Neill, 1994; see also McDonagh, in this volume).[5] Hence, 'Classes exist twice over, once objectively, and a second time in the more

---

[5] An example of how academics may inadvertently structure the exclusion of marginalised groups occurred at a conference organised in TCD on 18 July 1997 on 'Travellers, Society and the Law'. All the lecturers were professionals and there was no space in the programme for the Travellers' perspective. In addition, the fee for the day was £100, so only those with access to resources could attend.

or less explicit social representation that agents form of them' (Bourdieu, 1993: 37). While there are women, albeit upper middle-class women, who can challenge, mediate and redefine the images of women in the policy and academic arena, and while the same holds true for many other groups such as disabled persons, religious or ethnic minorities, this cannot happen for working-class people; by designation, working-class people are not part of the defining classes in society.

Within traditional positivist research, reflexivity is not a require-ment of the research task. The fact that the perspective of the expert is only one viewpoint, and one which is generally at least one step removed from the oppression, is rarely discussed. Researchers present what is a select viewpoint as one which is more comprehensive and epistemologically powerful than others; it is often presented as being superior to that of other researchers (especially ethnographic researchers), and to that of people living out inequality. The net effect of interpreting the world from the perspective of the 'expert' is that the viewpoint of the outsider is privileged over that of the insider who has experienced the inequality. The privileging of the expert produces perspectives on inequality and injustice, which are politically and emotionally detached from the experiences which generated their articulation in the first place.

While academic understanding involves abstractions, the abstrac-tions need not revisit the research subjects as 'expert opinions' which are superior to their own understanding.[6] It is possible to create knowledge and understanding through partnership between the researcher and the research subject, while recognising the differences between the two positions. Knowledge created in this manner is owned by the research subject in a way that non-

---

[6] At the Irish Conference on Civil and Social Rights in the European Union, Dublin, 7-8 May 1997, a number of working-class community activists were highly critical of one of the speakers who made no attempt to communicate his academic ideas in accessible language (the audience included community activists from various non-governmental organisations, researchers, policy-makers and administrators). The response to this criticism was (unfortunately) one of dismissal; the speaker justified his approach on the grounds that it was only possible to communicate (sic) his ideas in a particular type of language code.

partnership-knowledge is not. The fact that the subjects are co-creators of the knowledge means that they can exercise control over definitions and interpretations of their lifeworld. They are also in a position to be introduced to research practice through their ongoing involvement in the research process.

The normative and transformative tradition in feminist research

Feminist scholars have been especially effective in challenging the core epistemological and methodological assumptions of mainstream social scientific practice. They have challenged patterns of bias in research design, including the absence of research on questions of central importance to women; the focus on élitist research topics; the naïve understanding of objectivity; the improper interpretation and over-generalisation of findings; and inadequate data dissemination (Jayaratne and Stewart, 1995: 218).

Not only have feminist theorists been to the fore in the critique of positivism, they have also been leaders in developing a theory of emancipatory action through education and research (Harding, 1987; Humphries and Truman, 1994; Lather, 1991; Lentin, 1993; Mies, 1984; Smith, 1987; Stanley and Wise, 1983; Weiler, 1988). They have encouraged women to engage in action both in and through education, and through research. They have also attempted to document the type of procedures which must be followed in order to create an emancipatory research approach. Lather claims that:

> ... the development of emancipatory social theory requires an empirical stance which is open-ended, dialogically reciprocal, grounded in respect for human capacity, and yet profoundly sceptical of appearances and 'common sense'. Such an empirical stance is, furthermore, rooted in a commitment to the long-term, broad-based ideological struggle to transform structural inequalities (Lather, 1986: 269).

The challenge posed by feminist theories for research in terms of reflexivity, dialogue and co-operation with marginalised people, are considerable. An even greater challenge is how to establish collaborative practices between theorist/researcher and marginalised peoples, which will ensure that the understandings arrived at can work towards a transformative outcome. To confront the latter challenge is to confront the forces of interest within the academy itself.

Challenges and issues to be addressed in developing an emancipatory research model

While certain feminist theorists have engaged with the contradictions of their class position in relation to research production (e.g. Humphries and Truman, 1994; Lather, 1991; Reay, 1996), much of feminist theory ignores the logic of the sets of cultural relations within which academic knowledge is produced. Feminists, no more than other intellectuals, 'tend to leave out of play their own game and their own stakes'. Yet, 'the production of representations of the social world, which is a fundamental dimension of political struggles, is the virtual monopoly of intellectuals ...' (Bourdieu, 1993: 37). Academics create virtual realities, textual realities, ethnographic and statistical realities. These overhang and frame the lived existence of those who cannot name their own world; it is frequently in the context of these detached and remote realities that public policy is enacted. The frame becomes the picture in the public eye. Yet theoretical knowledge has serious limitations imposed upon it by the conditions of its own performance.

The relations of cultural production within which critical theory, feminist theory and egalitarian theory are produced are generally no different from those that operate for the study of nuclear physics, corporate law or business and finance. Although some academics may view themselves as radical, reforming, feminist or emancipatory, they occupy a particular location within the class system (Bourdieu, 1993: 36-48). They are part of the cultural élite of society. It is the designation of cultural elitism which provides them with the structural conditions to write; it gives them credibility over other voices and reinforces the perception of superiority which maintains the salary differentials between themselves and other workers. Being granted the 'freedom from necessity' which allows them to write and discuss is a privilege which academics (be they liberal, radical or conservative) in well-funded universities are rarely asked to reflect upon.

Yet, academics are also subordinate to powerful corporate interest groups in the business and industrial sector. In a sense they occupy a contradictory class location (Davies, 1995), being at once an élite in the cultural sphere and relatively subordinate in the industrial or financial sphere. Gender further compounds the relations of academics to the institution of the academy. While radical (and indeed conservative) women academics are part of the privileged class whose income and status differentials are maintained by well-established practices of social closure (Collins, 1979), women academics are simultaneously subordinated to men within this class. Not only do they occupy subordinate positions to men in terms of junior/senior, permanent/temporary posts, they are also heavily concentrated in disciplinary and research fields which are subordinate in terms of status and resources (Acker, 1990; O'Connor, 2000). Thus, while the concept of the 'free-floating, disinterested intellectual' may be part of the ideology of academia, it is not grounded in any sociological reality. In class terms radical intellectuals are culturally, and financially, privileged; in gender terms, women are subordinated within that class.

Operating within a contradictory state, of being personally radical and publicly privileged, makes it difficult for many politically left-wing and feminist academics to be progressive in cultural or university politics. It is much simpler to be progressive in general politics that do not touch the core values of one's own work. Bourdieu (1993: 45) suggests that there is no easy resolution to this dilemma for radical intellectuals. He proposes a radical, ongoing reflexivity wherein one prepares 'the conditions for a critical knowledge of the limits of knowledge which is the precondition for true knowledge' as the principal protection available. Lather (1991) suggests a similar option for feminists.

Even if academics do engage in ongoing reflexivity, this does not alter the structural conditions under which they work. The dilemma posed by unequal power between researcher and research subject is not readily resolved, even when the researcher works with emancipatory intent (Lentin, 1993: 128; Martin, 1996). It is generally the researchers who produce the final text, the written record of the research event. This gives them a power of definition which cannot be abrogated at will. Moreover, the very efforts of those interested in transforming the relations of research production (from those of dominance to those of partnership or emancipation) are deeply implicated in the exercise of power. One cannot escape the reality of power relations even within the language of emancipation.

In addition, intellectuals work in institutions which lay down working conditions based on the dominant meritocratic principles of our time – ostensibly at least, promotion is based on merit. The way in which merit is measured is in terms of conformity to the dominant norms of intellectual and academic discourse. This includes not only writing with the dominant paradigm (Kuhn, 1961) but writing about what is currently intellectually fashionable. Without at least a nodding recognition of the importance of the dominant discourses, one's work is not likely to be published.[7] And it is through their publications that intellectuals in universities are generally assessed. While 'there is something desperate in the docility with which "free intellectuals" rush to hand in their essays on the required subject of the moment' (Bourdieu, 1993: 43), the fact remains that the jobs and incomes of academics are often dependent on such conformity.

Not only does the academy generally only recognise those who conform to the intellectual norms of the day; it penalises those who attempt to redefine the purpose of the academy. Lectures, consultations and involvements with non-academic bodies do not count in terms of the enumerations of one's work or achievements.[8] This acts as a very effective control on academic work, limiting and containing interests within the safe confines of the university. It also works effectively to preclude intellectuals from involving themselves, and the university, in radicalising initiatives. While established or tenured academics can afford to indulge in such developments, sanctioning via limited promotional opportunities continues to exercise control even over these.

---

[7] While there are exceptions to this, most notably intellectuals who are in the position of defining what is or is not in fashion, most academics, especially those without tenure, are not in that position.

[8] An interesting example of this is the way in which inventories of academic activities and research publications are compiled; only lectures to one's academic peers are generally counted as being of high standing; the same principle applies to publications. While this is understandable from the perspective of the academy, it shows how the university systematically devalues dialogue with persons and bodies other than academics.

Yet, public lectures and involvements with voluntary, statutory, community and other organisations are essential if research findings are to be circulated outside the narrow confines of the academy. Given that the production of scientific knowledge generally is often legitimated on the grounds that it will contribute to progress, and to the ultimate general good of humanity, it is difficult to see how this can happen without the dissemination of the findings outside the academy in accessible contexts and language.

What is interesting about the boundary maintenance that goes on in universities is that it is not confined to any one field (Bernstein, 1971). It occurs within and between disciplines, and between the university itself and the 'outside community'. Academic knowledge is defined as 'superior' knowledge. The fact that the academic perspective is only one viewpoint, and that it may need to be complemented by other forms of understanding by non-academic research subjects is largely ignored (Lather, 1986). The parameters within which academic dialogue takes place therefore are narrowly defined, thereby inhibiting criticism of academic discourse itself, and prohibiting academics from understanding the world from the perspectives of the 'other' outside the academy.

Emancipatory methodology

Resolving the dilemma posed by the colonising nature of research has been addressed by several feminist scholars and researchers (Bowles and Duelli-Klein, 1983; Harding, 1991; Lather, 1991; Mies, 1984; Roberts, 1981; Smith, 1987), and more generally in the social sciences (Bernstein, 1983; de Koning and Martin, 1996; Oliver, 1992; Reason, 1988; Reason and Rowan, 1981). It is suggested that the alternative to illusory value-free knowledge is emancipatory knowledge. The aim of emancipatory research is to increase 'awareness of the contradictions hidden or distorted by everyday understandings', and in so doing to direct 'attention to the possibilities for social transformation inherent in the present configuration of social processes' (Lather, 1986: 259).

• *Ethical issues*
The research industry is a massive one across all fields and disciplines; it takes place not only in universities or research institutes

but also in government departments, private companies, local and national service agencies, and voluntary bodies. Cultural capital, of which research is a fundamental part, parallels industrial, financial and agricultural capital as a source of wealth and power. Unless it is shared with those who are directly affected by it, research data can be used for manipulation, abuse and control. The importance of democratising research arises therefore because knowledge is power.

Although conventional human rights thinking focuses on political rights in the more restricted political sense, there is also a need to recognise the importance of human rights in relation to the operation of public and private institutions and systems which exercise control over people's lives but which are not democratically appointed. Research-generating institutions and universities are such bodies, as they play a central role in validating and developing cultural forms and scientific knowledge which underpin social, economic and political policies in society.

Emancipatory research involves a recognition of the moral right of research subjects to exercise ownership and control over the generation of knowledge produced about them and their world. As Heron (1981) observes, this is a human rights issue. It constitutes part of people's right to political membership of their community. If people are structurally excluded from democratic engagement with research practice, they are precluded from assessing its validity in an informed manner. They are effectively disenfranchised from controlling the creation and dissemination of knowledge about themselves and/or about institutions and systems within which they live and work:

> For persons, as autonomous beings, have a moral right to participate in decisions that claim to generate knowledge about them. Such a right does many things: (1) it honours the fulfilment of their need for autonomously acquired knowledge; (2) it protects them from becoming unwitting accessories to knowledge-claims that may be false and may be inappropriately or harmfully applied to others; (3) it protects them from being excluded from the formation of knowledge that purports to be about them and so from being managed and manipulated, both in the acquisition and in the application of knowledge, in ways they do not understand and so cannot assent to or dissent from (Heron, 1981: 35).

Although the moral or human right to know applies primarily to research on persons, it is also of significance in other fields, including research in the physical sciences. The most obvious example arises in relation to research involving experimentation within the natural environment (as in the case of the nuclear industry) or the development of genetically modified foods. These, and indeed many other forms of research, much of which is not very high profile, have serious health and environmental implications not only for the living generation but for future generations. Concealment of the scope and impact of research may add to the power and influence of the companies and states that produce it, but it also creates a world order in which ordinary people are politically and informationally disenfranchised. Research and information enfranchisement must complement political enfranchisement.

Often a research information deficit can be the differentiating factor between having a meaningful or an alienating experience in an organisation. An immediate and concrete example arises in the field of education. Parents who know the basic research findings regarding such practices as streaming and ability grouping can exercise control over schools and teachers in a way that other parents cannot. Knowledge about the effects of different forms of ability grouping enables them to act in a way that protects the interests of their own child; they can exercise strategic choices such as moving the child to a more supportive school if they find her or him in the 'wrong' class. No such possibility exists for those who do not even know the implications of different forms of grouping in the first place. Similar examples could be taken from the health services where, for example, women and men are not aware of research findings regarding the long-term implications of taking different types of drugs and medication. Those who have access to (and can decode) the information are in control and can exercise choices in a way that those without it cannot.

Not only can people not make informed decisions if they lack information; they cannot participate effectively in public debates or policy partnerships. Even when and if people are given a partnership role, they may lack the technical knowledge to participate effectively. They can be physically present but technically absent, living in fear of a professional put-down from those who are part of the research-informed. What is at issue is not only the exercise of democratic procedures in research production, therefore; the effective democratic dissemination of research findings is also essential. Much research is closeted and used selectively by researchers, policy-makers or service-providers as the politics of the situation allows. Such practices ensure that people are managed and manipulated from the top and from outside.

• *Reciprocity in the research relationship*
Emancipatory research also involves developing a reciprocal relationship between the researcher and the research subject. This requires a democratisation of the research relationship so that the research process enables participants to understand and change their situation. This is especially important for research in the area of equality, as research which is not oriented towards transformation effectively reinforces inequality by default. It allows inequality to persist by diverting intellectual and public attention elsewhere.

Reciprocity involves engaging participants firstly in the research planning and design, as it is only through such participation that marginalised groups can begin to control the naming of their own world. If research participation is confined to the interpretation or theoretical elaboration stage, it may be too late; issues which are not central to the group or community may have become the focus of attention in the first place. Involving research subjects in planning poses numerous challenges to researchers and theorists, not least of which is the information and expertise differential between the researcher and the researched. Mutual education is at least a partial solution to this dilemma; there is an especially strong onus on researchers to facilitate and promote education, given the power differential between them and research subjects (Heron, 1981). However, integrating education with research imposes time and resource constraints on research, which cannot be easily set aside. And neither the funders nor the research subjects themselves may be interested in bearing the cost.

Reciprocity also demands that the research enables people to know and control their own world. This takes time, trust and negotiation; it is quite possible that researchers and participants may not agree on the definition of inequality, or indeed how it should be addressed. Kelly's (1996) research shows how working-class community groups themselves interpreted unemployment according to quite different socio-political frames – ranging from radical to reformist to localist – although the formal class identity of all twelve groups involved was the same.

Recognising the very real practical difficulties posed by reciprocal research relations is not a sufficient reason to discount them. Operating out of principles of reciprocity, albeit imperfectly, would radically alter the way in which research is planned and conducted; this is important in restructuring power relations and would be an important movement towards the democratisation of research.

•*Dialectical theory building*

Another feature of praxis-oriented research is its use of dialectical theory-building rather than theoretical imposition (Lather, 1991). Research respondents are not only involved therefore in the design of the research but also in the construction and validation of meaning. To undertake theory-construction in this manner represents an enormous challenge for researchers as it imposes a substantive educational commitment upon them (Heron, 1981). A dialogical approach to theory building is even more demanding than partnership in empirical research, as it involves the accommodation of two very different epistemological standpoints on the world, the academic, and the local or particular. It demands theoretical construction in a language which is recognisable and meaningful across disparate communities. The theorist can no longer construct a view of the world without knowing and recognising the view of the 'other', howsoever the latter may be defined. What dialectical theory building involves is the democratisation of theoretical construction, a reordering of power relations between the academy and the named world. Yet theoretical imposition is the natural predisposition of most researchers, given traditional academic training. Researchers-authors assume the superiority of their 'framework'. Grounding frameworks in the context of lived understandings challenges this tradition and informs and enriches understanding.

•*Reflexivity*

Systematic reflexivity is also a requirement for emancipatory research as it is only through the constant analysis of one's own theoretical and methodological presuppositions that one can retain an awareness of the importance of other people's definitions and understandings of theirs. Although reflexivity is necessary, it is not a sufficient condition for emancipatory research. An ethically disinterested reflexivity would not suggest any change in research practice. If reflexivity is to facilitate change it needs to be guided by principles of democratic engagement and a commitment to change.

Emancipatory research in practice: coalitions and partnerships

There are several practical problems posed by the emancipatory methodology, including the fact that it does increase the cost of the research. This is not necessarily something that will be supported by research funders, although it may change over time when the importance of dialogue and its educational outcomes are appreciated. There is also very little research training available in most educational institutions on emancipatory methodology, although there are exceptions to this (Reason, 1988), especially in feminist-led courses in recent years.

A further dilemma for the operation of emancipatory research is the establishing of procedures whereby radical understandings can be utilised for challenging structural inequalities. Even if radical understandings emerge from research, which for example, happened in Kelly's (1996) work, there may be no mechanism within the emancipatory method to move this understanding into discourses and political practices which would enable it to become active in the struggle for equality and social justice. Emancipation cannot be conferred by one group (academics) on another (oppressed or marginalised people) no matter how well-intentioned the researchers might be (Martin, 1994; 1996).

While Mies (1984) shows how particular research led to important policy changes in Germany in relation to policies on women and violence, it is not clear what makes it possible for this to happen. Is egalitarian development left contingent on a particular set of historical and political circumstances? One fact which does appear to be important is the involving of marginalised groups themselves at all stages of the research, including the policy-related implementation stage, if action is to be taken. For this to happen, research organisations have to enter into new relations of dialogue and co-alition with community or other groups which may be anathema to their organisational or cultural traditions. Certainly universities and research institutes have rarely established procedures for entering into dialogue with research participants in marginalised groups and communities. While liaison with such groups may be permitted, they are usually kept at the periphery of the organisation where they exercise marginal power, often in adult education departments or Women's Studies departments.

Within current emancipatory discourse, the choice as to whether or not to use emancipatory methods is left to the researcher; there is no serious attempt to identify the kind of structural conditions necessary to ensure that emancipatory methods are implemented on an ongoing basis. To institutionalise a truly radical approach to research, however, would require the development of new structures at both university and departmental level (and ultimately at central university and research planning level). Similar challenges would arise for institutes and bodies undertaking research elsewhere. Procedures would have to be put in place whereby those who are marginalised and oppressed in society can enter into dialogue about all research undertaken in their name. They would not simply be dependent on the good will of individual researchers allowing them to enter into dialogue on their own terms. Rather, community groups or other representatives of marginalised groups would be involved on an ongoing basis in planning, monitoring and commenting on research. They would play a very different and more powerful role than if they are simply research subjects being given the opportunity to participate or dialogue about research at the will of the researcher.

This would require a radical change in the structuring of departments in the university and in the management of research operations. It would involve the establishment of *research coalitions* with marginalised groups and communities who are so often the objects of research. Such groups would move from being objects to being subjects, from being respondents to being partners. They would have the opportunity to define research agendas relating to their own lives. No one would have the authority to name, codify and claim scholarly understanding and ownership of someone else's world without debate, negotiation and, ultimately, consent.

Under a research coalition arrangement, power would be shared. The researchers would have to explain and justify the nature of their proposed research and theory about marginalised groups to the groups themselves. This is not to deny the difficulties involved.

The academic voice is validated by virtue of its scientific origin; it is structurally defined as superior to the local or community voice. Thus any research partnership between researchers and the community is not an equal one, in the sense that prior cultural relations define it otherwise. To say this is not to suggest that the power differential in research coalitions cannot be managed and controlled. It merely highlights the importance of enabling those who are not full-time researchers to have the capacity and skill to name their research agendas in the partnerships. A further difficulty arises from the volatile character and composition of community groups themselves. Such groups are not necessarily constituted in a democratic or representative manner; they often lack formal procedures of accountability to their own constituency. Therefore their effectiveness as representative bodies has to be constantly monitored. While this is not essentially a research problem, it is nonetheless an issue that has to be addressed in partnership contexts (Sabel, 1996).

If research coalitions were to be established, it is evident that the onus of responsibility for setting them up rests initially with those who exercise control over the research process. Negotiations and discussions need to be set in train to identify the needs and interests of both parties, and to resolve the barriers which need to be overcome. These include barriers relating to differences in research expertise, language usage, life experiences, and attitudes to, and experiences of, research.

The experience of Local Area Partnerships in Ireland has shown that community representatives cannot be fully effective participants without resourcing (Lynam, 1997). If marginalised groups are to participate effectively in the research process, training, resourcing and support would be essential, although the knowledge differential is not only confined to them. Academics also experience a (frequently unacknowledged) knowledge differential concerning the daily-lived reality of the groups about whom they write. Such living knowledge represents an important resource which the community groups would bring to the research coalitions.

To be effective, research coalitions would need to be complemented by *learning partnerships*. Those would be mutual education forums for academics, researchers and community personnel, so that each could share their definitions and interpretations of issues and events. In this way research agendas could be assessed and prioritised. The research coalitions and learning partnerships would inevitably facilitate action for change, as the communities where action is required would be directly involved in defining and interpreting their own situations. The research understandings available to them would be a powerful tool in negotiations with politicians and policy-makers.

What is at issue here is the case for an extended epistemology within the academy (Heron, 1981: 27-31). Most empirical research is in the domain of propositional knowledge. The outcome of research is stated as a set of propositions, which claim to be statements of *facts* or *truths* about the world. However, these theoretical constructs or empirical statements are artefacts or constructs about the world; they do not constitute the world in and of itself. They provide a framing of the world, a context for giving meaning; they are not synonymous with the experiential knowledge of the world. Experiential knowledge involves knowing the world in a direct face-to-face encounter: 'it is knowing a person or thing through sustained acquaintance' (Heron, 1981: 27). Knowing poverty or racism through the medium of academic frameworks, and framing propositions about it empirically and theoretically, makes an important contribution to human understanding. However, it is but one window on reality; it can only offer a limited perspective. While it is clear that academics do not claim to offer a 'complete understanding' of any phenomenon, the reality is that academic definitions of situations have status and power over and above other understandings. The meaning of poverty or inequality as it is understood and acted upon at policy level is as researchers have defined it; it is not as poor people see it (O'Neill, 1992).

The need to democratise the creation of academic knowledge arises from the simple fact that such knowledge is acted upon as the defining understanding of a situation. With the advancement of information technology, the likelihood is that this trend will grow rather than retract. The scope for creating massive data bases on people of both a quantitative and qualitative nature has been greatly enhanced by computer developments in recent years. With this, the scope for researchers to colonise the life worlds of those who are marginalised is likely to increase considerably unless democratisation of the research process is introduced.

While the democratisation of the research process is necessary across all fields, it is especially acute in the equality field. In general, those who carry the burden of inequality are far removed from the life-world of researchers. By virtue of their personal experience, however, they have a better vantage point for understanding the totality of the social world that creates inequality than those who enjoy its advantages. They have a much deeper understanding of how particular laws, policies and procedures operate to promote inequalities than those who are advantaged by them (Connell, 1993: 39-41; hooks, 1994).

The importance of establishing learning partnerships between researchers and the community arises not only from the point of view of respecting the fundamental human rights of those about whom we write, but also as a means of realising change. While critical theorists place considerable store on developing theories, including theories jointly created by researchers and participants, they do not make clear how such understanding will lead to change. Most academic productions remain confined to a narrow community of readers and listeners. No matter how radical the knowledge may be, its transformative potential is far from self-evident unless it is available and disseminated in accessible form to those about whom it is written or whose lives are affected by it. Learning partnerships arising from research coalitions would allow this to happen. They would ensure that an avenue of communication is established so that those who have most to gain from transformative action have the knowledge to act. The learning partnerships would provide a forum for challenging biases and deceptions and thereby reinforcing the incentive to act. Those who have experiential knowledge of inequality and injustice can ally this understanding with academic knowledge to create a new and deeper knowledge of their world. This deeper understanding can challenge established 'wisdoms' and 'ideologies' around inequality and injustice. Learning partnerships would provide the opportunity to link analysis directly into a community of participants with the potential to act.

Knowledge, no matter how radical in intent, is not inherently transformative. Even if critical intellectuals shift from being 'universalising spokespersons' for marginalised groups to being 'cultural workers whose task is to take away barriers that prevent people from speaking for themselves' (Apple, 1991: ix), this does not guarantee change. It is not self-evident that deepening knowledge of injustices and inequalities among marginalised communities or peoples themselves will inevitably lead to transformative action outside of the research field; there is always an element of choice. Understandings need to be linked into a political forum so that knowledge does not become redundant and divorced from action. If learning partnerships are created between academics and community representatives, then it also seems necessary to develop *equality action plans* on a collaborative basis. Action needs to be planned and implemented for changing structures at the political and related levels. Without integrating planning for change into the entire process there can be no guarantee that it will happen.

A challenge to the academy

What is being proposed here in terms of research coalitions and learning partnerships would be seen by many academics as a challenge to their intellectual autonomy. And it does pose serious questions about the nature of independence for the universities and research institutes if taken seriously. However, the professional ideology of 'freedom and independence' within the universities is itself in need of deconstruction. As Bourdieu (1988; 1993) has noted, the nature of the freedom which academics exercise is in fact seriously circumscribed by numerous conventions and controls. There are many forms of subtle constraint and censorship which operate for intellectuals, although these are rarely named as such. To be published requires a high degree of conformity to the paradigmatic rules of the day within one's discipline, and breaking out to create new forms of knowledge, either within existing disciplines, or through the creation of new disciplines, can be heavily sanctioned.

> The secret resistance to innovation and to intellectual creativity, the aversion to ideas and to a free and critical spirit, which so often orientate academic judgements, as much at the viva of a doctoral thesis or in critical book reviews as in well-balanced lectures setting off neatly against each other the latest avant-gardes, are no doubt the effect of the recognition granted to an institutionalised thought only on those who implicitly accept the limits assigned by the institution (Bourdieu, 1988: 95).

Freedom of expression is allowed, but the publication and dissemination of that expression is often dependent on working within the received wisdom. And this is even truer when trying to establish new forms of knowledge or understanding. While resistance to innovation may be concealed within established disciplines, more open resistance has confronted new disciplines such as Women's Studies and Equality Studies. There is a need therefore to establish the procedures and practices of those who control academic knowledge and discourse. This would help clarify the power relations within which intellectual life operates, and may be necessary before dialogue can be satisfactorily introduced.

What is being suggested here is that the forces of conservatism within the academy exercise a power over academic freedom which is too rarely named. The forces countering innovation operate both within and between disciplines; the control which medicine has traditionally exercised over nursing is an example of the latter, while the marginalisation of feminist research within male-dominated disciplines is an example of the former. At other times, the forces of conservatism arise from the simple organisational dynamics of academic careerism itself. Although academics may have tenured posts (as most full-time academics do in Ireland), the freedom which flows from this does not always encourage people to think critically; rather people become beholden to the concept of the career – moving upwards promotionally within the system. All too frequently the line of least innovation is the line of ascent. Organisational recognition comes more readily to those who conform to the dominant norms and paradigms. This breeds a culture of conformity, silence and academic orthodoxy that belies the very freedom granted by the academy. While it is clear that people do innovate and resist the forces of conformity within the academy in many different ways, it is also evident that this often happens at considerable personal cost, especially when the innovations challenge traditional values and practices among dominant groups.

Giving a role to marginalised groups to set out the terms in which knowledge about themselves and their world is created is merely to recognise that such groups have hitherto exercised little power in relation to the definition of knowledge. If there is to be a serious attempt to decolonise the knowledge and understanding of oppressed groups in society, then it seems essential to put mechanisms in place to ensure that emancipatory methods are not always an optional extra, something to be granted on a case-by-case basis at the behest of experts. Without structures there can be no guarantee that partnership-based dialogue will happen.

The academy needs to be reconstituted in its structural relations with marginalised groups if resistance is to be effective. Otherwise systems of dialogue will be completely one-sided, with all the choices about initiating or ending dialogue being left to the researcher. Allowing researchers to decide on all occasions whether or not their interpretations of other people's worlds will be shared and/or challenged is to perpetuate the highly unequal power relations which now underpin the social construction of knowledge in academic life. This perpetuates a practice wherein the naming of one's own world, especially by marginalised people, is effectively in the hands of academic power brokers, no matter how well-intentioned these might be.

Conclusion

Radical researchers occupy a contradictory class location in relation to the academy. On the one hand, like all other academics, they are part of a cultural élite that receives salaries and work privileges in excess of many other occupational groups by virtue of their claim to expertise. On the other, they are working as agents for change and social transformation to create a more egalitarian society, one which may not endow their own groups with the same 'freedom from necessity' to research and to write.

A genuine and ongoing commitment to change cannot be guaranteed in this type of situation by simply relying on some form of subjective reflexivity. While reflexivity is essential, it is but one element in the process of creating an emancipatory research methodology. If the aim of critically inspired thought is to make theory, method and praxis inseparable from each other, then it is necessary to create structures which guarantee that this will happen rather than leave it to the good will or interest of individual researchers. Moreover, granting researchers a veto on whether or not to utilise emancipatory methods on equality issues is to disempower research participants in the very way that critical theorists have strongly criticised in other contexts. The only way in which people can exercise ongoing, systematic influence on naming their own world is by being centrally involved at all stages of the research process, including design, interpretation and outcome-implementation. For this to happen, procedures for research coalitions would need to be developed between research bodies, universities (and their departments) and communities and groups who are being researched. In addition, learning partnerships need to be established to enable researchers to learn (in the doing of research) about the role of experiential knowledge in understanding and to enable marginalised peoples to name their own world in their own words. Finally, if knowledge is to have transformative potential at a structural as well as an ideological level, then equality action plans need to be developed from the research findings.

For Equality Studies and other cognate fields to have moral, intellectual and political credibility it is incumbent upon researchers to implement emancipatory research methods as outlined. If it confines its emancipatory actions to the operational stage of the research and ignores the conceptualisation, design, interpretation and action stage, then it is belying the notion of emancipation in its more substantive sense. To operate a more radical form of emancipatory method does present many new and exciting challenges not only for research but also for other work in the university. Clearly if emancipatory methods are being employed in research this also calls into question the authenticity and suitability of current pedagogical and assessment methods, most of which are based on a strongly hierarchical view of both teacher-student relationships and indeed of knowledge itself.

Many Irish universities and colleges of higher education claim service to the community as one of their objectives. If this is the case, then there is a need to identify the many different communities with whom we are to work. In this chapter it is suggested that marginalised and excluded groups in our society are part of the community; indeed very often such communities comprise the subject matter of social scientific research, but are rarely the research designers or partners. The chapter suggests that it is time that research coalitions were established between the universities and socially excluded communities to enable the latter to control the naming of their own world.

References

Acker, Joan (1990), 'Hierarchies, jobs, bodies: a theory of gendered organisations', *Gender and Society*, vol. 5: 390-407.

Apple, Michael (1991), 'Introduction', in Patti Lather, *Getting Smart: Feminist Research and Pedagogy With/In the Postmodern*, New York: Routledge.

Barry, Ursula (1996), *Trends and Prospects for Women's Employment in the 1990s in the Irish Economy,* Manchester: Manchester University Press.

Bernstein, Basil (1971), 'On the classification and framing of educational knowledge', in Michael F.D. Young (ed.), *Knowledge and Control: New Directions for the Sociology of Education* (19-46), London: Collier-Macmillan.

Bernstein, Richard (1976), *The Restructuring of Social and Political Theory,* New York: Harcourt, Brace Jovanovich.

Bernstein, Richard (1983), *Beyond Objectivism and Relativism: Science, Hermeneutics and Praxis*, Pennsylvania: University of Pennsylvania Press.

Bourdieu, Pierrre (1973), 'Cultural reproduction and social reproduction', in Richard Brown (ed.), *Knowledge, Education and Cultural Change*, London, Tavistock.

Bourdieu, Pierrre (1978), *The Inheritors: French Students and Their Relation to Culture*, Chicago: Chicago University Press.

Bourdieu, Pierre (1984), *Distinction: A Social Critique of the Judgement of Taste*, London: Routledge and Kegan Paul.

Bourdieu, Pierre (1988), *Homo Academicus,* Stanford: Stanford University Press.

Bourdieu, Pierre (1993), *Sociology in Question*, London: Sage.

Bowles, Gloria and Renate Duelli-Klein (eds) (1983), *Theories of Women's Studies,* London: Routlege and Kegan Paul.

Breen, Richard, Damian Hannan, David Rottman and Christopher T. Whelan (1990), *Understanding Contemporary Ireland,* Dublin: Gill and Macmillan.

Brown, Philip, A.H. Halsey, Hugh Lauder and A.S. Wells (1997), 'The transformation of education and society: an introduction', in Albert H. Halsey et al (eds), *Education: Culture, Economy and Society*, Oxford: Oxford University Press.

Byrne, Anne (1992), 'Academic Women's Studies in the Republic of Ireland', *Women's Studies Quarterly,* nos. 3 & 4: 15-27.

Callan, Tim, Brian Nolan, Brendan J. Whelan, Damian F. Hannan and Seán Creighton (1989), *Poverty, Income and Welfare in Ireland,* General Research Series No. 146, Dublin: Economic and Social Research Institute.

Callan, Tim, Brian Nolan, Brendan Whelan, Christopher Whelan and James Williams (1996), *Poverty in the 1990s*, Dublin: Oaktree Press.

Chambers, Richard (1983), *Rural Development: Putting the Last First,* Harlow: Longman.

Clancy, Patrick (1988), *Who Goes to College*, Dublin: Higher Education Authority.

Clancy, Patrick (1995), *Access to College: Patterns of Continuity and Change*, Dublin: Higher Education Authority.

Collins, Randall (1979), *The Credential Society,* New York: Academic Press.

Connell, Robert W. (1987), *Gender and Power,* Cambridge: Polity Press.

Connell, Robert W. (1993), *Schools and Social Justice*, Philadelphia: Temple University Press.

Cormack, Bob and Bob Osborne (1995), 'Education in Northern Ireland: the struggle for equality', in Patrick Clancy, Sheila Drudy, Kathleen Lynch and Liam O'Dowd (eds), *Irish Society: Sociological Perspectives,* Dublin: Insitute of Public Administration.

Davies, S. (1995), 'Leaps of faith: shifting currents in critical sociology of education', *American Journal of Sociology*, vol. 100, no. 6: 1448-78.

Davis, Angela (1982), *Women, Race and Class,* London: The Women's Press.

de Koning, Korrie and Marion Martin (eds) (1996), *Participatory Research in Health,* London: Zed Books.

Dowling, Teresa (1991), 'Inequalities in preparation for university entrance: an examination of the educational histories of entrants to University College Cork', *Irish Journal of Sociology,* vol. 1: 18-30.

Drew, Eileen (1999), *Gender Imbalance in Irish Civil Service Grades at Higher Executive Officer Level* (Executive summary), Dublin: Institute of Public Administration.

Giroux, Henry (1983), *Theory and Resistance in Education,* London: Heinemann.

Habermas, Jurgen (1971), *Knowledge and Human Interests*, Boston: Beacon Press.

Halsey, Albert H. (1994), 'Sociology as political arithmetic', *British Journal of Sociology*, vol. 45: 427-444.

Hammersley, Martyn (1992), 'On feminist methodology', *Sociology*, vol. 26, no. 1: 187-206.

Hammersley, Martyn (1995), *The Politics of Social Research*, London: Sage.

Hannan, Damian F., Emer Smyth, James McCullagh, Richard O'Leary, and Dorren McMahon (1996), *Coeducation and Gender Equality*, Dublin: Oak Tree Press.

Harding, Sandra (ed) (1987), *Feminism and Methodology: Social Science Issues*, Bloomington, Indiana: Indiana University Press.

Harding, Sandra (1991), *Whose Science? Whose Knowledge?* Milton Keynes: Open University Press.

Heron, James (1981), 'Philosophical basis for a new paradigm', in Peter Reason and J. Rowan (eds), *Human Inquiry: A Sourcebook of New Paradigm Research,* Chichester: John Wiley and Sons.

Hill Collins, Patricia (1990), *Black Feminist Thought,* New York: Unwin Hyman.

hooks, bell (1994), *Teaching to Transgress: Education as the Practice of Freedom,* London: Routledge.

Humphries, Beth (1997), 'From critical thought to emancipatory action: contradictory research goals', *Sociological Research Online,* vol. 2, no.1: <www.socresonline.org.uk/socresonline/2/1/3.html>

Humphries, Beth and Carole Truman (eds) (1994), *Rethinking Social Research,* Aldershot: Avebury.

Jayaratne, Toby E. and Abigail J. Stewart (1995), 'Quantitative and qualitative methods in the social sciences: feminist issues and practical strategies', in Janet Hollan, Maud Blair and Sue Sheldon (eds), *Debates and Issues in Feminist Research and Pedagogy,* Clevedon: Open Universtity Press.

Kelly, Mary (1996), *Educational Television: Emancipatory Education and the Right to Learn Project,* Dublin: Radio Telefís Éireann in association with the Equality Studies Centre, University College Dublin.

Kuhn, Thomas (1961), *The Structure of Scientific Revolutions,* Chicago: Chicago University Press.

Lather, Patti (1986), 'Research as praxis', *Harvard Educational Review,* vol. 56, no. 3: 257-277.

Lather, Patti (1991), *Getting Smart: Feminist Research and Pedagogy With/In the Postmodern,* New York: Routledge.

Lentin, Ronit (1993), 'Feminist research methodologies – a separate paradigm? Notes for a debate', *Irish Journal of Sociology,* vol. 3: 119-138.

Lugones, María and Elizabeth Spelman (1985), '"Have we got a theory for you!" Feminist theory, cultural imperialism and the demand for the women's role', *Women's Studies International Forum,* vol. 6, no. 6: 573-581.

Lynam, Siobhán (1997), *Democratising Local Development: The Experience of the Community Sector in its Attempts to Advance Participatory Democracy,* unpublished Masters thesis, Equality Studies Centre, University College Dublin.

Lynch, Kathleen (1999), 'Equality Studies, the academy and the role of research in emancipatory social change', *Economic and Social Review,* vol. 30, no. 1: 41-69.

Lynch, Kathleen and Cathleen O'Neill (1994), 'The colonisation of social class in education', *British Journal of Sociology of Education,* vol. 15, no.3: 307-324.

McCullagh, Ciaran (1995), 'Getting the criminals we want: the social production of the criminal population', in Patrick Clancy et al (eds), *Irish Society: Sociological Perspectives,* Dublin: Institute of Public Administration.

Mahon, Evelyn, Catherine Conlon and Lucy Dillon (1998), *Women in Crisis Pregnancy,* Dublin: Government Publications Office.

Martin, Marion (1994), 'Developing a feminist participative research framework: evaluating the process', in Beth Humphries and Carole Truman (eds), *Rethinking Social Research,* Aldershot: Avebury.

Martin, Marion (1996), 'Issues of power in the participatory research process', in Korrie de Koning and Marion Martin (eds), *Participatory Research in Health,* London: Zed Books.

Mies, Maria (1984), 'Towards a methodology for feminist research', in E. Albach (ed.), *German Feminism: Readings in Politics and Literature,* Albany: State University of New York Press.

Nolan, Brian (1991), *The Wealth of Irish Households,* Dublin: Combat Poverty Agency.

Nolan, Brian and Dorothy Watson (1999), *Women and Poverty in Ireland,* Dublin: Oak Tree Press.

Oliver, Mike (1992), 'Changing the social relations of research production', *Disability, Handicap and Society,* vol. 7: 1011-114.

O'Connor, Pat (2000), 'Resistance in academia', Proceedings of the International Conference on Women in Higher Education, New Orleans, January 2000.

O'Neill, Cathleen (1992), *Telling It Like It Is,* Dublin: Combat Poverty Agency.

Reason, Peter (ed.) (1988), *Human Inquiry in Action: Developments in New Paradigm Research,* London: Sage.

Reason, Peter, and J. Rowan (eds) (1981), *Human Inquiry: A Sourcebook of New Paradigm Research,* Chichester: John Wiley and Sons.

Reay, Diane (1996), 'Insider perspectives or stealing the words out of women's mouths: interpretation in the research process', *Feminist Review,* no. 53, Summer: 57-73.

Roberts, Helen (1981), *Doing Feminist Research,* London: Routledge and Kegan Paul.

Ruane, Frances and J.M. Sutherland (1999), *Women in the Labour Force,* Dublin: Employment Equality Agency.

Sabel, Charles F. (1996), *IRELAND: Local Partnerships and Social Innovation,* Paris: OECD.

Smith, Dorothy (1987), *The Everyday World as Problematic: A Feminist Sociology,* Milton Keynes: Open University Press.

Siraj-Blatchford, Iram (1995), 'Critical social research and the academy: the role of organic intellectuals in educational research', *British Journal of Sociology of Education*, vol. 16, no. 2: 205-220.

Stanley, Liz and Sue Wise (1983), *Breaking Out: Feminist Consciousness and Feminist Research*, London: Routledge and Kegan Paul.

Tomlinson, Mike, Tony Varley and Ciaran McCullagh (eds) (1988), *Whose Law and Order? Aspects of Crime and Social Control in Irish Society*, Belfast: Sociological Association of Ireland.

Weiler, Kathleen (1988), *Women Teaching for Change: Gender, Class and Power*, Boston: Bergin and Harvey Press.

3

Naming our own World: Making a Case for Feminist Research

Cathleen O'Neill

Introduction

> We are the subject of books and papers
> Our lives recorded by the middle-class
> Who steal our stories, use our oppression
> To serve their own needs; they won't let us pass.
>   (*Class Attack*, 1990)

These lines accurately reflect my experience of being a research subject. I wrote them for *Class Attack,* a community drama and video produced by the Women's Education Initiative in 1990, to draw attention to the inequalities that were present within the community development and education sector during the 1980s. This era lingers in my mind as the decade of debate and poverty research, when a searching spotlight was focused on many working-class communities, with researchers and academics arguing about the causes and effects of poverty. The notions of 'deserving' and 'undeserving' poor came under a great deal of scrutiny as droves of researchers, media people and academics sought out the best case studies or sound bites. For a time I gave my views to anyone who sought them until I became disillusioned about the process. I decided to stop giving interviews and to learn more about research. This chapter will outline some of the lessons I have learned during that process.

As a feminist and working-class woman I learned to declare my bias and my way of working in the research process. I will do so now by saying that this chapter is as much about me and my social class perspective, as it is about why I feel so strongly about equality and inequality within the research process. As a feminist I would like research to be as accessible, discursive and representative as possible. This is something that I have rarely found in academic research, especially when I needed it for my own research purposes. As a working-class activist I believe that working-class culture is neither fully understood nor properly documented. The documentation which does exist has been written from the 'outside in', usually by middle-class researchers:

> Poor people ... and increasingly within Ireland, women, become the subject of books and papers in which their lives are recorded by professional middle-class experts who frequently share neither their culture nor their gender (Lynch, 1999: 48).

Working-class culture and the unique contribution made by women within that culture therefore becomes invisible, undocumented and misunderstood. In the past, my own social class was culpable; we have not always recorded or made visible the unique norms or networks that are vital to our daily lives and our understanding of the world.

My research methodologies have developed out of the need to change inequalities within the research process. When I am involved in a research process, whether as the researcher or the research subject, my main aim is to make the research process clear, under-standable and accessible. In much the same way, I am trying to write this chapter in an open and accessible style, because I believe that if the people I live beside and work with cannot read it, then I have failed them and allowed this work to 'become a further contributor to oppression' (Oliver, 1996).

I have constantly been dissatisfied with my experience and involvement in research projects, frequently feeling patronised, misrepresented and oftentimes used. As I have already stated, the use of academic language and the way in which research is written up and presented is another cause of my feeling alienated. These experiences have led me to try out new ways of working with people whenever I needed to produce research or to explain com-plex concepts. Feminist, emancipatory processes have suited me best in my work with women, both in the community where I live and in the projects I work with. I have used these processes when working on two important research projects. The first one was called 'Telling It Like It Is' – a research project about the Kilbarrack area where I live. This work was published by the Combat Poverty Agency (O'Neill, 1992). The second project was a study of women and drug use called 'Walk Tall and Dream Big'– about bringing women drug users in from the margins and the role of emancipatory education in that process (O'Neill, 1994). This work was the subject of my thesis for an MA in Equality Studies. Both of these projects will be featured in this chapter as I explain my research process.

Telling It Like It Is

The aim of this project was to examine the extent and the experience of poverty in the Kilbarrack area, and to assess the impact of state services on a working-class community on the Northside of Dublin. I was familiar with the area because it was my local neighbourhood. I knew all about the poverty there because of my own experience and I was anxious to document the unique coping strategies of the women who lived there. This anxiety stemmed from my dis-satisfaction with the way in which the 'experts' had understood and written about poverty. I wanted to develop and be a part of an equal research partnership, of a new process of obtaining the facts about poverty and of analysing the information with the very people who experienced it. I wanted the research process to become knowledge leading to transformative action. I did not want to reduce my neighbours to mere 'units of analysis'. In those days I was unable to articulate it fully but I did not want to lend myself to a project in which:

> the very owning and controlling of the stories of oppression adds further to the oppression as it means that there are now people who claim to know and understand you better than you understand yourself; there are experts to interpret your world and speak on your behalf (Lynch, 1999: 48).

There were several unique factors about the Kilbarrack research. The research project was developed with the support of an experienced researcher. She helped me to draw up a funding proposal and develop the initial research design. She also guided me and acted as mentor throughout the entire project. She read numerous drafts and guided me through numerous local discussions and questions about social class. She provided me with reading and reference materials that enabled me to understand culture, kinship and other questions connected with doing research in your own locality. In short, I felt that she provided me with a short, intensive course in social studies, something I had never had the opportunity of doing. Her advice, guidance and sensitivity was proof positive that it is possible to develop alliances between different social classes.

My own ability to develop a more equal research process was helped by the fact that I was a member of a local adult education centre that was actively involved in the Kilbarrack area. People knew me and trusted me and it was easy for me to hold local meetings and seek support. I was able to develop a collaborative research partnership when a group of ten local women agreed to assist me in drawing up the research guidelines and in supporting the process. For purposes of clarity I will call this group the research focus group. I was able to develop a collaborative process with this group, after holding a series of meetings in the education centre, explaining the reason for the research and seeking support from local women in doing the fieldwork. At these meetings great care was taken to ensure that the ten women were encouraged to ask any questions about the research process and research publications. It was agreed that the women would own the research. We discussed the reason why research was being done and the possible advantages of doing it in the Kilbarrack area. At this stage of the process it was agreed that none of the research would be written up or handed over until it was read and agreed by all members of the focus group and by the women who were writing case histories.

The research guidelines from the Combat Poverty Agency sought to obtain information about the extent of poverty in the area. In addition to this the focus group wanted to document the extent of unemployment and examine the link between this and the high incidence of ill-health in the area. The group also felt it was important to examine prejudice and discrimination within the social welfare and education systems. And finally we wanted to document working-class culture from the perspective of women. We drew up a questionnaire which reflected these issues and was agreed by the group. Two members of the group who were also involved in the KLEAR adult education centre agreed to assist me in doing the fieldwork and in conducting a random survey of one hundred houses

in the locality. The fieldwork took a number of weeks to complete
and the findings were shared with the research focus group. In
addition to this a number of focus group meetings were held during
the summer of 1990 on the following topics: life on social welfare,
including the 'discretionary nature' of supplementary welfare; the
role of Dublin Corporation in the design and maintenance of flats
and houses and the impact of this on family life; understanding
and writing up a description of working-class culture, from a
working-class perspective; the content, cost, delivery and design
of education; health service or sickness service? and managing
poverty.

The discussions around these topics took place over two months
with different members of the focus and support groups. They
were held in an informal way in an informal location, with tea,
sandwiches and child care provided. A small sum of money was
given to the women in recognition of their time and expertise. At
all stages of the research process regular meetings were held to
explain the progress of the research. During these meetings it was
my job to ensure that the findings were carefully and clearly
explained, and to check out whether people agreed with the analysis
that was emerging. It is important to reiterate that the work was
being guided by an experienced researcher who was acting as my
mentor. During these meetings many lively discussions and debates
were held about different aspects of the research. Finally, the
research was written up and handed over to the focus group for
comment. It was also given in its entirety to the women who had
participated in case studies. A number of case studies were written
to illustrate different aspects of women's lives including the
following: living on social welfare, managing poverty, a case study
on health, and the experience of education.

Comments were actively sought as I asked the women for their
first impressions; queries were patiently answered, and changes
and corrections were made as requested and as appropriate. A
second draft was written and I left this draft with the focus group
over the summer (a very long summer) and was relieved when the
final wrap-up meeting came. Some changes were sought by the
focus group at this stage, mainly to do with the issue of identifying
people. The group felt strongly that the area should be named
throughout the publication, particularly because they fully supported

the research results. Group members agreed with the analysis in terms of writing up the local culture and in relation to the impact of state agencies on working-class lives. Some changes were made in terms of the language that was used to make it more discursive. The biggest change at this stage was an agreement to change the names of those who were featured in the case studies (we had originally identified people by their own names). After agreeing a number of other small changes with the group I was finally given the go-ahead to hand up the research to the Combat Poverty Agency.

The feeling at the end of this process was of a job well done, of consultation and information dissemination having reached new levels of equality. This approach became an empowering process for all of those who took part; it was felt that the process strengthened people's social analysis skills and eventually led to their becoming involved in local action to redesign the local area. The evidence of this activity can be judged by how the area has since been completely redesigned: examples are the new spiral bridge over the railway line and the recent demolition of the high rise flats adjacent to the railway. These changes have been made as a result of sustained local community development activism.

Since the completion of this research process Kilbarrack has been assigned the status of a Designated Area of Disadvantage, which makes the area eligible for EU funding. This funding is accessed through the Local Area Partnership Programmes. In order to access this funding the community had to develop an Area Action Plan and this plan was produced with the support of the women who were involved in the Kilbarrack research. The action plan brought substantial funding into the area and this led to setting up a thriving local resource centre catering for a wide range of age groups, including a homework club, a jobs club, an active retired club, a craft centre and a creche. Funding has also been obtained for a community-based drug rehabilitation project and a Youthstart programme that supports young people. In addition there is a men's group as well as several other programmes dealing with long-term unemployment.

As well as the financial advantages mentioned above there were several other advantages to creating this type of feminist, collaborative research. Firstly it was clear that the project empowered local women to name their own world; they gave unique insider views into the rituals and norms of working-class culture from a woman's perspective. The women also took part in a journey to understand and to document their own social class and learn about social analysis. They were able to enter into more equal discussion about the area when we achieved the status of Designated Area of Disadvantage. The area has also been given funding to support a Community Development Programme.

The research process also meant that the story of Kilbarrack really was about 'telling it like it is' from an insider perspective. The relationship between local researcher as writer and the researcher/ mentor role was another useful development because it proved that collaboration is possible with local people without losing either the message or research integrity. From my own perspective I felt that the extent and experience of poverty was written well from a working-class viewpoint. And finally, a little thing that gave me a lot of pleasure: a local doctor who came in for a lot of criticism about the design and layout of his surgery because it wasn't child friendly, built a playroom and equipped it with toys and with books for all ages.

A disadvantage of this type of research is the amount of time it takes to include all the players on an equal footing and to conduct full consultation. Local rows and debates had to be facilitated because men in the area objected to our interviewing only female heads of households. Our explanation that we wanted to document poverty from a woman's perspective gave rise to some lively discussions about 'women's libbers' and so on. Finally, from my own perspective, I felt that I was always on duty explaining the process and the findings to local men who disagreed with our analysis about the extent of poverty and ill-health in the area.

The SAOL project[1]

In the SAOL project the research task was to understand and document the use of emancipatory education processes with a group of women drug users. The SAOL Project, based in the North Inner

---

[1] SAOL means 'life' in Irish and is an acronym for Seasmhacht, Ábaltacht, Obair, Léann (Stability, Ability, Work and Learning).

City of Dublin, was established in 1995, and specifically targets women drug users, providing a two-year programme of education, development and support. The programme is run five mornings a week and a creche facility is provided for participants' babies and toddlers. The SAOL programme is based upon community development principles and adult education techniques derived from what Paolo Friere calls a 'new pedagogy', or emancipatory education.

The aims of the SAOL Project are to provide women drug users with a safe, welcoming and challenging learning environment. It also aims to support their re-integration into their local community and the broader society. In addition, the project incorporates holistic health and art therapies as an integral part of the weekly programme. The most important aspect of the programme is the way classes are designed to facilitate a number of women who had very poor levels of literacy. The backbone of the SAOL teaching system is the use of emancipatory education through a unique system of team teaching. The SAOL project incorporates many aspects of Friere's emancipatory pedagogy into its programme, particularly the concept of placing the experience and culture of those who suffer social exclusion and social disadvantage at the centre of the education focus through discussion, stimulation and class work. The project takes its lead from Friere when practising community education, by encouraging an analysis of the social and political contexts which allow situations to occur; and also an analysis of the way these issues and experiences are ignored or dismissed by the dominant groups in society.

One participant who took part in the research has her own unique way of describing her situation and the area in which she lives:

> People live the best they can. It is the worst place for crime because it has the highest amount of unemployed people. In my area not one playground can be seen. Heroin is the main subject in my area. … When we wake up in the morning we open our windows to try and let fresh air come in – but it doesn't. We get the same smell over and over again. People don't realise that it's the smell of anger, fear and hate. It's like living in a graveyard, except the corpses are walking around (Anita Byrne, SAOL Project).

Community education in SAOL is designed for a group of stable women drug users whose experience, culture and world view are often ignored by the dominant culture, indeed, who are often demonised by the dominant culture. The Freirean approach to learning encourages a process where the SAOL participants are encouraged and supported to discuss and find the difference between 'reading words' and 'reading the world'. In other words, the women in SAOL are encouraged to develop a social analysis of their lives.

Researching the project for an MA in Equality Studies, I chose a feminist research method because I believed that it was an honest, open process and because it gave the best opportunity to involve the SAOL participants in all aspects of the research. This decision was made in order to ensure that they – the real experts – would name their own world. Examining the experience of drug use and its impact is a highly sensitive issue and it can only succeed where it is based on trust and co-operation. Moreover, as the researcher I felt the need to 'give something back' to the participants rather than take something from them. A feminist participatory approach was used because it allowed for a deeper understanding of the issues as it would provide knowledge and insight to the group and enable them to make a better case in their dealings with health boards and other agencies.

The study of SAOL set out to understand and document the use of emancipatory education processes and outcomes in a drugs rehabilitation context. It also set out to examine other SAOL developmental processes such as advocacy and relationship rebuilding and to assess the success, or otherwise, of its role in the rehabilitation of former and stable women drug users back into the immediate community and the broader society. Since the participants are the real experts when it comes to telling us about the effects of drug addiction and drugs misuse, it was essential that they should be the ones to articulate their experiences of drug addiction, service provision and rehabilitation options. Their voices are essential to any research or debate about education treatment or rehabilitation. Ongoing discussion and involvement became the keystone of the research process and it became evident that the research process would be a lengthy one. I was looking for greater equality between the researcher and the researched, not merely by changing labels from 'research subject' to 'research participant' without looking at the power dynamics. I wanted the SAOL study too to 'tell it like it is' and was anxious that the research process, its impacts and outcomes would be understood by everyone in SAOL. I hoped it would be a 'warts and all' analysis of drug misuse by problem drug users who would articulate their concerns about the services provided by SAOL, the Eastern Health Board, FÁS (Foras Áiseanna Saothair) and members of ICON (Inner City Organisation Network).

The fact that I was working full-time as education co-ordinator with SAOL was a big advantage because the group trusted me and because I had the time to fully engage in a participative research process with the group. The SAOL management group were supportive of the venture and felt they could also make use of the findings. Questionnaires and other remote survey methods were not appropriate for several reasons, mainly due to the sensitive nature and cultural background of the group and because such methods would be at odds with group processes and adult education methodology already established in SAOL.

My first task was to call a group meeting to ascertain participants' level of interest and raise other concerns. I outlined my ideas and explained why I felt the research would be useful. There was an immediate interest in the idea, even though there were expressions of doubt by some group members about their ability to 'do research'. Several group members had participated in various health studies which used more formal questionnaire styles of information gathering and they felt a bit unsure about their abilities. I explained my own vision of how we might create a new way of 'telling it like it is' and I offered to hold a number of workshops that would help us to develop a research style that would suit our particular situation. When organising the two workshops I was supported by several positive factors: firstly, the group was used to working in a collective way using group work processes and secondly, because of their involvement in creative writing workshops, a number of the women were confident about their writing skills: 'When we wrestle with words and get them to say what we want to say, what a victory that is!'

These words come from the SAOL publication *Resolute Women Recite* (Cardboard Box Writers Group, 1996) and they are the result of what Paulo Friere calls a 'process of conscientisation' (Friere, 1974). Emancipatory or community education, as described and analysed by Friere, focuses on the education of marginalised groups whose experiences, culture and worldviews are often ignored by the dominant culture and by mainstream education. Emancipatory education also encourages a process whereby adults can be enabled to discuss the difference between 'reading words' or 'reading the world'. The participants of the SAOL Project are actively encouraged towards 'reading the world' and are given the skills and support to name their own world. This experience was to prove invaluable when it came to doing the research.

Arising from the introductory workshops the following decisions were made:

- ten women would have an involvement in drafting questions for a number of workshops about drug use, health issues and educational experience
- focus group discussions around a number of themes relevant to the study – education, health etc – would be held with the whole group
- two case studies would be compiled around the topic of early drug use, its causes and effects.

As a result of the workshops a number of the women offered to write case studies based on their understanding of how and why they became involved in drug use. In addition, several taped interviews were held with SAOL members and their families, and with key community workers. These were written up and analysed with the relevant members of the study group. In addition, one participant has written a description of her experience of the SAOL programme, reproduced below. By encouraging the group to name their own world and to articulate inequality as they understand it, we obtained a rare insight and a more rounded analysis of the background to the drugs crisis in Dublin.

Case study

Anna participated in the first SAOL programme. Since writing this case study, she has become completely drug free. She undertook further training and was employed by SAOL as peer worker on the New Opportunities for Women (NOW) programme. As well as passing her Leaving Certificate English exam, Anna has also obtained a Certificate in Women's Studies from UCD. Her two-year contract with SAOL ended in early 2000 and she has recently obtained a job as a youth worker in a local youth service.

SAOL, for me, is a safe place that was set up for stable drug users. It is a women's training and education programme. I believe in my heart it is a good choice for me. Personally it gives me stimulation, education, training and support. We are also learning to know our rights. We work at different modules and have the full support of our tutors. SAOL is very important to me because it has given me back the support of the community. People are starting to look up to me now. It makes me feel good to be a part of society. I am proud to call myself a working-class person. My father loves to see me here. He is already wondering about what will happen when the two years are up. He is as scared as I am of finishing in this place. God, what will we do? People in the community are looking up to us now. It is a great feeling when all the older women and men say to me, 'Are ya off to work, love? See ya later!' It makes me feel great. Especially when I hear them say, 'She has come a long way, God bless her.' SAOL also gives other parents the hope that their kids will get up off the ground. Just like we did!

The work we have been doing lately has been great fun. It also gives me joy that it is a successful project. I have tried a number of projects and they have never worked for me before. I have to admit I did not think we would make it through one month, never mind twelve. However, we are a special bunch of women; unique in our own way. Sometimes we have our ups and downs with each other and with the staff. But we talk about it. That is what makes a group project and process work.

The members of SAOL give the group good energy. We deal with grief, sorrow and hope. I would hate to think what my life would be like without SAOL. I know I would be 'head wrecked' with nothing to do. I would be stuck in the house all day. I will feel very sad at the end, but I don't dare to think that far ahead. I feel like crying as I write this. I wish it would never happen but that is life. Maybe SAOL has given me the strength to go further; that is one of the things I came here for. Before I started here my sister had died. I know if I was not in the group I would be heading for a nervous breakdown. It's more than a project here; we are a little family to each other. I hope SAOL goes on after the two years to give others a chance. We are really being noticed now. The public wants to know how we are doing so well. I would love to tell them.

Maybe one day I will have a job like my tutors, helping young women or kids on drugs. I hope I will have their understanding and skill. I think people like us, who have been through addiction, can offer a lot to other people who are addicted. We might not be

able to change the community but we can make it a better place
for the kids. I will never forget this group. I would love to go on to
do outreach work. I could help other drug addicts and give them
the knowledge, strength and dignity SAOL has given back to me.
We are powerful women. We have become a strong army of women;
we can walk with our heads in the air and look back at where we
used to be. I will never forget SAOL. Long may it live.

Conclusion

The methodology I used with the Kilbarrack project was unique in
many ways. It allowed a group of women from the area to take
time out to understand and design a research package. The process
of *Telling It Like It Is* empowered them to become involved in
further local development. My role as local writer-researcher allowed
me to accompany them on that journey as they revealed the positive
and negative norms of working-class culture. In many ways they
were telling my story as well: I shared their experience of poverty,
poor services, ill-health, and the burden of managing too much
with too little. I have lived in the area for twenty years and the
opportunity to write as 'insider' along with my neighbours meant
that the story of that community was told with the permission,
support and active help of the women who live there. The study
speaks for itself in terms of being a hard, honest look at how a
working-class community was treated by the state.

The SAOL research project was much more challenging for me
and I took many lessons with me from *Telling It Like It Is*. The key
lesson was to be patient; it would take a long time to produce a
thesis using collaborative feminist research. It would take endless
sessions of telling and retelling how and why it was important to
write up the SAOL methodology of using emancipatory education
processes. And this time, I would not be the 'expert'. While I shared
an understanding of poverty in Kilbarrack, I knew nothing about
drug use or addiction, or of living with HIV. I could only offer my
expertise to enable the SAOL group to 'tell it like it is' for those
who were trying to detox and reintegrate in society.

Again and again the SAOL group read drafts and wrote up their
experience of obtaining an education that was meaningful for them
in the inner city. The key challenge for me was to write a thesis
that could be read and understood by the very people it featured.

I feel that neither piece of research would have been worth producing without using a feminist methodology and I would encourage more researchers to follow up such processes in the future.

References

Cardboard Box Writers Group (1996), *Resolute Women Recite,* Dublin: SAOL.

Class Attack (1990), A community drama and video. Dublin: The Women's Education Initiative.

Freire, Paulo (1974), *Pedagogy of The Oppressed,* Harmondworth: Penguin.

Lynch, Kathleen (1999), 'Equality Studies, the academy and the role of research in emancipatory change', *Economic and Social Review,* vol. 30, no. 1: 41-69.

Oliver, Michael (1996), *Understanding Disability: From Theory to Practice,* Basingstoke, Hamps: Macmillan.

O'Neill, Cathleen (1992), *Telling It Like It Is,* Dublin: Combat Poverty Agency.

O'Neill, Cathleen (1994), *Walk Tall, Dream Big: Bringing Women Drug Users in from the Margins,* MA, Equality Studies Centre, University College Dublin.

4

Analytical Action, Committed Research: What does a Feminist Action Research Partnership Mean in Practice?

Cynthia Cockburn and Marie Mulholland

Introduction

This chapter discusses an action research project involving a partnership between an academic researcher, Cynthia Cockburn, and the women of an activist organisation, the Women's Support Network in Belfast. Marie Mulholland was its co-ordinator at the time.[1] We share authorship of this review of our work together, each contributing those parts of the story we are best placed to tell. The action research involved two other activist organisations in addition to the Women's Support Network. Indeed the relationship between the three was the pivot of the project. They are the Medica Women's Association in Bosnia-Hercegovina, and Bat Shalom in northern Israel. Some of their observations are included here too. But in the interests of coherence and focus, this chapter deals mainly with the interactions between Cynthia Cockburn and the Women's Support Network.

The action research project began in 1995. We called it *Women in Bridge-Building Projects* – 'Women Building Bridges', or just WBB, for short.[2] The intention was to study the history and activities

---

[1] Cynthia Cockburn carried out this work from the Department of Sociology, City University London.

[2] We wish to thank the following funding support: The E. and H.N. Boyd and J.E. Morland Charitable Trust; the William A. Cadbury Charitable Trust; the Community Relations Council of Northern Ireland; The Global Fund for Women; Gresham College; the Lipman-Miliband Trust; the Network for Social Change; the Niwano Peace Foundation; the Scurrah Wainright Charity; and Womankind Worldwide.

of three cross-communal initiatives in areas of conflict, and to analyse the experience and feelings of individual women involved in them. WBB was based on the belief that there is probably no more urgent need just now than to find means of avoiding a future of injustice and war. So we were choosing to research the positive face of that coin: processes of social inclusion, integration and cohesion. We hoped the research would contribute towards an answer to the question: how can women organise and work productively together across the lines that divide us, whether these are differences of identity, rifts between ethnic communities or borders between nations?

The three activist projects involved in the research each had a distinctive practical focus. But they all involved this element of co-operation across politicised ethnic differences that had been made dangerously conflictual in processes of oppression and war.

- The *Women's Support Network* links a number of women's centres in working-class districts of Belfast (some of them strongly nationalist/Catholic, others strongly unionist/Protestant) and other women's organisations. It acts as a 'unified feminist voice affirming difference' and seeks recognition of women's needs and strengths, and a means for women's understanding of democratic process to reconstruct political life in Northern Ireland.

- *Medica Women's Association* was set up in 1993 to give medical and psycho-social care to the many women and children who were being displaced by the conflict in Bosnia. They developed a unique facility for responding to the trauma of rape. More recently they have turned their attention to the needs of local women, and to domestic violence and sexual abuse. Both staff and clients of Medica are predominantly Bosnian Muslim, but the presence of women of Bosnian Croat, Bosnian Serb and other backgrounds, and women in mixed marriages and of mixed parentage, affords a valued residual ethnic diversity.

- *Bat Shalom*, the third project, is a partnership of Israeli Jewish women, mainly living on kibbutzim, and Israeli Palestinian Arab women living in towns and villages in the same area of northern Israel. It is the local branch of a better-known organisation of the same name based in Jerusalem. They campaign together for justice for Palestinians within Israel and in the Occupied Territories, for a negotiated peace and for the creation of an independent Palestinian state. They also organise workshops, seminars and political and cultural events bridging the two communities.

The Women Building Bridges Project: aims, process and output

The Women Building Bridges initiative had three main aims. One was *research* – making and disseminating new understandings. We were asking in particular, what is it that women, as women, bring to these bridge-building processes? It was already widely understood that nationalism, militarism and racism are gendered phenomena. But how could gender be seen to be involved in the positive processes of bridge-building and conflict moderation? The aim was to draw on and contribute to theories of gender and national identities in relation to democracy. A second aim was *intervention*. We stated clearly, from the earliest version of the project proposal onwards, that by 'action' research we meant making a practical contribution to the work of the three organisations. The funders we approached were those we knew to have an interest in supporting 'peace and international relations' rather than academic research for the sake of scholarship alone. The third aim was *networking*. Although it was Cynthia Cockburn who identified the three projects, and negotiated research access with each of them separately, part of the incentive she offered them to participate was that they would be enabled to get in touch with each other, so as to strengthen their own practice by exchanging experience on their work, countries and conflicts.

The timetable and process of the action research, eventually completed in early 1999, was as follows. Case studies of the three projects, taken separately, were carried out between September 1995 and March 1996. They involved in total three months of fieldwork, interviewing and photography; and three months of writing up field notes. The following six months, from April to August 1996 (a period during which interviews were being transcribed), Cynthia worked specifically for the benefit of the three organisations. She prepared photographs for them to use in publicity. She made a five-panel display of text and photos to advertise the work of the Women's Support Network. A publicity poster promoting Medica's work was designed and printed in three languages, and this helped in a UK fundraising campaign that brought in more than £30,000. Dissemination in this period focused on non-academic audiences, and we wrote or inspired articles in fourteen magazines and newspapers.

Particularly successful in bringing the three projects to the attention of a wider public was a 13-panel display of Cynthia's photo-narratives on the three organisations. This was circulated between 1996 and 1999 to 27 different venues in 10 countries and has been translated into French, Catalan, Hebrew and Arabic.

During 1997 Cynthia Cockburn reported on the three case studies, analysing the organisations as small 'polities', exploring similarities and differences in the ways they handled identity processes and struggled not only to achieve their ostensible work, but also to create and maintain democracy. The book, *The Space Between Us: Negotiating Gender and National Identities in Conflict* (Cockburn, 1998), was published in October 1998. Cynthia presented the material during this period in around thirty academic and political venues, and prepared a number of articles for publication.[3]

In September 1996 representatives of the projects met each other for the first time, at a five-day residential workshop held in Mijas, southern Spain. Six women came from Northern Ireland, four from Israel and four from Bosnia. Together with two interpreters and four facilitators we totalled twenty-two. It was a very intense and greatly enjoyed encounter. The projects presented carefully-crafted histories of their projects and conflicts (not easily achieved when you come from conflicted national groups). The subsequent (very productive) discussion focused on the following questions: 'why are we women's groups? what are human commonalties?'; 'what is nationalism?'; 'what is the relation between women and nationalism?'; 'what is meant by tradition? ethnicity? culture? religion?'; and 'how

---

[3] The following are the publications that have appeared or will shortly appear reporting the action research project 'Women Bridge-Building Projects': Cockburn, 1997a; 1997b; 1998a; 1998b; forthcoming; forthcoming; Cockburn and Hunter, 1999.

can we build democracy out of differences – inside our projects and outside?'

At the Mijas workshop Medica, the Network and Bat Shalom conceived the idea of an exchange of visits. Funding was raised, and the visits took place in the summer and autumn of 1998. The lynch-pin in the exchanges was the Women's Support Network. They hosted a two-week visit from four members of the Medica Women's Association in June 1998, and four of their own women flew to Bosnia for two weeks the following month. In October the Network received four women from Bat Shalom for two weeks, and completed the exchange with a visit to Israel/Palestine in November.[4]

The conclusion of the research was marked by two one-day seminars held at Gresham College in London, at which we crossed yet more bridges. The first day, titled *Doing Transversal Politics,* was co-hosted by the Women Building Bridges Project (the researcher, and women from the Network, Medica and Bat Shalom) and Southall Black Sisters, a well known and experienced organisation of women of Muslim, Sikh, Hindu and other backgrounds who work cross-culturally for women in London. The invited audience included other black women's projects and a number of women's writing groups. The idea was to exchange experience of alliance-building, dealing with 'difference' in the midst of different kinds of violence, the violence of national war and that of urban racism. The presence of the writing groups foreshadowed the second seminar, which was called *Translating Words, Translating Practices,* when the participants from WBB and Southall Black Sisters heard presentations from women involved in arts and community projects who had had experience of working with words as a way of dealing with the difficulties of racial, ethnic, religious and social difference. These seminars resulted in a thematic edition of *Soundings,* in the summer of 1999 (see note 3).

---

[4] We did not include an exchange between Bat Shalom and Medica, partly for lack of time and funding but also because we felt that the differences in practical focus between those two organisations was greater than that between the Women's Support Network and either one of them.

Distinctive features of our method and methodology

In its research methodology this project was clearly *qualitative*. Qualitative research is multi-method in focus, involving an interpretative, naturalistic approach to its subject matter. This means that qualitative researchers study things in their natural settings, attempting to make sense of, or interpret, phenomena in terms of the meanings people bring to them. Accordingly, qualitative researchers deploy a wide range of interconnected methods, hoping always to get a better fix on the subject matter at hand (Denzin and Lincoln, 1998: 3).

Further, these 'interconnected methods' were framed within the study of 'cases'. We use this term advisedly, because, as Robert Stake has noted, *case study* is not a methodological choice, it is the choice of a subject (Stake, 1998). Our cases were organisations (the three women's groups) and a series of defined events (instances of interaction between them). The reasons underlying our choice to study 'cases' was no different from those given by other researchers. The decision usually arises, as it certainly did with us, 'out of the desire to understand complex social phenomena ... [it] allows an investigation to retain the holistic and meaningful characteristics of real-life events.' As Yin goes on to explain:

> case studies are the preferred strategy where 'how' or 'why' questions are being posed, when the investigator has little control over events, and when the focus is on a contemporary phenomenon within some real-life context. (Yin 1989: 13-14)

Case studies characteristically use an array of methods of data gathering, producing various 'takes' on the matter in hand. And this we did. Cynthia read *documentation*, including histories of the projects and their contexts, carried out *interviews*, and undertook *participant observation*. The interviews were, to an extent, characteristic of qualitative research, loosely structured around themes, but essentially exploratory and open-ended. However, the component of participant observation calls for some unpacking. It has been suggested that between the researcher who is the complete observer and the participant who is nothing but a participant there are two possibilities: the observer who participates; the participant who observes (Atkinson and Hammersley, 1998: 110). In this case Cynthia was the former, Marie (and other women in the projects studied) the latter.

The choice of participant observation, Danny Jorgensen believes, is most logical,

> ... when the research problem is concerned with human meanings and interaction viewed from the insiders' perspective ... It is a logic and process of inquiry that is open-ended, flexible, opportunistic and requires constant redefinition of what is problematic, based on facts gathered in concrete settings of human existence (Jorgensen, 1989: 13-14).

And indeed we were 'directly involved in the here and now' (p.9), 'building theories grounded in concrete human realities' (p.18). So much so that we conceived of the research as *action research*. But what, exactly, is action research? The term was around in the social sciences as early as the 1920s and 1930s, but it seems to have become a respected approach after its formulation by Kurt Lewin in 1946 as a way of generating knowledge about a social system while, at the same time, trying to change it. Lewin applied action research in business organisations (Lewin, 1948). Since then, however, it has more often been used to assist development of services such as health and education.

There is more than one point of view on the purpose of action research. John Elliott (1991), for instance, working in the educational field, suggests, 'the fundamental aim of action research is to improve practice rather than to produce knowledge. The production and utilisation of knowledge is subordinate to, and conditioned by, this fundamental aim' (Elliott, 1991: 49). Our own research aimed to produce knowledge as well as improve practice. Indeed we would believe that Elliott's formulation gives too much pre-eminence to the researcher as knowledge-maker and neglects the role of the actors in producing knowledge, which they do both when the researcher is present and when she is not. In this sense we prefer the definition of Elizabeth Hart and Meg Bond, who have applied action research in the health field.

> The emphasis is much more upon awareness-raising and empowerment and upon finding ways for researchers and practitioners to work collaboratively and for practitioners to become action researchers in their own right (Hart and Bond, 1995: 21).

Overall we feel confident in affirming that the research was an achievement, that it both contributed to the work of the three organisations and made a contribution to our understanding of the micro-processes involved in building and maintaining co-operation in democratic alliances. But in the remainder of this chapter we want to draw out some of the contradictions and difficulties we encountered, from our two starting points as university-based researcher and community-based activist, the things that at times became issues between us all, and the costs that were sometimes entailed in reaping the benefits of the methodology. We deal first with issues of action, second with issues of research. But it will be clear just how difficult it is, and perhaps inappropriate, to divide them.

Achieving action: pluses and minuses (written by Marie)

The burden to the projects. The WBB project called for a big expenditure of energy from the three activist organisations. Looking back, we perhaps were not very clear at the start what we were getting into. Early decision-making was more enthusiastic than careful. We tried to cover out-of-pocket expenses, but people's time (for instance time away from work to travel abroad), their attention and their goodwill (co-operating in interviews for instance) are impossible to recompense. The Women's Support Network perhaps suffered least from this effect, having a wider and deeper 'membership' to draw on than the other two organisations. But for Medica, especially, given its urgent practical work caring for traumatised women in Bosnia, we sometimes felt the involvement in the project made too big a call on project resources. And Sonia, speaking of Bat Shalom, admitted, 'It was very burdensome. We have few activists. Everyone is involved in other groups and organisations too. So it did interfere with other activities. We had to stop everything else to handle the exchange of visits.' 'But', she added, 'the benefit outweighs that cost.'

However, as the only project which has English as a first language and the one geographically closest to the researcher, the Women's Support Network bore most of the workload involved in liaising with Cynthia and producing feedback in the form of editing and commenting on the materials produced by the research. We also played host to both exchange visits and took part in two visits ourselves that necessitated a substantial commitment of human resources and time from the organisation. At times this was an enormous drain on our collective and individual capacities within the Network, accounting for at least one quarter of our overall activities, particularly in 1998 with the exchange visits and the publication, distribution and launch of *The Space Between Us* (Cockburn, 1998b).

The challenge of communication. The importance, and the difficulty, of clear communication across situational, national, cultural and language differences became more and more evident as the project progressed. First, there was the question of communication between organisations and individuals, which involved transfer of meanings across countries, conflicts and projects – for instance on the exchange visits. Within the Women's Support Network (and undoubtedly too for our sister organisations in Medica and Bat Shalom), we were fearful of over-simplification in the explanations, translations and documentation of our particular political context. How to summarise 30 years of complex political conflict in Northern Ireland without slipping into convenient labels and generalisations? Could the researcher not only understand but also convey the importance of nuance, the sophisticated intricacies of inter-relating across cultural and political boundaries, which are often delicately-balanced practices honed over years of experience? Certainly, our feedback structures and our frank relationship with Cynthia allowed us to challenge situations where inaccuracies occurred or more usually where the subtext was missing but, as in the case of the making of the videos (Cynthia discusses this further below), such pitfalls were not always avoided. New knowledge is seldom taken in on the first telling; it needs frequent repetition. That takes time – often more time than is available. Second, there is the question of actual language interpretation. This was a perennial difficulty. We had some professional assistance with interpretation, particularly in the main meetings. But much of our relationship with each other depended on the ability of women of Bat Shalom and Medica to speak English. Subtleties were often lost. We certainly budgeted too little for interpretation and translation. But money was not the only issue. To have had sufficient interpreters around would also have been an intrusion. Sometimes struggling to understand each other directly, the fumbling self-translations were part of the bonding process.

Processes. The most difficult and contentious element of our involvement with Women Building Bridges was the threat it sometimes posed to our own organisational processes of negotiation and decision-making. The research demanded a pace of response and reaction that was sometimes at odds with our own internal processes. At a number of meetings, both internally and with the project, concerns were voiced by members about the risks of pushing too hard or too fast to obtain either political views or actions from the organisation or individuals within it. The Network has established an instinctive feel for timing over many years that in my view is integral to its ability to hold diverse constituent parts together within a unifying embrace. At times, participation in WBB, particularly where interrogation of our practices and processes was required, clashed with our own organisational culture of process.

Expectations. To a large extent these were met: documentation of our organisation's work impact and vision was undertaken and produced to a standard not often available to an under-resourced, community-based women's organisation as was the promotion of that work over a wider audience. As a consequence of the quality of the research (and the researcher) the Network has had the opportunity to contribute to international debate and analysis with regard to women and conflict. Relationships between the three participating organisations were nurtured, deep friendships established and invaluable learning took place that has fired new activities, emphases and practices within our respective groups. Perhaps too there were other less articulated expectations of the research or, more specifically, of the research process that it could provide us with solutions to the dilemmas that we face in our daily work, traversing identities, political conflicts and women's survival. These were of course unrealistic and WBB, by identifying the actions we had already taken, confirmed (at least for me) that the Network is constantly finding its own solutions.

Planning the action. The content of the programme of each exchange visit was open to choice. The broad criteria were laid down in our agreed project design, but the decisions were made by the host group, in consultation with the visiting group. The programmes were packed with meetings and visits, inside and outside the host projects. This was enriching. But most of the participants afterwards said they wished they had had more peaceful time with their hosts, one to one. They would have liked to get deeper into their host projects. They would have liked a slower pace so as to be able to share more personal, painful, candid and meaningful stories. The ground had been prepared for this, women on all sides were ready for it, but the opportunity was partly missed.

Facilitating the encounters. This was in part an issue of facilitation. As we planned the Mijas workshop we were acutely aware of the heightened feelings that would be involved in it, the extraordinary complexity of the relationships and interactions and the likelihood of distress, pain and anger. So we provided for skilled, thought-through and consultative facilitation. In the exchange visits the facilitation was made the responsibility of the host projects. The events were spread out over two weeks in each case, were geographically scattered and involved encounters with continually changing individuals and groups.

The three projects habitually maintain their internal alliances between politically-charged ethnic identities by means of thoughtful limitation of agendas and extreme care in the use of differentiation and naming. They are very practised and successful at this within their own contexts. In meeting each other, however, the agendas were inevitably full of surprises. Sometimes tension was produced within the project teams, as relationships were exposed to this unaccustomed randomness and spontaneity. It was particularly liable to be generated by encounters arranged between visiting groups and *other* local groups, some of which were on one 'side' or the other of the conflictual line and were consequently less modulated in their representations of differences than the WSN, Bat Shalom and Medica customarily are. When hurt arose within the members of a travelling group they would brush it off: 'We're used to it.' But the fact was that, while on the journey together, they could not walk away from each other and were cut off from usual allies. Gillian, of the Network, had been at Mijas and then went to Bosnia on the exchange trip:

> The Mijas workshop was a hard act to follow, the way it was set
> up. Members of that workshop talked about it for a very long time

afterwards. When the idea of the exchange visits came to be put on the table of the Women's Support Network I don't think we fully took on the ramifications of what would be involved, what painstaking work you would have to put in to get out of them what came out of Mijas. Because this time the agenda was different. This was about two organisations showing off, showing what they'd got. Visitors coming, national pride, all sorts of things mixed in. What we got were great demonstrations of differences in ways of organising, differences in forms of hospitality.

Final evaluations of the project by the activists. The individuals who participated in the Mijas workshop and the exchange visits undoubtedly gained from participating. Nudzejma was one of Medica's group at Mijas, a Bosnian Muslim who had been obliged to think deeper about her co-operation with colleagues of different ethnic identities. She said afterwards, 'I've always advocated understanding and co-operation, harmony in humankind. But in some moments I feel an internal struggle. After the project I became completely certain of my convictions and my life wouldn't be complete without them.' Sonia, of Bat Shalom, said, 'Before the visit of the WSN to Israel I was part of the group but not sure I wanted to be very active. I was in the group, but not with all my heart. After the visit I feel I can never go back. I was so inside, so active, so intensely involved.'

But a question remains: did the benefit accrue to others in the project who did not travel or were not particularly involved in receiving guests? There was a possibility that some women may have felt excluded because they were not chosen to travel. Much depended on the way the selection was done. This was in some cases more and in others less sensitive and democratic. Something also depended on feedback from the active participants/travellers to others 'back home'. All the projects organised report-back meetings on their return.

The final evaluations provided by the projects as a whole were in fact positive. The Women's Support Network and Medica clearly intended to remain in touch and exchange skills. Indeed some of the women from the two organisations met again within weeks. They also felt that the experience of travelling together had strengthened relationships within the Network. And while in Medica, the Belfast women had found themselves speaking about things in their lives not uncovered before: 'That space must have been created for them to say things for the first time. There was trust there.'

Samira, of Bat Shalom, said something similar: 'The most important effect has been that *we* discussed matters together more. We debated, we got to know *each other* better.' And Sonia said, 'The benefit for Bat Shalom was it gave us another opportunity to look at ourselves and discuss things more. Because the project made us sit and discuss more than usual about the issues and our differences. For instance we don't usually see so clearly what different views of history we have. That's been the main benefit.' In addition, WBB had given Bat Shalom's work a higher profile: 'The photos and the book have contributed a lot to getting us known. It's added to our self-evaluation and the way we think of ourselves. ... Because we're all connected with communities, it has spread outwards. Everyone in our kibbutz heard about [the visit] and were asking, who are these visitors? They were asking us questions.'

Women of Medica said similarly positive things in their evaluation of Women Building Bridges. Rada said: 'For me I see only positive things out of our participation in WBB. The most important gain has been to know about the other projects. And it made us open more to ourselves. We got more awareness about ourselves and saw good things and bad things in our own experience. We got our problems more in perspective and got a feeling that they may be survivable.'

Achieving research: rewards, tensions, compromises (written by Cynthia)

Although we have divided the body of this chapter into two parts, one about action and one about research, it is not in reality easy to separate them. When I read what Marie has written I see most of what concerned her was also of concern to me. And the following, which are particular preoccupations of mine, likewise bear on the action as well as the research.

Researcher accountability. Arrangements were made concerning the researcher's accountability to the projects: I needed this for my legitimisation as a researcher and they needed it to protect themselves as activists. My agreement with the researched organisations involved two commitments. First, that I would show all material intended for publication to the agreed reference people in the researched group in time for them to comment and negotiate agreement on content. Second, if any conflict were to emerge between the needs and work of the researched group and the process of research, whether during fieldwork or writing up, I would prioritise the wellbeing of the group.

The second point did not present a problem in practice. Where material was sensitive I held back from reporting it. But the first was not as easy to implement as we had thought. For a research project to achieve its aims, a great deal of material has to be written and published. In this case a book was written, and many articles. Reading this material was very time-consuming (and eventually boring) for the three projects – especially for Medica and Bat Shalom where only the few English-speakers could do the work. It was sometimes impossible to have the material read even-handedly by a representative from each/all the ethnic groups represented within the projects. As for me, although I felt I continually gained by getting improvement to the texts, the 'clearing' process was frustratingly slow. I also found there were outputs I simply could not consult on: giving talks about the project I always have to *ad lib* about the researched women in a way I have sometimes felt uneasy about.

A problem of continuity. The WBB action research project had several phases, each involving the three organisations in different ways. There was a tension around continuity. On the one hand we wanted to gain the obvious advantage of involving overall a wide range of participants, changing the participation from one phase to the next. On the other, by doing so we lost coherence. Some of the women on the exchange visits for instance had not been among the women I originally interviewed, nor among those who had been to the Mijas workshop. They brought freshness to the action but lacked background knowledge and experience of the project and its purposes, a lack to which we did not have the time to give proper attention.

A difference of agendas. Cross-community alliances and the negotiation of identity differences was my research interest. But these are not the only or even the principal *raison d'être* of any of the three projects, all of which have other practical work to do. They do not at all times feel they gain by stressing politicised national difference. For one thing, not all the three organisations found it equally easy (or relevant) to arrange to send ethnically representative and fully balanced groups which I had established as a principle for the exchange visits. Rada said, speaking of Medica:

> The main focus of Cynthia's study did not apply to our day-to-day concrete project work, but to 'building bridges' between women who come from different ethnic groups in conflict. This formula may have meant much more to the other two projects than it does to Medica. Medica is a multi-ethnic team, but that is not a criterion for our activism. It happens in a more coincidental way. It reflects our previous experience of living together, which was normal for the women who are now in Medica. In the other two projects this is not the case.

Often members of the three projects flinched when, sometimes for necessary purposes, sometimes through carelessness, I used differentiating labels like 'Catholic' and 'Protestant', where they themselves would avoid marking a difference, or choose alternative differentiators.

Tensions between research and action. When interviewing project members I was quite clearly doing research. When fundraising for Medica or making publicity material for the Women's Support Network I was clearly sharing in action. But in the exchange visits I was acting in both modes at once. I was the contact person between the projects, their travel agent and, during the visits, their car driver. But I was also observing and recording all the time. At times tensions arose in this dual role both for me and for the activists.

On the Women's Support Network visit to Israel some members of the visiting group felt the programme had been insufficiently discussed with them, was too intensive and impossibly tiring. And I was seen as at fault, being the only one who they believed to be in full possession of the facts from both sides. Amanda, from the Women's Support Network, said:

> [The planning] wasn't perfect and I'm quite sad about it. Because I think it made me quite fraught, and it made me quite tired and

emotional. And at times I wasn't firing on all cylinders. And I feel quite cheated by that. ... Quite a lot of the time I felt I was being herded from one place to another, without being told what was going on. ... There were things that only you could have known. ... I feel you are the only one who could have helped us.

Others felt that the research role and my needs in filling it had not been made clear. 'You explained it a bit,' said May of the Women's Support Network, 'but I think you could have explained it more at the outset.' One matter that became a point of friction was that I had wanted to carry out interviews with the members of the travelling groups at the start of each visit and again at the end. Some of these interviews had to be scrapped and others curtailed because the programme of the visit and the participants' exhaustion allowed no space for them. May, who herself has an academic background, wished that I had stressed the research imperatives more strongly. In fact, in her final interview she said that she would have liked more, not less, interviewing to have been built into the visits. 'I'd have liked to be asked to reflect on the visit day by day. You'd have seen how my models were being applied, and how, when I found they weren't right, I shifted them a bit. And I can't tell you that now. You could have just taken the initiative and the authority. Set a time for it. You'd have got more from me that way.' This would have called for an entirely different pace to the visits.

But two of the group who went from Belfast to Bosnia felt, on the contrary, that the research factor had been too ever-present in the exchange visits. Gillian said: 'The first time [at Mijas] I felt very much into the WBB project. This time I felt torn between personal interests and the research. And at times it was frustrating. And it wasn't that I didn't want to be part of the research. But you felt there was a tension there.'

It was not that they wished me away: 'It's been nice to have you around, you're the connection between us after all.' But they would have preferred to have clearly demarcated research times and rest times during which, as Gillian said, 'You'd have been there, but switched off. ... We'd like to give you permission, by saying this day isn't research and you can leave your notebook in the house and just hang out.' She added, 'You should have had more faith in us and relaxed more and accepted that we would see you got it done. We've got used to you now. We know what you need. We can always switch back to work.' But I felt threatened by the idea of returning to the bad old days of covert research, when I had had to hide my note-taking in the toilet.

The issue of intervention. And just what could be seen as appropriate intervention by me into the action? I often wondered. That this project had been established from the start as action research was helpful. It legitimated my role as an actor. My initiation of the Mijas workshop and the exchange visits was quite clearly massive intervention in the first place. But endless questions flowed from this. For example, how much written information should I provide to the travelling groups by way of briefing before the visits? We wanted the travellers to be able to make the most out of the visit, and preparation could help in this. At the same time we did not want their expectations to be too shaped and coloured by my extensive prior experience of all three groups. Perhaps no input of information at all would be ideal? But this was impractical – I was inevitably conveying information conversationally between the groups. I had already written a book about all three groups which was available to the projects before the visits happened. Should I urge the organisations to read the relevant chapters? Summarise them? Get information directly from the projects translated?

A similar problem existed from moment to moment during the visits. A situation would arise when a piece of information slipped by me into a conversation could reveal and open up a connection between the two organisations, or introduce a new meaning into a dialogue. Yet I was meant to be studying precisely whether and how well they were able to make such connections. Should I withhold information in the interests of research, or contribute it in the interests of action? The answer was always a compromise.

An issue of control. There may perhaps always be an issue of control and 'author-ity' underlying action research. Transparency about who is in control of what, and why, is therefore of key importance. Here is an example of failure. I obtained the projects' agreement to my making videos of the exchange visits. I had two motives. One was to improve feedback about the visits to the women in the projects who had experienced them. The videos were intended to say in effect, 'this is what we did, who we met and what went on between us.' In the past I had tried giving the projects material I had written, but this had proved difficult for them to absorb and use. The content of a video, I thought, could be more casually taken in. It could, besides, be consumed more socially and would therefore perhaps be more likely to stimulate discussion in the organisations. The Sony Camcorder used for the purpose was my own and, with the participants' concurrence, I shot film at many moments of the exchange visits.

Amanda's (WSN) perception of this would have been shared to some extent by others: '[To me] action research would be *me* with the camera; this is what I'm seeing; this is it. Whereas this video will be you. ... I'll see something on the video that *you've* chosen.' And she was right. There were after all many moments in the journey of the four travellers when I was not even present. Why did I not simply hand over the camera to the visiting group and let them shoot what they wanted, when they wanted, as a 'snap-album' to take home?

Because – and it is something about which I was insufficiently clear at the time, with myself as with them – I had in mind a second use for the videos, a research use. They would help me to do my reports-back too, to my own community, a research community. For this purpose they needed to be not just casual snippets of film but as full and detailed a coverage as possible of the things we did and the people we met. More important yet, I wanted them to contain an analytical assessment of the issues debated between the projects, the differences and similarities they revealed in interaction with each other.

Not only filming, but also script-writing and editing are highly selective processes. I assembled the film on return to London, using the University's equipment. The script and the selection of images were cleared with the organisations before I went firm on them. But the videos of course recorded my interaction with the travellers' journey, not the travellers' journey as they lived it. The activists were right to feel 'these are Cynthia's videos'. And because they are not fully at ease with them I have been reluctant, in the event, to give them more than limited use in academic contexts.

Evaluating the project as research. As the researcher in this project, I have been candid about difficulties and compromise. But I do not want to give the impression of failure. On the contrary, I received unwavering co-operation from the three organisations. I was very satisfied with what I was able to learn and with the dissemination of results. The published output can perhaps be read as a measure of completion. In fact, for me it has been the single most rewarding research experience of my life. It seemed at each moment utterly politically relevant. And the warmth of the relationships made any tensions and complications that arose into a source not of crisis but of learning.

Reflexivity and commitment (written by Cynthia and Marie)

We said at the outset that this was 'reflexive' research. But it is worth remembering that reflexivity, as Martyn Hammersley and Paul Atkinson (1983) say, is not so much a matter of methodological choice as of existential fact. Whether we like it or not, the social researcher and the research act itself are an integral part of the social world that is being investigated. This being so, all social research must be seen as founded on participant observation. There is no escape from reliance on common-sense knowledge and on common-sense ways of finding things out. No matter how detached or 'scientific' we attempt to be as researchers, we cannot avoid having a role in shaping the action we observe. But there is one matter over which we do have a choice: how clear we are about it; how willing we are to make use of, rather than cover up, the ineluctible bias of reporting from inside the action (Hammersley and Atkinson 1983).

In this chapter we have tried to come clean about research relationships and processes, aspirations and compromises. It is especially important, and especially pleasing, to make the attempt because as feminists, as researchers and as activists, we share a political purpose: empowering women and their organisations, and strengthening cross-national and international co-operation between women. It has not been a question of Cynthia doing research in a way that does not harm Marie and the Network and other organisations. It has been about producing knowledge-out-of-action together, stating it more explicitly and publishing it more widely than might otherwise be the case, so as to further their shared political agenda. So here is one final descriptor of our methodology:

this was *committed* research. And it is in partnership for specifically feminist work that the methodological decisions discussed here were shaped. We know what Ann Oakley meant when she wrote, of all such feminist research, 'Personal involvement is more than dangerous bias – it is the condition under which people come to know each other and to admit others into their lives' (Oakley, 1981: 58).

References

Atkinson, Paul and Martyn Hammersley (1998), 'Ethnography and participant observation', in Norman K. Denzin and Yvonna S. Lincoln (eds), *Strategies of Qualitative Inquiry,* Newbury Park, London, New Delhi: Sage Publications.

Cockburn, Cynthia (1997a), 'Different together: women in Belfast', a photo-narrative, *Soundings: a Journal of Politics and Culture,* no. 2, Spring: 32-47.

Cockburn, Cynthia (1997b), 'Refusing ethnic closure: a women's therapy centre in Bosnia-Herzegovina', a photo-narrative, *Soundings: a Journal of Politics and Culture,* no. 3, Summer: 62-78.

Cockburn, Cynthia (1998a), 'Wrong and wrong again: women for peace in Israel', *Soundings: a Journal of Politics and Culture,* no. 5, Spring: 52-67.

Cockburn, Cynthia (1998b), *The Space Between Us: Negotiating Gender and National Identities in Conflict,* London: Zed Books.

Cockburn, Cynthia and Lynette Hunter (1999), 'Transversal politics and translating practices', thematic edition of *Soundings: a Journal of Politics and Culture,* no. 12, Summer: 88-190.

Cockburn, Cynthia (forthcoming), 'Choreography of a social movement: women's boundary-crossing steps on terrains of conflict', in Robin Cohen and Shirin Rai (eds), *Social Movements in a Global Age,* London: Routledge.

Cockburn, Cynthia (forthcoming), 'The anti-essentialist choice: constructions of nation and gender in two women's projects', *Nations and Nationalism,* Special issue on gender, ed. Deniz Kandiyoti.

Denzin, Norman K. and Yvonna S. Lincoln (1998), 'Introduction: entering the field of qualitative research', in Norman K. Denzin and Yvonna S. Lincoln (eds), *Strategies of Qualitative Inquiry,* Thousand Oaks, London, New Delhi: Sage Publications.

Elliott, John (1991), *Action Research for Educational Change,* Milton Keynes and Philadelphia: Open University Press.

Hammersley, Martyn and Atkinson, Paul (1983), *Ethnography: Principles in Practice,* London and New York: Routledge.

Hart, Elizabeth and Meg Bond (1995), *Action Research for Health and Social Care: A Guide to Practice,* Buckingham and Philadelphia: Open University Press.

Jorgensen, Danny L. (1989), *Participant Observation: A Methodology for Human Studies,* Newbury Park, London, New Delhi: Sage Publications.

Lewin, Kurt [1946] (1948), 'Action research and minority problems', in G.W. Lewin (ed), *Resolving Social Conflicts: Selected Papers on Group Dynamics by Kurt Lewin,* New York: Harper and Brothers.

Oakley, Ann (1981), 'Interviewing women: a contradiction in terms', in Helen Roberts (ed.), *Doing Feminist Research,* London: Routledge and Kegan Paul.

Stake, Robert E. (1998), 'Case studies', in Norman K. Denzin and Yvonna S. Lincoln (eds), *Strategies of Qualitative Inquiry,* Thousand Oaks, London, New Delhi: Sage Publications.

Stanley, Liz and Sue Wise (1983), *Breaking Out: Feminist Consciousness and Feminist Research,* London: Routledge and Kegan Paul.

Yin, Robert K. (1989), *Case Study Research: Design and Methods,* Newbury Park, London, New Delhi: Sage Publications.

5

Researching One An-other

Anne Byrne

Introduction

This chapter details collaborative research practices in a research project on women's self-identity. As the researcher, I am not a member of the participant group. Though I too am a woman, I do not share the characteristics which shape the collective identity of the participants and which define the research sample. An extensive number of research dilemmas are posed in utilising a feminist research paradigm; their resolution invites reflection and ultimately hard decisions. The issue of Othering is one of the most challenging. Given the social construction of woman as Other (see de Beauvoir [1949] 1993), as the oppressed relation, the challenge in a feminist research practice is to 'interrupt Othering' (Fine 1994) as much as is feasible. This chapter describes my attempts to develop a collaborative, non-oppressive, research design which builds on the researcher-researched relationship. Considering feminist theoretical concerns of Othering, I describe a 'relational' research design, developed for the study of single women's identities in contemporary Ireland.

Self and Other

Many of the demands exacted in using a feminist research framework are brought together for me in and through the issue of Othering. Consideration of being Other or engaging in acts of Othering, invites decisions about participation, representation and interpretation, provoking keen self-reflection as well as critical examination of all interactions, all analyses, all acts of knowing, all texts produced in the research process. I wish to detail here my engagement with issues of the Other in researching single women's identities.

Throughout my research the concept of Other includes Self-as-Other, the act of Othering and the experience of being Othered. I try to identify and represent the consequences of being Othered through the exclusion and marginalisation experienced by single women in contemporary Irish society. I listen to how single women have been represented as Others, as 'outsiders', as different to the mainstream and I learn about myself, I learn about those of us who do the Othering. I listen to single women speak about married women, about their mothers and fathers, their siblings, their friends, about work colleagues, about us. I know that the self cannot be composed without the Other; that Othering is deeply implicated in self-composition, in knowing boundaries, in relationship, in separating me from you. In Othering and being Othered, I know myself. But Othering is also a practice of domination and women are always Other.[1] Female identities are commonly constructed as Other and I want to understand how we survive this.

And what of my own relationship to this research project, to this topic? Where has it come from? I am not a single woman. I have a partner and am mother to two children. I am also an academic, a sociologist, a researcher with the attendant status, power and distance that these labels confer. I am another Other at the level of self and social identity in relation to single women. The location and meaning of Other is also ambivalent; in one place, moment and relationship it can be conceptualised as a position of power and authority. In another place, time and social setting to be Other is to be weak, impotent, marginal. And in the same moment, same location, same setting, one can be aware of the power and the weakness of the Self-as-Other. Self and social identity are composed of often contradictory layers of Otherness, some of which become more significant, more sensitive, depending on the interactional context, on the social, 'raced', classed, gendered relationship between the individual and her society, for example.

---

[1] Some critics argue that the construction of women as other is ethnocentric, particularly in relation to de Beauvoir (1949). See Elshtain, 1981; Tong, 1993. Thank you to Ronit Lentin (1997) for these references.

An awareness of difference, an interest in feminist ideas as well as a concern with the treatment and perception of women in Irish society are intertwined in the development of the research topic. I have chosen this research topic, not in partnership or with the permission of single women. In so doing, I may be judged as not fulfilling the requirements of a model of participatory research, but I am motivated to do this work not only for intellectual reasons but also because I believe it exposes a previously invisible wrong and practices of injustice. I have also been supported to continue with the work through the responses of single women in workshops and from letters that women have written to me on learning about the research. I cannot absolutely say where this topic has come from, but only that it is connected to me. My interest in singleness reaches back to my childhood, peopled by three spinster grand-aunts, one of whom was adopted into the family.

As the eldest child in a family of nine children, with both parents in paid employment, my two sisters and I spent school holidays in the company of Nonie Byrne and her companion Maggie. This household was very different to the one in which we were growing up. Nonie was single, worked for the Department of Agriculture as a poultry instructress and managed her own farm. Maggie too was single, having been placed by her mother as a domestic servant in Nonie's household at the age of 14, where she remained until Nonie died sixty years later. Both of these women were boundless in their affection and care for us. My other grand-aunt was Nonie Ba (Bastible) who lived all her life with her brother, a Catholic priest, moving from presbytery to presbytery. She was a National School teacher and a formidable, opinionated, deeply kind woman. Somewhere in my consciousness I became aware that not all women married and had children, that single women led interesting, varied, self-supporting, sometimes physically demanding lives, and this has made a difference and is part of the present story. All three of these women earned their own living, though there were distinct class divisions between Maggie and the two Nonies.

A similar thread was woven by my own mother who spent much of our growing years working outside the home as a teacher. She had to give up her permanent teaching post on marriage in 1955 because of the marriage bar, and spent the intervening years as a temporary teacher until the bar was eventually removed in July

1973.[2] Her constant message to the women in the family was 'get your piece of paper; never depend on a man for money – earn your own living.' So somehow, for me, singleness, educational qualifications, economic independence and difference became part of the fabric of growing up in Irish society in the 1960s and 1970s. I observed that singleness was regarded as a very poor second best to marriage, every young girl's ambition. In stories and talk I learned that to be a single woman beyond a certain age was suspect; but I was suspicious of marriage and motherhood as the only possible future.

In being drawn to researching single identities, I notice that many research publications on single women are authored by single women. The works are often celebratory of their lives, demonstrating the strengths and survival skills of single women or strategies used to combat a marginalised and stigmatised status (see for example Adams, 1976; Allen, 1989; Peterson, 1981). Being a member of a marginalised group and writing about that experience may well be a powerful way of overcoming the stigma of being Other, of giving voice to those who have been silenced; it challenges the supposed objectivity of the researcher and the emphasis on maintaining distance from research subjects. Such writing is very much part of a sociology 'for' rather than 'about' women, but it also poses a number of theoretical and ethical dilemmas for feminist researchers. For example, there is a view that only 'insiders' or those who have direct experience of a topic should research that topic (see Spivak, 1988 and hooks, 1990): any other relation between researcher and topic is regarded as an act of oppression, continuing to displace the voices of those at the margins. This argument is derived from a feminist criticism of traditional research relationships in which it is presumed that the objective, expert researcher would have little in common with research participants and that this is desirable for the production of value-free, neutral, scientific research.

The construction of women as Other has long been a critical concern of feminist sociological theorising which variously has

---

[2] The marriage bar was imposed in 1935 as part of restrictive employment legislation whereby on marriage, women had to leave full-time permanent employment in the civil service, in banking and financial institutions and in teaching. Some women chose to remain working on a temporary basis, which subsequently affected pension entitlements.

sought to bring women from the margins into the centre of academic discourse or has recognised the radical strength of being an outsider, of being Other in disrupting, de-stabilising, changing the centre, challenging the discipline (see Wilkinson and Kitzinger, 1996). But, critically, attention to Otherness reflects theories of power and domination, of exploring the relationship between oppressor and oppressed, of undoing the construction of woman as inferior and silent and of revaluing women's experiences, voices and knowledges of the world. Also, a focus on representations of the powerful or theorising from the position of the Other offers the potential for both transformed and new understandings as well as more enlightened ways of knowing and 'undoing' the social. This is the basis of empancipatory research.

Othering is ultimately about relationship, generating a sharp awareness of processes of exclusion. Othering maintains positions of power and control, since the powerful regulate which representation is permissible and which is not; which voice has authority, which voice is deemed expert. Feminist researchers are acutely aware that research practices are scrutinised for any residue of Othering, any sign of acts of hegemony over other women. My choice of topic to investigate, my sampling procedure and my interpretation can exclude some and silence other research participants; my voice can displace the voices that speak the data; my account will transform what is said and my research act can be an act of colonisation. This is what I do not want to do. Neither do I want to abandon doing investigative social science as I believe that research writing can contribute to the alleviation of oppression and that other people's lives can be represented in written research (see Game, 1991; Stanley, 1996). Yet I realise that solutions to the problem of the Other are a compromise and are at best used to undo oppression. Social research is intrusive of people's lives, may be harmful and may not directly or immediately benefit research participants.[3] Much of the advantage may accrue to the researcher

---

[3] This is not to deny the very many beneficial collective effects of research, manifest through policy or legislative change, for example. The point here concerns the research participant who has agreed to be interviewed; though many feminist accounts claim that women report satisfaction having been listened to with great attention by another person, I ask is this enough?

either in economic rewards, career promotion, expert status or academic qualifications.

There are always partial resolutions available to the problems of Othering. Some solutions will be rejected out of hand, depending on one's ideological stance. For example, Spivak (1988) and hooks (1990) are clear that Othering must stop, now.

> I am waiting for them to stop talking about the 'Other'. ... It is not just important what we speak about, but how and why we speak. ... Often this speech about the 'Other' annihilates, erases: 'No need to hear your voice when I can talk about you better than you can speak about yourself. No need to hear your voice. Only tell me about your pain. I want to know your story. And then I will tell it back to you in a new way. Tell it back to you in such a way that it has become mine, my own. Re-writing you, I write myself anew. I am still author, authority. I am still the coloniser, the speak subject, and you are now at the centre of my talk.' Stop (hooks, 1990: 151-152).

Wilkinson and Kitzinger (1996) review ways feminists have negotiated the problems of Othering: speaking only for ourselves; speaking of Otherness only to celebrate it; attempting to destabilise Otherness, and interrupting Othering (p. 10). In a criticism of speaking for oneself, they note that all representations and all theorisation of Others are not permitted; the powerful no more than the powerless are immune from the Other's point of view. Wilkinson and Kitzinger maintain that 'speaking only for ourselves' does not serve the interests of feminist theorising which seeks to disrupt the exclusion and silencing of women. They are equally critical of feminist work that concentrates on celebrating Otherness on the grounds that we tend to romanticise the resistance of Others, projecting our own political ideals onto oppressed women as we appropriate them to our cause. Strategies which seek to 'destabilise Otherness' in contrast, call into question the rigidity of identities, the construction of research participants as oppressed, of researchers as members of the dominant, powerful group. Post-modernist reflections on Othering illuminate the diverse locations, the contrary positions that we can occupy in the same moment. The category of Other is examined and is seen as ... 'constructed – by those who do the Othering, by those who reflect upon that Othering, and by the Others' own representations of themselves' (Wilkinson and

Kitzinger, 1996: 15). Presenting women's accounts and voices 'as they really are' is regarded as problematic in this view, as the researcher has created, constructed, transformed voices, in producing the research narrative. Others' voices do not speak for themselves. The implication here is that, in hiding my own voice I also misrepresent the voices of Others. Undoubtedly this is the case, as I choose quotes, themes, voices which fit or stand out from the work that I write.

Alcoff (1994), cited in Wilkinson and Kitzinger, recommends four 'interrogatory practices' useful for evaluating why and how we speak for others in our research: analyse and perhaps resist the impulse to speak at all; interrogate the relevance of our autobiographies to what we say; maintain an openness to criticism and analyse the effects of speaking on the discursive and material context (Wilkinson and Kitzinger, 1996: 16). Similarly, Fine (1994) has suggested ways of 'interrupting Othering' for feminist, qualitative research practice, through a focus on the relationship between self and Other, engaging in '… the contradictions that percolate at the Self-Other hyphen' (Fine, 1994: 70). She describes the importance of looking at what is between self and Other, that blurred area at the boundaries of identities between 'researchers and informants'. Her solution to Othering is 'to work the hyphen'.

> By *working the hyphen,* I mean to suggest that researchers probe how we are in relation with the contexts we study and with our informants, understanding that we are all multiple in those relations. I mean to invite researchers to see how those 'relations between' get us 'better data', limit what we feel free to say, expand our minds and constrict our mouths, engage us in intimacy and seduce us into complicity, make us quick to interpret and hesitant to write. Working the hyphen means creating occasions for researchers and informants to discuss what is, and what is not, 'happening between', within the negotiated relations of whose story is being told, why, to whom, with what interpretation, and whose story is being shadowed, why, for whom and with what consequence (Fine, 1994: 72, italics original).

Fine advises those engaged in doing qualitative work to first create and then continually negotiate with 'communities of friendly, critical informants' (p. 80) who can assist us in representational and analytical choices about whose voices and which location should be privileged throughout a text. Wilkinson and Kitzinger, acknowledging Fine's contribution to their thinking, suggest the following ways of working the hyphen: checking the validity of our representations of Others with them; showing how Othering works by listening to others' accounts of 'us'; listening to powerful representations and constructions of Others and developing opportunities for dialogue between Others and us (see p. 16). Many of these suggestions can be applied during data collection and analysis and I have attempted to use these strategies in researching single women's identities.

However, issues of representation, participation and interpretation come together in a textual form in the completed research text, which despite following 'good' feminist research guidelines remains a piece of academic, distant writing aimed at a limited, privileged audience and is not intended to be read by research participants. A case in point is research produced for a doctoral dissertation. How can I reduce Othering in and through the text that I produce for an academic qualification? Is it even possible?[4] In following a feminist, qualitative, interpretative paradigm of emancipatory research, I am motivated to transform ideological aspirations into concrete opportunities to reduce the effects of being Othered in the research process for research participants, and to open myself to hearing criticism of the interpretations that I make.

Researching with women: creating a 'relational' research design

I consciously decided to use researcher-researched relationships as a foundation for my research design. Since I am not a single woman I have little sense of the personal and private meaning of singleness. I have not experienced insult, hurt, discrimination, exclusion nor am I the object of attention from curious strangers

---

[4] Stein produced two versions of his research work on single people in the US. One is an academic account (1981), while the other (1976) is aimed at single and married people, sharing his sociological interpretation of singleness with a view to creating greater understanding of the choice and circumstances of living the single life.

because of my 'marital' status. In this sense I do not know what it
is to be single, to be Other. But in consciously 'working the hyphen',
developing the researcher-researched relationship to the fullest
extent possible and permissible, the design of the research project
and all research decisions can be altered so that Othering is 'inter-
rupted'. I detail the research practices which in their entirety
contribute to what I call a relational model of research, one which
gives primacy to the researcher-researched relationship.[5]

A cautionary note, however. I do not pretend that by so doing,
I have given research participants control over the final research
product which, in this example, is a post-graduate dissertation. As
the sole and final author I take responsibility for the interpretation.
But there are other options available to me and to participants in
the production of written texts; for example a few participants indicated that in the future they would be interested in co-authoring a
work based on women's accounts of singleness.

The research strategies that I used to build a collaborative,
relational research design in the context and limits of a post-graduate,
academic dissertation, were as follows:

- Devising interview schedule with participants
- Collaborative style of interviewing
- Using the voice-centred relational analytical method
  (Mauthner and Doucet, 1998) for analysis
- Sending a complete copy of the interview transcript to partici-
  pants, inviting comments, corrections, deletions, additions
- Sending each participant a copy of a summary report of the
  main themes of the work and inviting a written evaluation
- Providing a workshop/seminar on my interpretation of the
  findings – an opportunity for participants to meet each other,

---

[5] I stay with convention in referring to the researcher-researched relationship
(rather than researched-researcher relationship) as it is accurate. I am the person
writing and reporting the account. I am the researcher and it is my point of
view that is being expressed. While I did ask participants to write, comment
and make observations about the various aspects of the research process, the
feedback was more often in the context of how they experienced or felt or
responded to various events such as the interview itself, the workshop, reading
the summary report, meeting other single women. Establishing a good working
relationship with participants leads to the development of a variety of research
practices which contribute to an overall model of collaborative inquiry.

discuss the work, provide their own interpretations and raise other issues
- Inviting participants to read and comment on the complete draft account
- Co-producing a text.

I will now report briefly on various aspects of these strategies.

• Devising interview schedules with participants

Concerned with contemporary women's identities, and using a network of friends, I asked four single women to write about themselves, about being single, after which, if they wished, we could talk. I did not want to overly influence the potential form or shape of the content, except to say that I wanted to learn about the meaning and experience of being single and was attempting to set up a doctoral research study for this purpose. All four women wrote accounts varying in length from one to ten written pages, describing with elaborate, moving and intimate detail their reflections and thoughts on being single. One account was in the form of a letter to me with accompanying artwork representing her single self and her feeling of isolation from the rest of society. Another account followed the format of a brief life history, starting with childhood reminiscences and ending with thoughts on her future as a single woman. Another account begins with life as it is lived now, describing many strategies invoked to cope with the constant curiosity of others about her single status and the energy she has to devote to negotiating familial demands and expectations because she is not married. All the women retained a copy of their account for themselves as it was the first time that they had consciously put into writing feelings and thoughts about being single.

Asking for written accounts was an experimental technique aimed at assessing the range and type of information generated by this process of data collection. I knew that a written account was dependent on the ability and willingness of a woman to express thoughts about herself in writing. But what I did find was a rich and varied source of information about the meaning and experience of singleness. The women wrote about the significance of independence, the hurt of stigma, family reactions, the choice whether to be single or not, relationships with men, feelings of loss, childlessness, the search for intimacy, thoughts on marriage, personal development, feelings of anger, social isolation and the lack of complexity and satisfaction that living alone invites. The written accounts provided a starting point from which to begin to understand what it is to be single in Irish society.

I interviewed two of the women who had written lengthy accounts of singleness, using a draft schedule which was in the process of composition, based on topic areas that had surfaced in all of the written accounts. In face-to-face talk with women about their experiences of singleness, I understood that there were many stories to be told and I felt women's strong emotions about being single. I learned that I needed to be with women when they were telling their stories, I needed to be able to listen to what was being told. I wanted to hear women's representations of themselves as single women. I wanted to know if and when singleness became an issue for women's sense of self, to talk about women's conscious-ness of their single identity and to learn how women managed their single status in everyday interactions. I wanted to hear the stories, events, and turning points which marked being single for women. I wished to be an insider, to abandon preconceptions as much as possible, to move beyond the single stereotypes and to sensitise myself to the significance of being single in the present moment. I wanted a lot.

I learned from these beginnings that singleness may be, but is not necessarily, problematic for single women, and that conceptualis-ing it as such masked the complex composition of singleness. I also learned that singleness was implicated in how women viewed themselves and how others perceived and treated them. Issues of public and private perceptions of identity began to come to the fore. The interview guide itself was prepared in consultation with single women, based on issues women felt were important to talk about as relevant to their singleness; the guide also draws from themes and topics identified in the pilot interviews and written accounts. The intention in using a guide was to provide a focus for women as they related a multitude of experiences about living as a single woman. As the guide neared completion, I offered it to five single women for further comments, additions and clarifications. The interview guide begins with the question 'Who are you? Describe yourself to me', an invitation to tell a life story. The guide allowed women to speak about themselves, becoming/being single; the attitudes and perceptions of others; one's own ambitions on marriage and children; the meaning of home, work, religion; relationships with family and friends; thoughts on sexuality, intimacy, leisure, and on voluntary and political activities.

• *Collaborative interviewing*
In reflecting on interviewing, it is clear that there are several elements involved in the process: interviewing as a social relationship, as a method of gathering data, and as reflexive talk (see Oakley, 1992; Giddens, 1991; Birch, 1998). Following Chase (1995: 2), I regard qualitative in-depth interviews as '... occasions in which we ask for life stories' precisely because I also share the view that '... people make sense of experience and communicate meaning through narration'. My primary task as interviewer, Chase suggests, is to invite others to tell their life stories of experiences that are of 'deep and abiding interest' and that this invitation to tell life stories may need to be constantly re-iterated throughout the interview. The purpose of the life story is to acutely focus on the participants' own experiences in the first instance, rather than on the researcher's interests. The participant is regarded as a narrator rather than an informant/reporter. Chase asks what does it mean to invite the other's story and what is a good life story question?

> Unlike sociological questions, questions that invite the other's story encourage a shift of responsibility for the import of the talk. Our task as interviewers is to provide the interactional and discursive conditions that will arouse her desire to embrace that responsibility. We are more likely to succeed when we orient our questions directly and simply to life experiences that the other seeks to make sense of and communicate ... (Chase, 1995: 12).

I take the view that the stories of a life told in a qualitative interview setting, stories of a person in relationship with others, is as much a process of self-exploration as a process of telling, of narration. In speaking about being single, women talked about themselves and who they were/are, in the past, present and future. For some, much of what was said was tentative, a trying on of words to describe the self, helping to bring the self into knowledge. Other women described a more firm, fixed view of themselves. I found that I did not have to listen very hard for evidence of reflection, self-reflection, consciousness. What is evident from women's stories of singleness as narrated in the interview setting is that most had thought about being single, were conscious and aware of the ongoing meaning and impact of singleness on their sense of self, and had much to tell about their own experiences of being single in contemporary Ireland. In the telling, in the talk, substantial identity work was going on.

A great deal of feminist theorising and methodological writing has been concerned about the researcher-researched relationship, with a focus on reducing power differentials between researcher and researched, rejecting researcher objectivity and encouraging the active participation of interviewees in engaging in the interview process and in ongoing analysis. In this context, feminist researchers have written about the problems and benefits of using unstructured interview guides, sharing personal information about themselves, sharing written interpretations of other people's lives with them, encouraging interviewees to initiate and structure the dialogue; about providing help, assistance, counselling and offering friendship to research participants (Oakley, 1981, 1992; Finch, 1984; Stanley, 1990; Reinharz, 1992). Acker et al (1991) acknowledge the benefits of using principles of feminist research in a project, but are more sceptical about the possibilities for erasing 'the contradictions in the relation between researcher and researched' (p. 150). Their particular difficulties concerned the effects of sharing written interpretations of women's lives in which there was not only 'lack of agreement on the meaning of experiences' but the material was 'potentially threatening and disruptive to the subject's view of the world' (p. 142); therefore they chose not to share with women whom they judged would be upset.

> We have not solved this problem; we believe the solution lies in accepting the dilemmas and maintaining an awareness of when and why we are not able to make the research process a true dialogue, thus giving full legitimacy to the subjectivity of the other as well as our own. At least then we can articulate the difficult balance between granting respect to the other's interpretation of her reality, while going beyond that interpretation to comprehend its underlying relation (Acker et al, 1991: 142).

In the development of the interview guide and in building a relationship with single women, issues of participation, representation and interpretation are brought together. I wanted to be as inclusive as possible, while also pursuing my own research interests. Building relationships began as I wrote to and spoke with women on the telephone. These relationships continued throughout the research process precisely because I invited women to participate in the ongoing interpretation of singleness in dialogue with me. While this is ideologically driven, I am also concerned with interview data as such and the meaning of accounts produced in the interview situation. I am aware of the many factors that can affect what occurs in an interview (see for example Fontana and Frey, 1994), but I am more concerned about making interpretations of people's lives based on an intense two to three hour conversation with them. Interviews need to be followed up, checked not only for accuracy, but also to offer women an opportunity to add what may have been initially held back or deemed unimportant at the time, as well as to remove or clarify information which they now regard as incorrect or unsafe in some way.[6] Another issue of which I was aware is the support a woman may need after the interview is over, particularly when the material is sensitive. I always mentioned to women participants that if they felt the need and if I was the most appropriate person to provide assistance, I was available and willing to give them listening support.

Within the setting of the interview, which was always held in locations of the women's own choosing, where they felt most safe, comfortable and in charge of the process, I began with a lengthy explanation of my own view of interviewing.[7] This was necessary as most people's expectation of an 'interview' is to answer questions according to a particular order. Focusing on participants'

---

[6] In a number of instances transcripts were added to for informational and clarification purposes. Only one woman asked that I do not include any of her interview material in publications as quotes; another needed extra assurance from me that anonymity would always be provided as she did not want people about whom she spoke to be identified.

[7] Interviews took place in a variety of locations; in an interview room in the university which I set up as a 'sitting room' with comfortable armchairs, side-lighting and tea-making facilities; in my office; in women's own work places and in women's homes and on one occasion sitting outside on a warm, sunny afternoon.

experiences, exploring issues together, participants asking questions, inquiring into what the other thinks, as one often does in conversation with a friend or colleague, needs to be explained.

I made it clear that the participant had control over the time, duration, pace, responses, interaction, and topic order, and that I was essentially at her command. I wanted to communicate that women had some sense of ownership of the process. Thus many of the women specifically chose where they wished the interview to be held; requested a copy of the interview guide to hold and consult while speaking; chose which topics they wanted to explore in more detail; sometimes asked me to comment on what they were saying, sometimes asked for advice, guidance, affirmation; took breaks, asked me back, invited me to lunch, asked me to leave. On occasion women commented that I had not asked them a specific question or did not probe enough into a particular relationship and offered me an opportunity to do so. And I did. After that I always concluded the interview with the question, 'Anything else I need to know? Is there anything I have not asked you about that you feel is important to tell me or that I need to know about?' How I opened and closed the conversation was crucial to building dialogue. On completion of the interview I also talked with women about the possible personal effects of the interview in the days and weeks following. I mentioned that recalling past, painful events and provoking uncomfortable reflections about oneself could bring further distress. I said that I could be contacted at any time following the interview if women felt I could be of support to them. In the event, nobody did contact me for this specific reason.

• *Transcript feedback*
At the beginning of the interview I also explained that on completion I would ask the woman to sign a consent form, showing that she had agreed to be interviewed, was aware that the interview was being taped and that the material was being gathered for a PhD thesis, but that it might also be used in other publications and in other settings. Guarantees of anonymity were contained in the letter. I also gave the women a transcript agreement form which I signed, detailing that I would return the transcript of the interview to them for verification and accuracy. I also verbally promised to send

women a written summary of the research findings. In due course *verbatim* transcripts were prepared for each interview, sent to all participants and returned, with some amendments. Five women amended their transcripts; amendments included deleting references to personal names or places, correcting misrepresentations, clarifying and adding information to the original transcript. Two of the five women substantially expanded on particular areas addressed in the interview, providing more detail, other relevant information.

• *Using the voice-centred relational analytical method for analysis*
Qualitative data, based on women's narrative accounts of their lives, is, I found, particularly challenging to analyse. Challenges are analytical, ideological and organisational, calling upon a vast repertoire of skills, none of which I was sure I possessed. Distinguishing between themes and sub-themes, finding categories that were essential and fruitful, identifying key words and phrases, connecting theoretical concepts written about in the literature with women's own way of talking and experiencing single identities, developing and instituting participative, interpretative, feminist analytical frameworks and managing the hundreds of typewritten pages of talk is all potentially overwhelming and disabling. Qualitative analysis requires a huge investment of time and good data-management, as well as the development of a systematic and theoretically meaningful analytical method. For me this had to be based on a combination of my own understanding of gendered social relationships, women's accounts of their own lives, social scientific models of the relationship between the self and the social – all woven to build either a mutual or a parallel interpretation of the meaning, making and organisation of singleness and women's identities in Irish society.

Mauthner and Doucet (1998) note that writing about the activity of data analysis is still largely neglected in the qualitative literature. Reasons for the neglect, they write, may be due to fear of exposure and criticism; fear that we have not followed analytical procedures in the correct way; that in data analysis we are confronted with the subjective, interpretative nature of what we do and that this is difficult to articulate and may be uncomfortable, unsettling; and that the initial stages of analysis are 'messy, confusing and uncertain' (p. 122), as we intuitively reach for meaning, categories and themes buried in a mass of words. Mauthner and Doucet outline their adaptation of a voice-centred relational approach to data analysis which involves four readings of interview transcripts, writing case studies and sharing qualitative interpretations with research peers in a group setting. The basis of the approach is relational, a view of individuals situated in a web of complex and social relationships:

> The voice-centred relational method, and our version of it presented here, represents an attempt to translate this relational ontology into methodology and into concrete methods of data analysis by exploring individuals' narrative accounts in terms of their relationships to the people around them and their relationships to the broader, social, structural and cultural contexts within which they live (Mauthner and Doucet, 1998: 126).

Mauthner and Doucet describe the different emphases required in four readings of interview transcripts. The first reading concerns the overall story being told and the researchers' own intellectual and emotional response to the narrative. The second reading is for the 'I' voice, tracing how the respondent experiences, feels and speaks about herself. The third reading is devoted to listening for how participants speak about relationships, familiar and unfamiliar, while the fourth reading involves placing people within cultural contexts and social structures (Mauthner and Doucet, 1998: 126-33). The first reading, they claim, encourages reflexivity in the data analysis examining and documenting how theoretical interpretations of the participants' narratives are made. The second reading helps the researcher to listen to how the participant speaks about herself, before an interpretation is made. Attention is focused on when, where and how the participant uses the personal pronouns 'I', 'we', 'you' in talking about themselves. While Mauthner and Doucet pay less attention to reading for relationships and placing people within the social structure, I regard this reading as crucial to understanding the importance of interaction in the composition of self-identities, crucial to listening for connection to and separation from others. I found the overall approach attractive as it offered a way of listening to, hearing and paying attention to the various layers and elements involved in women's stories. It offered a partial resolution to the conflicts over voice and representation, though Mauthner and Doucet are as sceptical as others (see Acker et al,

1991) about a truly participative and equal research process.[8]

I wanted to experiment with creating possibilities for a more collaborative approach to interpretation through dialogue and textual engagement with participants. While mindful of the experiences of other researchers concerning differences over meaning and status and power distances between researcher and researched (Fine, 1994), I remain interested in a method focused on emancipatory research outcomes and on providing a setting for sharing analyses beneficial to those who offered the information in the first instance. I used four strategies in order to involve participants in the overall analysis of data: assisting interviewee reflexivity in asking for explanations of their own or others' behaviours, relationships and interactions while the interview was going on; asking for written feedback on the interview transcript; asking for a written evaluation of a summary report of the main themes of the research; and setting up a seminar/workshop for all participants.

• *Summary report*

A summary report of the main themes and issues identified in the research was sent to participants, together with an evaluation form. Eleven women returned written evaluations of the summary report, two adding two to three type-written pages to the evaluation form. The 17-page summary report consisted of the following:

- an overview of the research topic and a written explanation of the participatory model
- substantive quotes and commentary on the meaning of being single
- others' perceptions of the single status

---

[8] Mauthner and Doucet write that '(d)espite the attempts we might make to ensure that the voices of our respondents are heard and represented, and in the process trace our research journeys and make our own thinking and reasoning explicit, we must also recognise the impossibility of creating a research process in which the contradictions in power and consciousness are eliminated. ... We have to accept that the entire research process is most often one of unequals, and that as researchers, we retain power and control over conceiving, designing, administering and reporting the research' (Mauthner and Doucet 1998: 139). They also comment that the power differential is greater when we research private lives, as people have less authority to regulate research output compared to those in public, institutional positions.

- explanations women offered for their continued single status
- women's own typology of acceptable and unacceptable singles
- advantages and disadvantage of singleness
- relationships with working colleagues, friends, intimates, family members
- dealing with coupledom, living celibately, making decisions about childbearing/rearing with more attention paid to the lack of validation for the single lifestyle in familial relationships
- the connection between single social identities and the lack of ascription of adulthood
- a commentary on the importance of social support and of choosing significant relationships to enable independent living.

Women responded to the material in the report, offering additional insights, asking further questions, communicating interest and support for the work.

I am struck by the commitment the women showed to the study and the time they gave in response to my requests. For example, the report evaluations focused on issues that interested women most, aspects of the report with which they agreed or disagreed and how they felt after reading the report. The women shared the view that to be single remained unacceptable. As one women wrote, 'Being single in the West of Ireland is a stigma and women still need to be approved of by marrying somebody.' A number identified with the quotes used in the report, one woman writing 'as if I said them myself'. Another commented that she agreed with the presentation of singlehood as 'undervalued, pitied, taken-for-granted when it is useful to a family, but also misunderstood and invisible; that social structures are lamentably disinterested in supporting single women in anything other than the marriage goal'. Women wrote that they were pleased that someone else felt 'this was a subject worthwhile studying' and 'that I am not alone in my perceptions of how I feel about my status and in the way society as a whole see and judge me, e.g., odd, different, not having our views and ideas taken on board at work or by family'. Similarly, another woman said she was 'relieved' on reading the report 'as others feel the same and are treated in the same manner as myself, because they are single'. All of the women who responded to the report mentioned that their singleness was not accepted by others and that it was a matter of some consequence. Despite this, two women said that the report had provoked reflection: '... it made me think about my situation and ask would I change. My answer was no. I am happy with my lot.'

The women supported the focus on the importance of relationships to single women and identified with the pain that can result because of the lack of reciprocity in familial relationships. One woman described the many hurtful things said to her by family members. 'After my father's funeral one sister, in full earshot of loads of people, commented, "Catherine, you are the only one of us not married; can you not find yourself a man?" and later that evening, "You don't have any children, and at the age you are now, you f———— bitch, you won't have any either."' Some women wanted to learn more about coping with the 'attitudes of couple society' and overcoming the 'power of socialisation, convincing most of us that marriage is our destiny ... and the difficulties of dealing with the failure to meet that expectation'. Others were interested that women would actively choose to be single and wanted to understand that viewpoint more. A woman wrote, 'I see that (choosing to be single) as requiring a strength that I simply don't have, as well as cutting off a source of happiness which I hope for – many friends whom I respect very much are married and have got married recently as mature adults – and so on this I rest my belief that I am not foolish for even thinking of getting married.' Another woman feels frustrated by women's unequal status and wondered how much further she has to go to show that there are other ways of being a woman, besides marrying and having children, in contemporary Ireland. She feels 'annoyed that I ever implicitly lied or apologised for having the courage to be different'. She asked a number of questions about the isolation of single women from society. 'Is it self-imposed, necessary or useful? Do we have to be tough, self-protective as we get older? How can we convey to the world at large that it is none of people's business whether we're married or not?'

Two women had difficulty with the perception that singleness impacted on working relationships with colleagues, impeded career advancement, or resulted in being asked to work longer hours and holiday periods. Another woman found 'it hard to stomach women blaming themselves for not being married. ... It is sad that now as free adults they must still suffer in society.' One woman used the opportunity in the evaluation form to tell me that 'I am a much happier person than I was when I did the interview with you. I am clear that I want love in my life; to have someone to love and be loved by in return, and I am working on myself to achieve this goal. The result may come as a man or a child or both. I am not desperately seeking a man like I used to. I am quite content to take whatever is in store for me.'

The summary report of the themes and issues around which I was writing my account of single identities, a copy of which I provided to women participants, was not only an opportunity to share my interpretation of women's lives with them, but also a potent medium for dialogue and a beginning point for our discussions in the workshop.

● *Single women study workshop*

All of the women who received a copy of the summary report were invited to participate in the single women study workshop. I made the decision to introduce a facilitator into the setting as I was aware that the material shared contained deep emotions and long-held feelings and I needed a skilled person present to care for all of the women in a collective setting. The workshop was designed in collaboration with the facilitator to meet a number of research requirements. It would provide more detailed information to participants on the main themes and issues from which the research was developed. The workshop was an opportunity to discuss my representation of singleness with women and for women to reflect back on the representations being made. Women would also meet and speak with each other, a desire expressed to me by some women. Finally the workshop would provide a collective setting in which the participation of the single women in the study could be negotiated and formally closed.[9]

---

[9] I met with the facilitator for three two-hour periods in which we clarified intentions and outcomes in the workshop. The facilitator was familiar with feminist, participative research methodologies and had read the draft methodology chapter for the thesis on single identities. In addition to helping me prepare and run the workshop, she also wrote a detailed report of her observations of the workshop.

I believe it is important in involving others in the research process that the invitation is made on a formal, explicit and clear basis – likewise the act of participation must be bounded and ended at a particular moment within the life of the research project. If boundaries are not drawn, if beginnings and endings are not marked, then it is no longer clear whether immediate obligations to participants have been fulfilled or not. The workshop marked the ending of my face-to-face relationship with the participants as a group and was personally significant in helping me to separate from them. I also wanted the evening to be a celebration of women's participation and to appreciate their interest in and attention to the work. Six women attended the workshop which was of five hours duration. I was pleased that the women had chosen to attend and were willing to engage further with the study, with each other and with me.

To share more of the research findings with participants, I designed 'posters' on themes which best informed aspects of single identity in which I am interested and which underpinned themes of the research: exploring the relationship between self-identity and social-identity; examining single self-identity, and the relevance of women's dominant social identities for single women in contemporary Ireland. The poster themes were chosen to complement themes already referred to in the summary report so that participants could engage with the material in greater depth. Each poster carried extensive commentary from me and quotes from participants on stigma, choice, independence, home, childlessness, marriage, sexuality, and sociological categorising of singleness. The use of posters was one way of making my representation of singleness visible and accessible to women. Participants spent the first hour of the workshop moving through the exhibition, meeting with each other, chatting and taking some food and refreshments.[10]

The facilitator's observation of this stage of the workshop was: 'The categories of singleness generated quite a bit of debate and

---

[10] The posters were placed on both sides of large storyboards and suspended from the ceiling of the room, above head height, in a spiral from one corner of the room to another. Women moved between the posters, reading, talking and reflecting on the material. It was easy to strike up a conversation and this setting did help women to feel more comfortable and involved in the workshop.

response. The whole area of home also seemed particularly charged.'
The next stage of the workshop involved discussing with women
participants the labels/categories sociologists (myself included) had
devised in studying single identities. The use of categories to fix
identities is an analytical practice which I was deeply ambivalent
about, marking the power of the researcher to name others without
consultation – a practice which seems inimical to collaborative
interpretation. I resolved the issue to some extent by presenting
and talking about the categories I had devised to the women in the
workshop; single women as rejectors, acceptors, resisters, and rebels.
I also talked about my ambivalence in using the categories. The
women present neither rejected nor accepted the categories; rather
they worked them for their own purposes. We used the categories
to generate discussion on single identity. Using crayons, women
also drew their interpretation of the categories, and drew themselves,
using words and brightly coloured images to represent themselves,
choosing their own location between, in, and beside categories.

The discussions and play around the category work was followed
by a body/mind focusing exercise. The facilitator's intention was:

> to give an opportunity for participants to become quiet and
> reflective; to sense what are the most significant issues for them
> being represented in the study. Also to focus on what is important
> for them to hear, have heard and be witnessed with. Participants
> were invited to share issues that immediately came up. These
> included isolation in the form of being stigmatised and stereotyped,
> e.g. going to a wedding and having your sexual practices questioned
> by your nephew, who is being naturally curious. Relationships
> with mothers came up in this, also homelessness and bereavements
> ... (extract from facilitator's report).

This was followed by a collaborative sharing of symbols of valued
aspects of singleness for all of us involved in the study. Each woman
shared what she valued most about her singleness, using a symbol
to do so.[11] The themes of independence, freedom, mobility, achievement of ambition in a career, being self-reliant, having experienced
a loving relationship, caring for another, having time for reflection

---

[11] The use of the symbol was suggested by the facilitator to help women speak
about the significant aspects of singleness for them. It seemed to work well in
that the symbol provided a focus for the discussion.

and creative expression and the influence of role-models were symbolically represented in a photograph of carer and cared for, in car-keys, a driving license, house and work keys, a comb and writing set, a silver locket, a glass peach. The last stage comprised workshop participants working in pairs, talking with each other about meaningful aspects of being single, then bringing the essence of this shared experience back to the group. The facilitator introduced this exercise in response to an expressed need in the group to talk with each other. We finished with a closing circle, marking the deliberate closure of the workshop. Each woman stood inside the circle '... and was held there until she was ready to let go'. The facilitator decided '... to use this formalised ending, because of my felt sense of the deep intimacy and bonding with the researcher and with the other participants in the research. This was a time of marking the ending of this relationship and allowing the story of each woman's intimate lived experience to become public knowledge ...' (extract from facilitator's report). She observed that there was a reluctance in the group to finish, that there was a strong, mutual connection among the women, which was collectively recognised.

Concluding comment

The workshop affirmed for me the suitability of the themes I had chosen to represent single identity and provoked me to re-examine the usefulness of identity categorisations. I was impressed with the women's engagement with the material that I presented and their commitment to exploring single self-identity in the workshop. As part of a participatory model for data analysis, working with materials such as quotes from interview transcripts, the summary report, and written evaluations in the workshop setting, not only provided an opportunity for participants to engage in dialogue with the researcher on the material, but was also an opportunity to witness the impact of the representation of singleness on and with other single women. One woman wrote on her evaluation form prior to the workshop that she was 'fascinated by other women's responses to being single and that she was looking forward to meeting with the other women in the workshop'. Women began to build relationships with each other during the workshop and afterwards a few exchanged names and addresses. One woman asked if anybody was interested in setting up a Single Women's Support Group. There was a strong sense of bonding in the group, women asking when we can see each other again. For my part, I told them I would write to each of them on completion of the work. Finally, the completion of the workshop was also important for me. I felt that I could now separate from the women as my promises to them had been fulfilled. In the context of this study, the researcher-researched relationship could now be ended.

References

Acker, Joan, Kate Barry and Johanna Esseveld (1991), 'Objectivity and truth: problems in doing feminist research', in Mary M. Fonow and Judith A. Cook (eds), *Beyond Methodology: Feminist Scholarship as Lived Research,* Bloomington, Indiana: Indiana University Press.

Adams, Margaret (1976), *Single Blessedness: Observations on the Single Status in Married Society,* New York: Basic Books.

Alcoff, Linda (1994), 'The problem of speaking for others', in Susan Ostrov Weisser and Jennifer Fleischner (eds), *Feminist Nightmares – Women at Odds: Feminism and the Problem of Sisterhood,* New York University Press: New York.

Allen, Katherine R. (1989), *Single Women/Family Ties: Life Histories of Older Women,* Newbury Park: Sage.

Birch, Maxine (1998), 'Re/constructing research narratives: self and sociological identity in alternative settings', in Jane Ribbens and Rosalind Edwards (eds), *Feminist Dilemmas in Qualitative Research. Public Knowledge and Private Lives,* London: Sage.

Chase, Susan (1995), 'Taking narrative seriously: consequences for method and theory in interveiw studies', in Amia Lieblich and Ruth Josselsohn (eds), *Interpreting Experience: The Narrative Study of Lives,* Newbury Park: Sage.

de Beauvoir, Simone ([1949]1993), *The Second Sex,* New York: Bantam Books.

Edwards, Rosalind and Jane Ribbens, 'Living on the edges. Public knowledge, private lives, personal experiences', in Jane Ribbens and Rosalind Edwards (eds) (1998), *Feminist Dilemmas in Qualitative Research: Public Knowledege and Private Lives,* London: Sage.

Elshtain, Jean B. (1981), *Public Man, Private Woman,* Princeton, New Jersey: Princeton University Press.

Finch, Janet (1984), '"It's great to have someone to talk to": the ethics and politics of interviewing women', in Colin Bell and Helen Roberts (eds), *Social Researching: Politics, Problems, Practice,* London: Routledge, Kegan and Paul.

Fine, Michelle (1994), 'Working the hyphens: reinventing self and other in qualitative research', in Norman K. Denzin and Yvonna S. Lincoln (eds), *Handbook of Qualitative Research,* Newbury Park: Sage.

Fontana, Andrea and James Frey (1994), 'Interviewing: the art of science', in Norman K. Denzin and Yvonna S. Lincoln (eds), *Handbook of Qualitative Research,* Newbury Park: Sage.

Game, Ann (1991), *Undoing the Social: Towards a Deconstructive Sociology,* Milton Keynes: Open University Press.

Giddens, Anthony (1991), *Modernity and Self-Identity: Self and Society in the Late Modern Age,* Cambridge: Polity Press.

hooks, bell (1990), *Yearning: Race, Gender and Cultural Politics,* Boston: South End.

Lentin, Ronit (1997), *Re-occupying the Territories of Silence: A Feminist Auto/biographical Exploration of the Gendered Relations between Israel and the Shoah,* PhD dissertation, Department of Sociology, Trinity College Dublin.

Mauthner, Natasha and Andrea Doucet (1998), 'Reflections on a Voice-centred Relational Method: analysing maternal and domestic voices', in Jane Ribbens and Rosalind Edwards (eds), *Feminist Dilemmas in Qualitative Research: Public Knowledge and Private Lives,* London: Sage.

Oakley, Ann, 'Interviewing women: a contradiction in terms', in Helen Roberts (ed.) (1981), *Doing Feminist Research,* London: Routledge and Kegan Paul.

Oakley, Ann (1992), *Social Support and Motherhood,* Oxford: Blackwell.

Peterson, Nancy (1981), *Our Lives for Ourselves: Women Who have Never Married,* New York: G.P. Putnam and Sons.

Reinharz, Shulamit (with the assistance of Lynne Davidman) (1992), *Feminist Methods in Social Research,* New York: Oxford University Press.

Ribbens, Jane and Rosalind Edwards (eds) (1998), *Feminist Dilemmas in Qualitative Research: Public Knowledge and Private Lives,* London: Sage.

Spivak, Gayatori Chravorty (1988), 'Can the subaltern speak?', in Cary Nelson and Lawrence Grossberg (eds), *Marxism and the Interpretation of Culture,* Chicago: University of Illinois Press.

Stanley, Liz (1990), 'Feminist praxis and the academic mode of production: an editorial introduction', in Liz Stanley (ed.), *Feminist Praxis: Research, Theory and Epistemology in Feminist Sociology,* London: Routledge.

Stanley, Liz (1996), 'The mother of invention: necessity, writing and representation', in Sue Wilkinson and Celia Kitzinger (eds), *Representing the Other: A Feminism and Psychology Reader,* London: Sage.

Stein, Peter J. (1976), *Single,* New Jersey: Prentice-Hall.

Stein, Peter J. (1981), 'Understanding single adulthood', in Peter J. Stein (ed.), *Single Life: Unmarried Adults in Social Context,* New York: St Martin's Press.

Tong, Rosemary (1993), *Feminist Thought,* London: Routledge.

Wilkinson, Sue and Celia Kitzinger (1996), 'Theorising representing the Other', in Sue Wilkinson and Celia Kitzinger (eds), *Representing the Other: A Feminism and Psychology Reader,* London: Sage.

6

Extending Feminist Methodologies: Researching Masculinities and Technologies

Maria Lohan

Introduction[1]

The chapter extends feminist epistemologies beyond a specific focus on women's lives by researching men's lives. Specifically, this chapter explores feminist epistemological issues in interviews with men in the context of their relations with an everyday technology: the domestic telephone. With few exceptions (Ferguson, 1996, 1998; Ferguson and Synott, 1995; McKeown et al, 1998; Lohan, 1998, 2000a, 2000b), feminist scholarship in Ireland has been slower than in other countries to re-cast gender studies to incorporate the study of men and masculinities. It has been slower to appreciate that unlocking limitations on life-spaces for women means opening up the means by which *both* masculinities and femininities are constructed in everyday-life to be 'different' from one another – complementary but, at the same time, unequal. Studies of masculinity confront patriarchy by presenting a mirror to the male gaze. The reflection reveals not the lives of gender-free human beings or a singular masculinity but, as others have argued, a complex of masculinities and a complex of power between masculinities (Connell, 1987, 1995; Brittan, 1989; Hearn and Collinson, 1994; Kimmel, 1994).

The objective of opening up diversity in men's lives is to break down the very oppositions between male and female on which patriarchy relies (Brittan, 1989; Connell, 1995; Edley and Wetherell,

---

[1] I would like to acknowledge the contribution of Prof. Ann R. Sætnan, NTNU, Trondheim, Dr Brian Torode, Department of Sociology and Dr Gráinne Collins, Employment Research Centre, Trinity College, for their helpful comments on this work.

1996). Men's studies is an important part of the feminist project since it is not about presenting men as the self-declared representatives of humanity but, rather, the very processes by which men have been able to achieve this status. Gender, as Anne-Jorunn Berg says, 'sticks more easily to women' (Berg, 1998: 35). 'Yet it is precisely men's status as "ungendered representatives of humanity" that is the key to patriarchy' (Johnson, 1997: 12) or the 'ruse to hold on to power' (Easthorpe, 1986: 1). The argument here is that to open up the way men create and sustain gendered selves is an important way of examining how gender is implicated in power relationships. It is to theorise men's lives in a way that does not re-exclude women and femininities (Hearn and Collinson, 1994).

Apart from the question of *why men,* the second question must be *why feminist methodologies?* Feminist methodologies mark a significant departure from mainstream social science methodologies, most particularly in the ways in which the subjective and the objective are not taken to be distinct and fixed but, rather, as developing simultaneously and fluidly in the research process (Berg, 1998; Harding, 1991; Haraway, 1991; 1997; Lentin, 1994, 1997; Stanley, 1990; Stanley and Wise, 1991, 1993). Such an epistemology that problematises the 'subjective' and the 'objective' is of special significance to researching the lives of women – since women in our culture have come to signify one half of this equation: the subjective, the emotional and the body. Yet, feminist epistemologies not only challenge us to think about women differently, but also to think about *science* differently (Harding, 1991, 1996; Stanley, 1994; Stanley and Wise, 1993; Haraway, 1991, 1997). Namely, feminist epistemologies challenge us to think about *how* we know what we know when engaging in science – rigorous empirical investigations of natural or social phenomena.

However, feminist studies is not unique in problematising the production of knowledge and, so, the question remains, why feminist epistemologies? In straddling research of both technologies and genders, my work is informed equally by science and technology studies (STS) and feminist theory. As I will explain below, I have found both feminist epistemologies and constructivist studies of STS to be reflexive in the sense that both STS and feminist epistemologies depart from positivist approaches and understand knowledge as politically contested. In this chapter, I set up a conversation between the reflexivity of the sociology of science and technology and that of feminist epistemologies in order to illustrate points of intellectual overlapping and points of tension. I conclude, however, that the 'responsible reflexivity' (Lohan, 1998, 2000a) of feminist epistemologies is more intellectually rigorous than that of STS.

The final part of this chapter involves an illustration of the use of feminist epistemologies for my research on men, masculinities and technologies. In this, I draw on my experiences of *interviewing* men in relation to their changing experiences of a domestic and 'feminised' technology – the domestic telephone (Lohan, 1998). In so doing, I point to some 'lessons' of feminist epistemologies for my research. In particular, using feminist methodologies draws analytic attention to the interview process as a site for the co-construction between researcher and researched of gender difference, the performance and maintenance of gender identities and the co-construction of reflexivity.

Conversing between STS and feminist epistemologies – choosing responsible reflexivity

The empirical aim of much of science and technology studies, following the work of Kuhn (1970), is to point to the role of the 'social' in the creation of scientific facts and technological artefacts (see, for example: Bijker and Law, 1991; Bijker, 1995; Latour, 1987; Law, 1991; Lie and Sørensen, 1996; Mackenzie and Wajcman, 1999; Pinch and Bijker, 1987). STS recognises scientific claims to be value-laden and constructed through social processes and, thus, to be a form of politics (Latour, 1987). In studies of science and technology, this epistemological view is rooted in a grounding principle – the principle of symmetry – from the sociology of scientific knowledge (SSK) as outlined by Bloor (1973, 1976). According to this principle, the sociologist should be impartial to the supposed truth or falsity of (*a priori*) scientific beliefs and, instead, trace empirically the social processes and forms of politics through which a particular technology or scientific fact came into being. Thus, STS is, more directly than feminism, informed by a post-Kuhnian 'reflexive' epistemology that questions how, where, and by whom knowledge is produced.

Nonetheless, I feel that this reflexivity of STS lacks a 'rigour' in terms of *epistemology*. Here, I use Berg's definition of rigour as 'systematic attempts to make clear how and why I do as I do when conducting research' (Berg, 1998: 37), thus disembedding rigour from its usual bed-partners of positivism and quantitative research. As noted above, the principle of symmetry in STS requires a *detachment* on behalf of the researcher to map impartially the scientific claims of truth and falsity. Feminist epistemologies, by contrast, have generally eschewed detachment in favour of participation. 'Feminist theorists have been suspicious of attempts to escape (metaphorically, methodologically or theoretically) from the concrete particularity of bodies and social relationships' (Rouse, 1996: 205). Instead, feminist science calls for 'recognition of partiality, openness to criticism and to alternative practices of inquiry'... [and] responsibility for one's actions and position as inquirer and authoritative knower' (Rouse, 1996: 209).

This 'responsibility for one's actions and position as inquirer and authoritative knower' is what I refer to as the difference between the responsible reflexivity of feminist epistemologies and the plain reflexivity of STS. STS lacks rigour precisely because it is inadequate to constantly stress that it (the scientific fact or technology) *may have been otherwise* (Law, 1991, 1995), and that it is socially constructed between different actors, without taking into account the involvement, or the account, of the researcher him/herself (Sætnan, 1997). It remains essentially an 'objectivist' account in which the others are marked, whilst the narrator is allowed the only innocent position (Berg, 1998: 41). By irresponsible reflexivity in research, I mean being unable to be called to account or, as Haraway writes it: the *God-trick* – 'ways of being nowhere and claiming to see comprehensively' (1991: 191).

Taking reflexivity seriously in scientific work leaves researchers with two alternatives. One is that we abandon any realist discourse in our research – since our claims are also socially constructed – for an epistemological anarchism or 'post-post essentialism' (Grint and Woolgar, 1995; Woolgar, 1991 [see Collins and Yearley, 1992 for arguments against this route within science studies]). The other option is to integrate this point of the non-value-neutral – but otherwise legitimate – position of the researcher and the research account as part of the research project. It is the latter which I have tried to do in my research, and it is the latter that I have learned from feminist epistemologies (Berg, 1998; Harding, 1991; Haraway, 1991; Lentin, 1994, 1997; Stanley, 1990; Stanley and Wise, 1991, 1993). I believe that the incorporation of responsible reflexivity in scientific research need not lead us into a relativist vacuum (see also Finlay, 1999). It is not an abandonment of our skills to define social (or as in my case socio-technical) relationships but, rather, a more critical understanding of the strengths and limitations and, in particular, a positioning of our own claims. Incorporating responsible reflexivity can lead to a more reasoned objectivity.

Harding, for example, argues that the principle of objectivity is too integral to the philosophy of science and to feminism to be dismissed. Instead, she argues we need to develop the concept to a form of *strong objectivity* through the use of *strong reflexivity*. Strong reflexivity is about unravelling and making explicit the cultural and historical values of the project and removing the category of 'privileged knowers' (Harding, 1991; Berg, 1998). Haraway (1991) also argues this viewpoint in an epistemology of *situated knowing* as an embodied and partial objectivity that accommodates paradoxical and critical feminist science projects.

'Situated knowing', as I read it, shares with constructivist studies of science/technology the principle that all knowledge is produced somewhere by somebody. But situated knowing also adds the *responsibility* rooted in feminist epistemologies: that knowing must also be placed in the context of *inter-relationships* between knower and known (Rouse, 1996; Berg, 1998). That is, it incorporates the rigour of inclusion and positioning of the researcher and research project as a precondition for scientific knowing and thus takes responsibility for transforming 'knowing' into knowledge. There are, in Haraway's own words, no 'innocent positions' between the God-tricks of relativism and totalisation. The knowing self is always partial, seeking understandings of others (Haraway, 1991: 190).

Studying men in relation to a 'feminised' technology – methodology

My study of gender and technology concerned the domestic telephone and a group of men living in the Republic of Ireland. It was the puzzle of looking at men and masculinity in relation to an apparently 'feminised' and everyday technology that attracted my attention. Technologies and masculinities are typically regarded as being symbolically aligned in our culture. Images linking men and technologies – for example, men and heavy and sophisticated technology (nuclear science, high-spec computers) prevail in the everyday, to the extent that some of the qualities of masculinity and technology are regarded as co-terminus – for example, 'advanced', 'skilled', 'remote', and 'dangerous'. My study looked instead at how meanings of masculinities and technologies are both deconstructed and reconstructed around a domestic technology which is familiar, 'easy-to-use', and which previous research has suggested is predominantly used by, and associated with, women – namely a feminised technology (Moyal, 1989, 1992; Rakow, 1986, 1992; Noble, 1987; Schabedoth et al, 1989; Claisse, 1989; Lange, 1993; Dordick and La Rose, 1992; Fortunati, 1995; see Haddon, 1997, for review). Such a study of masculinities and a domestic technology had not previously existed in the literature. The apparently contradictory stance of looking at men in relation to a feminised technology is a useful research perspective in that it opens up spaces for examining the processes of variation and change in gender-technology relations.

In particular, I wanted to examine what the telephone (a technology introduced at the beginning of this century) might mean in the everyday lives of a group of men living in the Republic of Ireland in the late twentieth century. I wanted to look for explanations of the statistics of difference (between men and women's usage of the telephone) which went beyond sex roles. I wanted to be able to draw relationships between culturally-generated stereotypes, media inscribed messages, and the ways in which people perform usage (or perform descriptions of their usage) of the telephone, and, thereby, also of gender. In short, I wanted to explore how we engender machines and engender masculinities simultaneously.

An important objective of my methodology was to capture some of the *diversity* in the possibilities of masculinities and technological identities. The primary source of analysis for this research was the description by male narrators of the integration/non-integration of the telephone in their lives. From November 1995 to June 1996, I interviewed 21 men living in Ireland (the exception being one narrator who was living in London). I sought to include diversity not only in traditional 'background variables' such as age, class and, to a limited extent, ethnicity, but also in the narrators' adoption of masculinities. Thus, I interviewed one priest, one transvestite, 'new men', as well as elderly bachelor farmers, 'family patriarchs', and so on. The interviews were based on a non-random snowball sample of men, such that whatever variability I may have found represents at least the minimum variability of masculinities and the technology found in Ireland at the time. The interviews were not designed to measure the maximum extent of that variability or the number and distribution of variants.

In this chapter, I want to point to my own demands for a responsible reflexivity in this research through the incorporation of 'situated knowing' (Haraway, 1991) from feminist epistemology – namely situating the researcher in the research process and incorporating analyses of the subjective to create 'strong objectivity' (Harding, 1991). My own demands for responsible reflexivity, however, did not occur through (research) design, but rather by accident and it was this accident which led me back into an exploration of feminist epistemology, as described above. The 'accident' I refer to was my decision to conduct a pilot case study of gender and domestic telephony in my own home. I had asked my male flatmate (Seán) if he would mind acting as a 'pilot study', to which he agreed. The interview followed a format I hoped to pursue with other narrators. This, generally speaking, involved asking men to explain how they used the domestic telephone in their everyday lives. Questions also tried to tackle this question from another direction – namely discussions about the narrators' relationships with friends and relatives and how the telephone was integrated into these social networks. However, intrigued by some of Seán's answers, I also decided immediately after the interview to interview myself. That is to say, I also turned a mirror on the researcher's gaze. I integrated my own personal narrative in the research process by sitting in front of my computer and posing similar questions to myself, transcribing my answers as I went along.

The inclusion of personal narrative became a means of practising 'situated knowing' in my research. The inclusion of personal narrative has partial precedents in the work of Liz Stanley (1993) and especially Stanley and Wise (1991). Stanley (1993) refers to work where she analysed taped conversations with her mother and the diary she kept from the time her mother suffered a serious stroke to the time of her death. Stanley and Wise (1991) recount the authors' analysis of abusive phone calls which they had personally received on a help-line they had constructed. The use of autobiography, based on feminist epistemologies, works to include the position of the life of the researcher into the research analysis. However, the inclusion of autobiography ought not to be merely referential. It is 'much less a narrative (I am this kind of person, I did this and that and the result was) and much more a teasing out how the research processes are understood so as to produce the particular product' (Stanley, 1990 quoted in Lentin, 1994: 49). In this sense, the inclusion of autobiography is about creating situated knowing or 'intellectual autobiography' (Stanley, 1994; Stanley and Wise, 1993): an analysis of the 'processes by which "understanding" and "conclusions" are reached' (Stanley and Wise, 1993).

As Stanley (1994) has argued, the inclusion of personal narrative is a powerful way of illustrating – especially for the social scientist him/herself – that there is a mutual shaping of the readings of our own lives and the lives of others; and that works or knowledge cannot be separated from experience (lives). According to Stanley and Wise, the inclusion of autobiography shaped their analyses differently. They went through a process of 'seeing differently': 'Our own seeing differently was involved in a symbiotic relationship with our "experiences" both first order in the phone calls and "second order in analytic attempts"' (Stanley and Wise, 1991: 280). The inclusion of autobiography also shaped my analysis differently. I came to recognise that in looking for variation and performance of gender identities in men's lives (the researched), I began to recognise the co-production of difference, performance of gender identity and reflexivity between researcher and researched in the interview context and its implications for the research process. In the next section, I try to point out some of the ways in which this occurred whilst interviewing men.

Reflections on interviewing men

• *The co-construction of difference and performance and main-tenance of identity boundaries*
Being a woman is thought to be an advantage in talking to men

about their private lives and relationships. This is well documented in the literature on men's friendships (Allan, 1989; Stein, 1986; Nardi, 1992), and testaments to this view were also espoused by narrators in my study. Many of them expressed the view that it is easier to talk in detail about their personal lives to women than to men. For example, according to Brendan, a tradesman in his mid-thirties:

> Fellahs are hard … when it comes to time to talk. Like I said, fellahs find it very easy to speak to a woman. You can speak to a woman today about anything – embarrassing things – no problem and they will listen. And if you have a problem with a girl, speak to a girl about it. When you bring it to a fellah's attention, they speak in a different language. The whole story gets f——d out the window. Women are more level-headed than men. Women will take it down piece by piece and say maybe you are going wrong here, maybe this is something you should do (Lohan, 1998: 217).

In expressing the view that women are 'naturally' interested in the personal and the emotional and are even possibly capable of being 'rational' (see Brendan above, 'women are more level-headed') in relation to the emotional, it was easier and more acceptable for the male narrators to discuss personal matters with me. Not only, however, was I arguably benefiting from this gender norm through the construction of a safe space for men to talk about their relationships, but I was also actively maintaining this perceived difference between men and women. As researchers, I think it is important to understand that in the social construction of gender, class, ethnic differences and bodily differences, we are not neutral observers and the interview context is not a neutral event. My interviews with the male narrators occurred in a site in which they and I could reconstruct safe spaces of gendered discourses and maintain this difference between men and women. It may be that, at times, as researchers we find ourselves entangled in, and possibly fortifying, the very ideas we might set out to challenge.

The second point relates to the performance of gender identities and this remains with me most clearly. The construction of gender identities also occurred in a much more fluid and dynamic way in the interviews than described above. In particular, I noticed that I was performing *multiple* gender identities in the context of the interviews which, in turn, generated different sorts of relationships with the interviewees. This was most pertinent in terms of the interviewees' age but also in terms of their socio-economic positioning. I was particularly conscious of my 'multiple-gender identity' whilst interviewing elderly men, especially those who had retired and were no longer part of the 'bright young thing' population. Elderly men are people to whom I felt one ought to show most respect. Some readers with research experience are probably already replying to me, as others have, with suggestions such as, 'Oh, but the elderly usually very much like to have company and to talk about their everyday lives and in particular to reminisce.' But my interview experience was not quite like that. I had first of all set the agenda concerning their private lives, conversation that some enjoyed and some didn't. Secondly, older men know the world is changing too and by asking them about gender – and about using the telephone for non-instrumental ends – I felt I was also challenging ways of life to which they were accustomed. It is not quite the same as interviewing middle-aged men who still feel influential in the world.

I know I was different in other interviews also. For example, in an interview with a middle-aged priest who expressed strong views against feminism, I felt I could confidently wear my feminism on my sleeve. Similarly, I chose to interview a psychologist in his chair with his alarm clock facing me and not him. By contrast again, in interviews with young men, especially with men in similar occupations to mine, the interviews were always relaxing, much like pub talk. That is to say, the diversity between men and masculinities was very tangible in my encounters with the narrators in my study and hence also the variation of gender power which men hold as a group in society (Brittan, 1989; Hearn and Collinson, 1994; Kimmel, 1994; Connell, 1995; Edley and Wetherell, 1996; Segal, 1997). There is, as Connell (1995) pointed out, a politics *within* masculinities. Within the interview context, I was also responding to this diversity within masculinities through a complex performative spectrum of femininities. This, in fact, leads me to my third point – namely how boundaries are actively co-maintained within the interview context.

McKee and O'Brien (1986: 158) have noted in their interviews with lone fathers that the 'boundaries between women as "scientific observer", confidante and sexual being are sometimes finely negotiated and often conflated' (See also Warren, 1988). It was, in fact, the border between scientific observer and confidante which, at least in my mind, was being most contested in my interviews and this was especially so in interviews with young men of approximately my own age. In this situation, the 'chatting' about men's personal lives, their friendships and family networks seemed altogether too akin to 'chatting men up'. In their interviews, McKee and O'Brien have referred to this as 'a wooing process' (1986: 149) in which their male interviewees attempted to attract the interviewer's sympathy and concern. Equally pertinent to the maintenance and fragility of the boundary between scientific observer, confidante and sexual being was my own feeling that it was I, as interviewer, who was doing the 'chatting-up' and that this might also have been the perception of some of my narrators.

This flexible interpretation of the interview process meant that, among other relations, power in the interviewer/interviewee situation was not at all fixed, but rather varied from one interview to the next. On the one hand, I could lead the discussion and could take my information and run. On the other hand, interviewees could withhold or alter details of their telephone friendship networks, which I now realise happened on at least one occasion. This was when a young man who, despite having talked at length about his (telephone) relationships with ex-girlfriends, made no mention of his current girlfriend at all at the time of the interview. He had decided instead that this relationship was entirely irrelevant to his usage of the phone or to the interview – and only told me about it by chance in a much later meeting. In such moments, it is clear that the interview process is, overall, an intricate and fluid web of gender and power relations.

• *The co-construction of reflexivity*
As each interview progressed, I usually had ample material on the narrators' integration of the domestic telephone into their everyday lives with much scope for the analysis of the mutual shaping of gendered and technological identities. In particular, I often became able to draw on theories of gender construction that could approximate the ways in which the narrators were making sense of their lives. During the interview, I could already hear things that I would say about them later. However, I felt a little uncomfortable about this. I wanted the narrators to also be able to 'defend' themselves later in the face of my descriptions of how gender-technology

relationships were being performed here. As I have described above, the inclusion of my 'intellectual autobiography' made me aware of my own partial perspective. Thus, in being reflexive about my own performances of gender, I also invited the interviewees to be reflexive of theirs. I realise that within feminist methodologies, there are some well-worked ways of doing this – for example, to have returned to the interviewees with the analysis would have been a more thorough way to have addressed this question (see Lentin, 1997; and Byrne, in this volume). However, I decided this would be inappropriate due to a perceived lack of interest on their part.

Instead, I entered into a stage of what might be referred to as interactive interviewing. I had already asked men about the technology – in which case, gender became relevant. But, I also asked men about gender, which frequently introduced technology as a site of changing gender negotiations. More specifically, in my research I have sought the narrators' own conceptions of what social changes (such as feminisms, new men's movements or generational differences) meant in their daily lives. This is because I wanted an insight into how the narrators were reading their own performances of gender and technology.

Thus, the interview also became a site for such reflexivity. For example, Senan was an elderly man living with his wife in a rural part of Ireland. In the course of the interview, he described how he and his wife had integrated the domestic telephone into their every-day lives in completely different and opposing ways. His attitude to the domestic phone is best summarised by himself: 'One I don't like it and two she loves it so why interfere?' For Senan, this division is a product of men and women being '*completely* different'. He regards this gender difference as being 'instinctive', that 'maybe society reinforces it but they [men and women] are born with this difference'.

Yet people's biographies are pluralised and, during our life-course, changing circumstances might also call us to question values and knowledge. What we regard as natural and right in gender orders can take unexpected turns in our lives, creating contradictions between ideologies and practices. This was also true of Senan. Paula, Senan's wife, developed a serious illness and now has limited mobility. Consequently, Senan actually did most of the housework. Our interview, in fact, was finally drawn to a close when he had to go and make the dinner. This disruption to the traditional or stereotypical division of labour between Senan and his wife – which Senan saw as a product of the natural differences between men and women – was a source of disturbance to him.

The interview became a context for him to express and rationalise this contradiction. His necessity to renegotiate this labour – *doing* 'women's work' – made him worried about his natural difference from his partner – *being* a man: 'You know, I look at myself doing all this women's work and I wonder which side of the fence I'm on.' When I asked him if he was sure there was such a fence, he said: 'Of course there is. Men and women are completely different. But I don't know, I've got to do it anyhow.' For my purpose, it was an interesting moment as it showed the construction of biography and thereby of a gendered identity.[2] It showed the interaction between private experiences and public discourses and the tension we sometimes experience in reconciling the two as life-experiences change. In effect, the 'subjective' making of 'objective' realities was being performed before my very eyes. I have also found reassurance in such an 'interactive' approach to interviewing in feminist epistemologies, but particularly *situated knowing* as outlined by Haraway:

> Situated knowledges require that the object of knowledge be pictured as an actor and agent, not a screen or a ground or a resource, never finally as slave to the master that closes off the dialectic in his unique agency and authorship of 'objective' knowledge. ... Actors come in many and wonderful forms. Accounts of a 'real' world do not, then, depend on a logic of 'discovery' but on a power-charged social relation of 'conversation'. The world neither speaks for itself nor disappears in favour of a master decoder (Haraway, 1991: 198).

Conclusion

This chapter elaborated the scope of feminist epistemologies beyond an exclusive focus on women's lives by researching men's lives. Within gender studies in Ireland, there is a notable paucity of

---

[2] See also Personal Narratives Group (1989), on women's personal narratives as 'a vital entry point for examining the interaction between the individual and society in the construction of gender' (Personal Narratives Group, 1989: 5).

research on men and masculinities. Yet, the lack of scholarship on how men construct their gender identity in modern-day Ireland serves to accentuate the perception of men as norm and ungendered and women as Other and gendered. Internationally, feminist-informed scholarship of men's studies has opened up research into men's everyday lives, the gendering of these experiences, diversity of masculinities, and variations in the power within masculinities as well as between femininities and masculinities. Such research is profoundly political in terms of seeking equitable gender-relations. Exploring diversity in masculinities can serve to break down the very gender dichotomies on which patriarchy relies, as well as opening up space for coalitions between men and women across sexual, ethnic, class, able and disabled identities, and other categories which we are only beginning to care about (cf. Law, 1991).

The extension of feminist methodologies beyond a focus on women's lives is a logical step since feminist epistemologies not only challenge and augment knowledge in the substantive area of women's lives but in the very practices of *doing* science. Chiefly, I have argued that feminist methodologies achieve this contribution by problematising simplistic accounts of the construction of 'objective' knowledge in the research process. Feminist epistemologies are, however, not unique in their questioning of the relationships between science and society in the construction of knowledge. The sociology of scientific knowledge (SSK) and science and technology studies (STS) have also consistently focused on questions of 'the political economy of knowledge production' (Bhavnani, 1993: 96), namely, how knowledge is produced, who produces it, and how certain knowledge systems become privileged.

The second question addressed in this chapter is, why feminist epistemologies? I have argued that both schools of thought (STS and feminist epistemologies) are reflexive about the ways in which 'objective' realities are constructed. However, I have also argued that the reflexivity of feminist epistemologies is more scientifically rigorous, in that it includes the role of the researcher and the research project as a legitimate and necessary part of the analysis of the political economy of knowledge production. Thus, the reflexivity of feminist epistemology becomes *responsible* reflexivity, as the researcher must also become accountable for his/her knowledge claims.

Furthermore, I have drawn on feminist writers, most notably Harding (1991, 1986) and Haraway (1991), to suggest that feminist reflexivity is responsible reflexivity, since, unlike much of the debate on reflexivity within STS, feminist reflexivity does not amount to a denial of the opportunity to make scientific claims from our research. Rather, feminist methodologies present opportunities to the researcher to recognise, and account for, our claims as being created through the social processes of research and, consequently, embodied and partial – or 'situated knowing' (Haraway, 1991). Our claims can, nonetheless, be legitimate claims, and all the more so when theorised in the context of situated knowing.

In the second half of this chapter, I have discussed how the inclusion of 'intellectual autobiography' (Stanley, 1994; Stanley and Wise, 1993) became a means of practising situated knowing in my research. The analysis focused on my reflections of interviewing men and theorising the relationships of interviewer/interviewee as a stage in the construction of knowledge. In particular, the analysis pointed to, one, the co-construction of difference, and performance of maintenance of identity boundaries and, two, the co-construction of reflexivity within the interview context – all of which had a bearing on the data from which I could later work.

I have tried to highlight ways in which the interview context is not a neutral space but rather an instance in which gender, class, ethnic and bodily differences may be re-constructed or, conversely, an instance in which they can be challenged. For example, I had set out in this research to challenge dominant representations of male reticence towards a feminised machine, and thus look for variation in masculinities amongst men. Yet, in reconstructing a space, in the process of my research, for men to talk about their personal lives (friendship and family networks), I was also re-constructing a space for gendered stereotypes and gendered conversations – as the woman who was interested in the personal, and the interview as a safe space for a man to talk to a woman about the personal.

I also became aware of how gender was being re-constructed in a much more fluid and dynamic way in the research process – especially in coming to see performances of my own multiple gender identities within the interview context. This, of course, was a relational construction, since my performances were almost always

in response to the encountered performative variation of masculinities. The interview context is clearly considered not merely as a
representation of gender identities within the research process, but
rather as a context for the *performance* of gender relations, with
the consequent possibility of changing gender relations. Furthermore, since gender-relations were being performed, so too were
power-relations. Thus power could not be represented in my study
as a static relationship between men and women or between
researcher and researched. Rather, power was being negotiated
constantly within the interview context. The interplay of negotiated
gender and power relationships was also apparent in the struggle
I experienced to maintain boundaries between scientific observer,
sexual being and confidante during the course of my interviews.

Finally, my interviews illustrated the co-construction of reflexivity.
Although I did not follow the practice of allowing interviewees a
right of reply, I did engage in a process of interactive interviewing
in which I not only encouraged the narrators to tell their stories,
but also invited them to reflect on their own reading of their stories
within the interview context. I have found men's reflexivity on
what it means to be a man in everyday life to be a significant
source in adding to the richness of my data and in connecting the
material (gender relations in everyday life) with symbolic levels
(ideologies of masculinities) of gender. It was my attempt to research,
as Haraway has highlighted, with the explicit assumption that my
research results rested less on a logic of 'discovery' and more on a
power-charged social relation of 'conversation' (Haraway, 1991:
198).

Feminist methodologies help us to focus on the in-between
spaces, the processes through which knowledge is constructed,
and to include in this the role of the researcher and the relationships
between researcher and researched. In so doing, the research
process is not so much a means to an end but an integral part of
that end.

References

Allan, George (1989), *Friendship: Developing a Sociological Perspective*,
    Boulder CO: Westview.
Bhavnani, Kum-Kum (1993), 'Tracing the contours: feminist research

and feminist objectivity', *Women's Studies International Forum,* vol. 16, no. 2: 95-104.

Berg, Anne-Jorunn (1998), 'Feminist methodology: how might we link rigour and situated knowledge in practice?', in Roger Silverstone and Marin Hartmann (eds), *Methodologies for Media and Information Technology Research in Everyday Life,* EMTEL Working Paper, no. 5, University of Sussex, UK.

Bijker, Wiebe E. (1995), *Of Bicycles, Bakelites and Bulbs. Towards a Theory of Sociotechnical Change,* Cambridge, MA: MIT Press.

Bijker, Wiebe E. and John Law (eds) (1991), *Shaping Technology/ Building Society: Studies in Sociotechnical Change,* Cambridge, MA: MIT Press.

Bloor, David (1973), 'Wittgenstein and Mannheim on the Sociology of Mathematics', *Studies in History and the Philosophy of Science,* vol. 4: 173-191.

Bloor, David (1976), *Knowledge and Social Imagery,* London: Routledge and Kegan Paul.

Brittan, Arthur (1989), *Masculinity and Power,* Oxford: Blackwell.

Claisse, Gerard (1989), 'Telefon, Kommunikation und Gesellschaft: Daten gegen Mythen', in Ulrich Lange, Klaus Beck and Axel Zerdick (eds), *Telefon und Gesellschaft: Beitrage zu einer Soziologie der Telefonkommunikation,* vol. 1, Berlin: Volker Speiss.

Collins, Harry and Stevan Yearley (1992), 'Journey into space', in Andrew Pickering (ed.), *Science as Practice and Culture,* Chicago IL: University of Chicago Press.

Connell, Robert W. (1987), *Gender and Power,* Cambridge: Polity Press.

Connell, Robert W. (1995), *Masculinities,* Cambridge: Polity Press in association with Blackwell Publishers.

Dordick, Herbert and Raymond La Rose (1992), *The Telephone in Daily Life: A Study of Personal Telephone Use,* Philadelphia: Temple University.

Easthorpe, Anthony (1986), *What a Man's Gotta Do: The Masculine Myth in Popular Culture,* London: Paladin.

Edley, Nigel, and Margaret Wetherell (1996), 'Masculinity, power and identity', in Máirtín Mac an Ghaill (ed.), *Understanding Masculinities,* Buckhingham, UK and Philadelphia, USA: Open University Press.

Ferguson, Harry (1996), 'Men's issues and changing experiences of masculinity in Ireland', in David McCarthy and Richard Lewis (eds), *Man and Now: Changing Perspectives,* Cork: Togher Family Centre.

Ferguson, Harry (1998), 'Working with men and masculinities', *Feedback, Journal of the Family Therapy Association of Ireland,* vol. 8, no. 1: 33-36.

Ferguson, Harry and P. Synott (1995), 'Intervention into domestic violence in Ireland: developing policy and practice with men who batter', *Administration,* vol. 43, no. 3: 57-81.

Finlay, Andrew (1999), '"Whatever you say say nothing": an ethnographic encounter in Northern Ireland and its sequel', *Sociological Research Online,* vol 4, no. 3, http://www.socresonline.org.uk/socresonline/4/3/finlay.html.

Fortunati, Leopoldini (1995), *Gli Italiani al Telefono,* Milano: Franco-Angeli.

Fuller, Steve (1991), *Social Epistemology,* Bloomington and Indiapolis: Indiana University Press.

Grint, Keith and Stephen Woolgar (1995), 'On some failure of nerves in constructivist and feminist analyses of technology', in Keith Grint and Rosalind Gill (eds), *The Gender-Technology Relation: Contemporary Theory and Research,* London: Taylor and Francis.

Haddon, Leslie (1997), *Empirical Research on the Domestic Phone: A Literature Review,* CulCom Working Paper, no. 2, Falmer, Brighton: University of Sussex.

Haraway, Donna (1991), *Simians, Cyborgs and Women, The Reinvention of Nature,* London: Free Association Books.

Haraway, Donna (1997), *Modest Witness@ Second Millenium. FemaleMan© meets OncoMouse™: Feminism and Technoscience,* New York: Routledge.

Harding, Sandra (1986), *The Science Question in Feminism,* Ithaca: Cornell University Press.

Harding, Sandra (1991), *Whose Science? Whose Knowledge?,* Milton Keynes: Open University Press.

Hearn, Jeff and David Collinson (1994), 'Theorizing unities and differences between men and between masculinities', in Michael Kaufmann and Harry Brod (eds), *Theorizing Masculinities,* Newbury Park, CA: SAGE.

Johnson, Sally (1997), 'Theorizing language and masculinity: a feminist perspective', in Sally Johnson and Ulrika H. Meinhof (eds), *Language and Masculinity,* London: Blackwell Publishers.

Kimmel, Michael (1994), 'Masculinity as homophobia: fear, shame and silence in the construction of gender identity', in Michael Kaufmann and Harry Brod (eds), *Theorizing Masculinities,* Newbury Park, CA: Sage.

Kuhn, Thomas (1970), *The Structure of Scientific Revolutions,* Second Edition, Chicago: University of Chicago Press.

Lange, Ulrich (1993), 'Telefonkommunikation im Privaten Alltag und die Grenzen der Interpretation', in Sybille Meyer and Ewa Schulze (eds), *Technisiertes Familienleben: Blick zurück und nach Vorn,* Berlin: Sigma.

Latour, Bruno (1987), *Science in Action: How to Follow Scientists and Engineers Through Society,* Cambridge, USA: Cambridge University Press.

Law, John (1991), 'Introduction: monsters, machines and sociotechnical relations', in John Law (ed.), *A Sociology of Monsters: Essays on Power, Technology and Domination,* London: Routledge.

Law, John (1995), 'Traduction/Trahision: Notes on ANT', Paper presented to EASST workshop, Social Theory and Social Studies of Science, Bielefeld: May 9-13 1995.

Lentin, Ronit (1994), '"I'll be a post-feminist in post patriarchy": reflexivity is a feminist issue', in Roland Tormey, Anne Good and Carol MacKeogh (eds), *Post-Methodology? New Directions in Research Methodologies in the Social Sciences,* Dublin: Trinity College Dublin Sociology Postgraduates Group and Dept. of Sociology, Trinity College Dublin.

Lentin, Ronit (1997), *Re-occupying the Territories of Silence: A Feminist Autobiographical Exploration of the Gendered Relationship Between Israel and the Shoah,* PhD Thesis, Department of Sociology, Trinity College, Dublin.

Lie, Merete and Knut H. Sørensen (eds) (1996), *Making Technologies our Own? Domesticating Technology into Everyday Life,* Oslo: Scandinavian University Press.

Lohan, Maria (1998), *The Transvestite Telephone: A Male Technology Dressed Up in Women's Clothes,* PhD Thesis, Department of Sociology, Trinity College Dublin.

Lohan, Maria (2000a), '"Come back public/private (almost). All is forgiven": using feminist methodologies in researching ICTs', *Women's Studies International Forum,* vol. 23, no. 1: 107-118.

Lohan, Maria (2000b), 'Men, masculinities and "mundane" technologies: the domestic yelephone', in Alison Adam and Eileen Green (eds), *Digital Gender,* London: Routledge.

Mackenzie, Donald and Judy Wajcman (eds) (1999), *The Social Shaping of Technology,* Second Edition, Milton Keynes: Open University Press.

McKee, Lorna and Margaret O'Brien (1986), 'Interviewing men: taking gender seriously', in Eva Garmanikow, David Morgan, Jane Purvis and Donna Taylorson (eds), *The Public and the Private,* Aldershot: Gower.

McKeown, Kieran, Harry Ferguson, and Dermot Rooney (1998), *Changing Fathers? Fatherhood and Family Life in Modern Ireland,* Cork: The Collins Press.

Moyal, Ann (1989), 'The feminine culture of the telephone', *Prometheus,* vol. 7, no. 1: 5-31.

Moyal, Ann (1992), 'The gendered use of the telephone: an Australian case study', *Media Culture and Society*, vol. 14: 51-72.

Nardi, Peter (1992), '"Seamless souls": an introduction to men's friend-ships', in Peter Nardi (ed.), *Men's Friendships: Research on Men and Masculinities*, Newbury Park, CA: Sage.

Noble, Grant (1987), 'Individual differences, psychological neighbour-hoods and the use of the domestic telephone', *Media Information Australia*, vol. 44, May: 37-41.

Personal Narratives Group (eds) (1989), *Interpreting Women's Lives: Feminist Theory and Personal Narratives*, Bloomington: Indiana University Press.

Pickering, Andrew (ed.) (1992), *Science as Practice and Culture*, Chicago IL: University of Chicago Press.

Pinch, Trevor and Wiebe Bijker (1987), 'The social construction of facts and artefacts; or how the Sociology of Science and Technology might benefit each other', in Wiebe Bijker, Thomas Hughes and Trevor Pinch (eds), *The Social Construction of Technological Systems*, Cambridge, MA: MIT Press.

Rakow, Lana F. (1986), 'Rethinking gender and communication', *Journal of Communication*, Autumn: 11-26.

Rakow, Lana F. (1992), *Gender on the Line, Women, the Telephone and Community Life*, Urbana and Chicago: University of Illinois Press.

Rouse, Joseph (1996), 'Feminism and the social construction of scientific knowledge', in Lynn H. Nelson and Jack Nelson (eds), *Feminism, Science and the Philosophy of Science*, UK: Kluwer Academic Pub-lishers.

Sætnan, Ann. R. (1997), 'Standing one's ground requires finding some ground to stand on', in B. Berner (ed.), *Gendered Practices, Feminist Studies of Technology and Society*, Sweden: Linköping University, Department of Technology and Social Change.

Segal, Lynne (1997), *Slow Motion, Changing Masculinities, Changing Men*, Revised Edition, London: Virago Press.

Schabedoth, Eva, Dieter Storrl, Klaus Beck and Ulrich Lange (1989), '"Der kleine Unterschied", erste ergebnisse einer repräsentiven Befragung von Berliner Haushalten zur Nutzung des Telefons im privaten Alltag', in Ulrich Lange, Klaus Beck and Axel Zerdick (eds), *Telefon und Gesellschaft: Beitrage zu einer Soziologie der Telefonkom-munikation*, Berlin: Volker Speiss.

Stanley, Liz (ed.) (1990), *Feminist Praxis: Research, Theory and Epistemology in Feminist Research*, London: Routledge.

Stanley, Liz (1993), 'The knowing because experiencing subject – narratives, lives and autobiography', *Women's Studies International Forum*, vol. 16: 205-215.

Stanley, Liz (1994), 'Introduction: lives and works and auto/biographical occasions', *Lives and Works Special Double Issue of Auto/Biography*, 3.1 & 3.2: 3-15.

Stanley, Liz and Sue Wise (1991), 'Feminist research, feminist consciousness and experiences of sexism', in M. Fonow and J. Cook (eds), *Beyond Methodology*, Bloomington: Indiana University Press.

Stanley, Liz and Sue Wise (1993), *Breaking Out Again: Feminist Ontology and Epistemology*, London: Routledge.

Stein, Peter (1986), 'Men and their friendships', in R. Lewis and R. Salt (eds), *Men in Families,* Newbury Park, CA: Sage.

Warren, Carol A. (1988), *Gender Issues in Field Research*, London: Sage.

Woolgar, Stephen (1991), 'The turn to technology in social studies of science', *Science, Technology and Human Values,* vol. 16: 20-50.

7

Writing between Worlds

Ricca Edmondson

Qualitative research methods are developing constantly in sensitivity and rigour; we now see sociological work as a multi-faceted, multi-level form of endeavour in which the effort to grasp what is salient about a social setting involves many forms of action by many types of human being. But these very nuances raise new questions about how we are to write sociological texts. Writing a text in sociology imposes obligations of accuracy and loyalty to both subjects (or subject-matter) and readers: there are constant tensions of judgement about what liberties one should take in representing the world one is describing, and how much impact to make on the reader to get her to appreciate what is going on in that world. Moreover, in qualitative research the investigator is her own main instrument, and feminist research traditions emphasise the notion of reflexivity especially strongly to reflect this. The instrument of research, clearly, must be examined, and her influence on her work considered: this is part of her responsibility to preserve her integrity towards both the world she is reporting on and the world she is reporting to.

This chapter argues that reflexivity does not entail importing the author's personality into her text as much as examining, step by step, which of her claims are likely to be valid, and what justifies her audience in taking her seriously. It introduces a tradition which aims to do just this – the ancient Greek rhetorical tradition. This tradition takes seriously the roles both of communicator and of the recipient of communication, examining how each contributes to making a piece of writing make sense. It also allows writers to become sensitised to their personal role in creating a text without personalising it in a way which restricts the reader's freedom. In fact, writers always attempt to make an impact on readers, but examining this tradition allows them to become aware of the processes involved rather than using them indiscriminately. It enables them to recognise that they need to make an impact on readers in order that the latter can take in the essence of a text – but that this need for impact should not prevent readers from participating in helping the text make sense. Writing between worlds means constantly balancing the claims of each.

Writing is a borderline activity, one poised between powerfulness and futility, torn between the worlds of the subjects, the author, and a plethora of readers, most of them unknown to the person writing. Sociological writing characteristically tries to mediate between worlds, to translate experiences, processes, structures at work in one world into a form which contributes to what is happening in another. Thus it is an essentially intercultural process, subject to all the risks attendant on trying to act within several worlds at once. There is often some type of distance between the author's world and her subjects' world, but it is often less than the gulf between subjects and readers. Feminist sociologists are celebrated for paying sensitive and responsible attention to the subjects of their research; this preoccupation itself sometimes obscures the reader's role in what happens to the text as an instrument of communication when it is brought into the world of the reader.

Because of the challenges and the dangers of distortion involved in writing as mediation, many sociologists try to flee the tensions it brings, situating themselves among a certain group of people and writing for that group only. This approach may be adopted for motives that range over the entire moral and political spectrum. Writing like this includes technical accounts written by and for experts, as well as politically and socially co-opted writing which is composed in the interests of some dominant group which forms its main audience. It also includes the writing of those political activists – including some feminists – who belong to a certain group or who 'participate as subjects' within it, and who compose texts intended to convey the views and experiences of that group in a manner whose validity the group helps to define (Smith 1992: 96). But in the last case, the writer is already doing more than simply enabling the group to say what it already knows about itself. People who need to name their experiences have this need as part of a social and political process in which, inevitably, others are involved. The language they choose to describe these experiences is a mediat-

ing language – interworld language: it tries to make sense both to
its subjects and, they hope, to some of the others who read it. The
language of sociological theory is a mediating language in a special
sense: it translates the reader's world to him or her. Even deliberately
hermetic language, secret to all but its users and rare though not
unknown among feminist sociologists, is part of a process involving
external readers; it just chooses – for whatever reasons – to shut
them out. This chapter is concerned with what happens when they
are allowed in.

Bestowing interworld language on the experiences of particular
groups of people is crucial to our ability to understand how we
live; if it is not done, sociology will be barren of the human beings
who make up the world. Yet there are great complexities involved
in trying to make the nature or the experience of one type of social
situation meaningful to those who inhabit another. Richardson
(1994), for example, is anxious to explore these problems inno-
vatively, and her work casts light on the sorts of distance which
exist between accounting for a setting either in its inhabitants' or in
conventional sociological terms and making it genuinely accessible
to strangers. She leaves no path untravelled in her quest for a
means of bringing to the hearts and minds of those who do not
know it, the precise experience of a particular way of being in the
world at a particular time. The reasons for which this is difficult
include the contextuality of language and of the rest of human
behaviour. Words, gestures, habits, attitudes, beliefs, possess the
meanings they do in terms of the network of other words and
habits, to which they belong.

If we take words from one setting and use them in another, they
do not mean the same thing any more. It is not enough, therefore,
to enter someone else's world and remove from it representative
terms used there to account for what people are up to – some way
must be found to give this language meaning for the reader who
has no access to that world except via the text. And some way
must be found to get that person to respond to the text. Sociologists
who quote 'telling' phrases and 'graphic' details from the settings
they are describing do so – whether they are conscious of it or not
– because these phrases and fragments of behaviour seem to have
the potential of enticing and allowing the reader to enter an
unfamiliar world. Almost literally, they are 'key' details which have

the capacity to extend the subjects' world (or the theoretical world) outwards or the reader's world inwards – in a way which will get the reader to permit this move. Comments made by nurses which allow us to enter into the special nature of their way of viewing professional 'success' (Lewin and Olesen, 1981), details from the lives of Japanese American domestic workers which bring them closer to the understanding of contemporary readers (Nakano Glenn, 1990): these are recorded not only because of their meanings for the people in question but because of the impact they are expected to have on the reader.

Hence, the kind of language sought by writers such as Richardson is intended to heighten the impact of conveying original meanings in a form which has been transformed so as allow them to function in another world. Rather than leaving readers unaffected, exactly as they were before they read anything, it seeks to stretch their capacities for social participation so that, in intellect and imagination, they are able to relinquish embeddedness in their own settings and visualise at least part of what it means to inhabit another. Thus Richardson is prepared to use literary or any other means – not to bestow speech on people who were previously dumb, but to force the terms in which they already express their experience to take on meaning in the reader's context. People's everyday speech is 'closer to poetry than it is to sociological prose' (1994: 522), she says, and thus we should consider poetic forms of connecting with readers. But:

> there is no single way – much less 'right' way – of staging a text. The same material can be written for different audiences – positivists, interactionists, post-modernists, feminists, humanities professors, cultural studies scholars, policy makers, and so on … Like wet clay, it is there for us to shape (1994: 523).

It is Richardson, note, who intends to do the shaping; she is prepared to confront the responsibility of acting as mediator for other people's meanings. She wishes to heighten the author's sense of self as a writer rather than efface it in the service of the world which is being described. Her work thus contrasts with the practice of those sociologists who write with a group, closing the gap with them so that the writing relationship is no longer threefold: subjects – author – reader, but dual: subjects/author – reader. But both these views

of writing focus on a phenomenological sociology whose preoccupation is with finding words so that readers can encompass the
experience being conveyed to them. This preoccupation, demanding
as it is, focuses on just one aspect of what needs to be done by
both writers and readers in order to understand the social world.

In this article, the category 'feminist sociologist' is meant to be
drawn as widely as possible, to include the very broad church of
those who consider it both unreasonable and unjustifiable to try to
analyse social processes in ignorance of their gendered nature (as
unreasonable as to ignore issues of class or military power), or to
envisage the production of knowledge in terms of a technicist model
of objectivity, or to be indifferent to the contribution which knowledge about the social world makes to that world. But these are all
theoretical claims about how the world should be understood;
phenomenological sociology is important to feminist sociologists
for many reasons, and especially because it is impossible to take
the experience of oppressed people seriously – wherever or whoever they may be – and still construct theories which minimise the
processes bringing that oppression about. The theories, accounts
and explanations which are needed go beyond the mediation of
experience; they involve different types of mediation.

The second half of the twentieth century in particular saw a
burgeoning of critical approaches to sociology – interpretive
accounts of social interaction which grappled with the problems of
construing meaning, a concern for emotions as joined with thinking
and acting, exploration of the theoretically and evaluatively contextualised nature of social knowledge, the vision of a committed
social science which aimed at producing reliable and insightful
accounts of how the socio-political world works. Feminist sociologists both supported these developments and expanded them
distinctively in some areas – not least in their care for their relations
with their subjects and their conscientiousness about their own
roles in producing research. Following the example of writers in
the American tradition of the early twentieth century among others,
feminists were conscious of pitfalls in their research involvement
with vulnerable individuals, but knew how much these had to say
about the world: more, in many cases, than could be learned elsewhere. They knew that the subjects of research are important: not
only do they have important things to say, what happens to them

personally is also important (see Lynch's contribution to this volume). But writing is only part of a process in which care is owed: texts are also intended for readers.

In their implicit relations with readers, feminists tend to oscillate between circumspection and vehemence. Feminist scholarship tends to be highly cautious about the processes by which accounts of the social world are written, partly because so much that passed for knowledge in the past has come to be seen as illusion arising from a specific social context, like Victorian claims about the fragility of women's intelligence and their unsuitability for public life. Hence their attention to the subtleties of gaining knowledge, their emphasis on knowledge as a processual development rather than the instant result of applying techniques (Tanesini, 1999). But for feminists, as Linda Nicholson (1990) remarks, pointing to the influence of social settings on thought is ambiguous in its implications. Feminists argue that much of what in the past had the reputation of objective knowledge is actually hopelessly biased (Lloyd, 1993), and that some criteria of truth and falsity may on occasion be considered merely local. But they still want to claim validity for their own accounts: to write valid analyses of reality, constructed with ethical integrity, contributing constructively to what goes on in the world.

This means that relationships with readers need to be constructed with special care. The process of enhancing understanding of social processes makes multiple demands. Since feminist sociology is not only concerned with getting readers to take in its subjects' experience, and is not always defensive of its subjects' points of view, it does not involve just one way of writing or just one set of responses. Writing stretches over such a variety of discourse forms that what is common to them is more likely to be their ethics than their content. The women about whom research needs to be under-taken are not always right, and reconstructing their point of view is not always central to the work – as in the case of Finnegan's (forth-coming) demonstration that middle-class Irishwomen of former decades were happy to use the labour of the utterly repressed and exploited women who were forced to work in Magdalen laundries. Secondly, feminist sociologists may need to criticise other feminisms, such as versions of feminism which have been co-opted into economic and ideological settings to the detriment of vulnerable people – children or the disabled or old. But, thirdly, sociologists need to understand social systems in a way which does not interest everyone. It is in the service of the world to understand theoretical technicalities of economic production, but not all the resulting writing needs to be addressed to everyone: to reach genuine rigour, some of it needs to be discussion between colleagues. Fourthly, understanding social systems implies understanding how cultures function. We can hardly discover this simply by asking their inhabitants (Edmondson 2000). Cultural interaction fails to work if its participants are aware of all the deep structures underlying their interaction, and many people justifiably prefer to remain unconscious of them. Thus, despite the fact that the people know great amounts about their settings, these settings still retain aspects which sociologists need to know but participants need not know. Fifthly – and these are only instances – feminist sociologists struggle to comprehend the field of knowledge production itself. This, like any other field in which experience and reflection are important, takes years to understand. Not everything written about it can be written on the principle that every reader should be able to understand it instantly. We do not expect to understand other people's settings at a glance – their intellectual settings included. A writer's commitment to human emancipation means that she should reflect on the relation her work has to it, but this need not entail persuading all readers to like and approve of her straight away. Ann Oakley's acclaimed book, *Social Support and Motherhood* (1992), for example, deals mainly with the research process itself. Its main mediating functions take place among the worlds of other academic researchers, including funders and controllers of academic research, feminists in general and health researchers in particular. It is not particularly accessible to non-academics and its subjects do not in fact figure particularly largely in it.

Sociological writing, therefore, is an intercultural process which can take many versions as it mediates between human beings situated in particular cultures, see with particular points of view, and interpret according to particular theoretical and political predispositions, all of which change over time. Mediation of some sort is inevitable, even between allies. In the case of feminism, such allies do not inhabit a worldview which is complete in itself, but one which uses other theories of politics, ethics, and social process in order to establish how the social world functions. Characteristically, it transforms them when they obscure gender issues, but it is hard to imagine that anyone could be only a feminist, and feminist convictions play different roles in the lives of individual sociologists. Hence it follows that feminist audiences are not homogeneous, as Iris Marion Young remarks in a different context:

> Where women group, their womanliness will not be the only thing that brings them together; there are other concrete details in their lives that give them affinity, such as their class or race position, their nationality, their neighborhood, their religious affiliation, or their role as teachers of philosophy. For this reason groupings of women will always be partial in relation to the series ... feminist politics must be coalition politics (Young, 1995: 212).

Sociological writing cannot, therefore, but be compromised as it attempts to be faithful – in some sense – to the world it is interpreting as well as to make that world impinge on readers of different hues and types. It creates something new – hence Richardson's description of it as 'a method of inquiry' in itself – and that something belongs fully neither to the world of subjects nor to the world of readers. Historically and mythologically speaking, figures who try to live in two worlds tend to be disapproved of. Though currently we romanticise them, they have more often been imagined as dangerous and malign, or severely punished for their lack of fidelity to one setting only – like Bridget Cleary of County Tipperary, who was burned to death at the end of the nineteenth century with the intention of restoring her from being a changeling, reputedly the last woman in Europe to suffer this fate (Bourke, 1999). Those who belong neither to one setting nor to another need, therefore – as the feminist emphasis on reflexivity would urge – to give special thought to the divided loyalties their position entails.

The personal and political conscientiousness of feminist writers and their responsiveness to process in research make them careful of their subjects and their intellectual processes. At the same time, they are involved in interpreting, arguing, making cases: trying to impinge on readers so that they become genuinely aware of what is being said. Neither the theoretical nor the empirical aspects of sociological writing are composed with the aim of leaving readers' worlds exactly as they were. Yet writing with integrity demands care for the autonomy of the person addressed. An account of arguing which responds to just this dilemma can be found in a version of Aristotle's analysis of rhetoric, which both justifies and regulates the introduction of people, politics and ethics into the process of acquiring and communicating social knowledge. Not only does this explicitly incorporate responsiveness to the possible reactions of the other (subject or reader) and recognise feeling as part of reasonable thought; it responds to the contextual nature and the fluidity of what can be grasped and conveyed about the social world, and enjoins care for co-arguers engaged with the writer in reflecting about this world.

A rhetorical analysis of the type I am commending in this chapter is not primarily a dissection of the manipulative qualities of communication. It examines the ways in which reasoning depends on a web of argumentative interaction, within a given socio-political context, between writer and reader (originally, in the time of Aristotle's *Rhetorica*, speaker and hearer: here, I am only dealing with aspects which apply to both). It specifically explores the functioning of social and personal practices with regard to reasoning as they develop through time. Time and setting have significant impacts on attempts to gain and convey knowledge about human social behaviour, which changes and develops constantly, sometimes of its own volition. As feminist sociology characteristically does, this type of rhetorical analysis acknowledges that the social origins of knowledge are integral to understanding social and political affairs, but does not see them as determining it so entirely that only relativism can result. The essential incompleteness of knowledge about society makes it tentative and subject to the need for constant revision, but does not undermine the validity of attempts to distinguish between what is more likely to be true and what is more likely to be false. This position is consistent with the contemporary 'fallibilism' which also acknowledges the sociality of knowledge without endorsing relativism. It retains the idea of truth as a guiding value (Popper 1959), rather than as something we can expect to achieve by the objective application of technical methods. It also, I shall argue, tells us much more about how to write politically and ethically responsible and responsive sociological texts than any other epistemological approach.

Ethos and ethics

In Aristotle's analysis, trying to reach any conclusion about public affairs inevitably involves our seeking to make reasonable judgements about the character, competence and intelligence of the person who tells us about them. Conversely, if we are telling others about public affairs, it behoves us to demonstrate the appropriate character, intelligence, and fitness to convey conclusions about the matter in hand. This analysis enhances our understanding of the sociality and ethics bound up with knowledge. It sees forming, and communicating, justified beliefs about the socio-political world as a social and personal matter. It emphasises a writer's responsibility to his or her audience, and that readers are behaving reasonably and rightly by paying attention to the person who is addressing them. It does not, however, imply that all writing should be autobiographical, nor that the social location of knowledge about society can either guarantee or cancel out its validity.

Aristotle uses the term 'ethos' to refer to a speaker's suitability to argue. This does not refer to the conduct of this person's life in general (which we cannot usually know), but to what he or she is able to communicate in the argument at hand (Wörner, 1990). Again linking knowledge with ethics, this concept stresses that we depend for our knowledge on the probity and dedication of others: for example, on the fact that they both become accomplished in and allow themselves to be restrained by the practices for gaining knowledge which are supported by the best forms of reasoning currently available. Knowledge is truly personal and social, not in the sense that it needs to contain personal accounts of how it was acquired – though sometimes it may do this – but because it depends on interaction between individuals as well as on shared practices which are both sustaining and open to criticism. By demonstrating that she possesses ethos, a writer shows readers that she can be trusted as offering what, in the light of the arguments available, she genuinely believes to be the case, and for good reason. Ethos endorses the active presence of an author as a moral agent in her own text, and guides her inclusion of personal experience – which should be present (only) insofar as it helps readers to assess her claims to knowledge and understanding.

According to this view, authors certainly need to appear in their own texts – in the sense that they should not pretend that their texts were written by no-one, by a neutral conjunction of methods in which human beings were not involved. But the way they appear is not, as a rule, by writing about themselves; rather by dealing as well as they can with issues their subjects raise or their readers need to know about. Directly autobiographical accounts, to the contrary, can manipulate readers by dazzling, cajoling, eliciting sympathy. They may or may not enhance the type of responsibility in which the writer is pledged absolutely to do her best for both her subjects and her readers. Exceptions arise where the author's experiences are part of her subject-matter: in Ann Oakley's case, for example – though this by no means causes her to adopt an effusively personal writing style – or in the different case of, for example, lesbian feminists who want to act against the silencing of entire ways of being a person. For them, writing autobiographically can both practise and legitimate an aspect of being human which was formerly supposed hardly to exist at all.

Yet their anxiety not to evade authorship sometimes leads writers to a form of self-description which is almost inevitably distorting: the biographical account. In place of criticising self-presentations in other texts, I offer the following example, based on a version of my own life:

> I have grown up in a series of different countries and settings, and came to philosophy, translation, then sociology and ethnography through never feeling entirely familiar with any set of events around me. Everything seemed divided, seemed insecure, everything needed to be questioned. Thus I have never been a native of any particular country. I was born in South Africa, but was a foreigner there because I had English parents; in England, I had not been born in England. Then I spent a dozen years in Germany, and a dozen in Ireland. I became accustomed to being puzzled about what people would do next.

Not a word of this is false in relation to myself, but as a piece of self-presentation it is entirely manipulative. It solicits the reader's approval by romanticising social duality; it exploits the implicit though dubious magic of standing between settings – currently considered glamorous, however much distrusted in the past. If necessary, I could augment the tale by true allusions to further themes which are favourites in this type of writing: I could, for example, highlight ancestors expelled from their homelands because of their race or poverty, or ostracised for marrying people of different faiths. Accounts such as these are almost impossible to compose honestly; almost all cultivate the impression that the author has triumphed over some form of marginalisation rather than being raised in socially conformist comfort. Most importantly, they do not really show how the writer came to regard any particular position as knowledge. But they do attempt to charm the reader into belief.

Autobiographical fragments almost always undermine readers' freedom of judgement by offering to replace the authority of professional success with the authority of specialness. Examples which resist this tendency more strongly are glosses which focus on stating intellectual convictions, like Olesen's (1994) note at the end of an article summarising approaches to feminist theory, helping the reader to interpret her emphases in the article:

> What you, the reader, will see here is constructed by and filtered through my research experience as a socialist feminist sociologist interested in women's health and women in health and healing systems. I have worked primarily within the emergent or Blumerian wing of the interactionist-social constructionist tradition ..., though I also start with a keen interest in the study of cultural products by virtue of a long-ago career in journalism and early graduate study in mass media of communication ... (Olesen, 1994: 169).

Writing about the research process itself also involves reference to the author's experiences; this can sometimes take the form of an appeal to the reader about moral and emotional dilemmas, as in Eileen Fairhurst's (1990) account of 'stressful' aspects of fieldwork in a geriatric unit.

> My notes began: It is with the utmost effort that I am writing today's notes. I really feel like walking out of the hospital and never going there again. I might even go as far as to say that I have arrived home tonight feeling the most depressed that I have ever felt.

> On that day, three events relating to three separate individuals, which disturbed me, occurred. The first concerned a woman whose sister, without asking her but on the advice of her GP, had given up the tenancy of her home and sold her furniture. I was distressed by this because the woman was due for discharge a few days later. .... The second incident focused on a woman whom I had got to know very well ... she had been discharged to an old people's

home. ... I asked her how she was finding the home. She told me she was very unhappy there. ... She detailed the conduct of the manageress of the home and how, all in all, she did not like it.

Finally, ... (o)ne of the men I had asked to take part in my study of patient carers refused for 'everything gets back to the nurses'... I found our conversation very distressing not only because of the content but also because he was stammering when talking to me. My dilemma in this case was twofold. On the one hand, I had great sympathy with the man for I found it intolerable that he should be treated in the way he had been by nursing staff. On the other hand, however, I realised that informing a ward sister or nursing officer ... might have had exactly the opposite consequences for the man than I had intended: my action could have been interpreted as confirming him as a 'troublemaker' (Olesen, 1990: 147).

This is writing which uses the autobiographical stance, not to encourage readers to understand the author specifically, but to understand studying a social setting and its problems. This, it seems to me, is not dissimilar from the approach taken by Dorothy Smith, who insists that writing should include the author's position in order that no-one should forget the contextual nature of knowledge – not in order that the author should appear as a personal presence in her text.

Riding a train not long ago in Ontario I saw a family of Indians – woman, man, and three children – standing together on a spur above a river watching the train go by. I realized that I could tell this incident – the train, those five people seen on the other side of the glass – as it was, but that my description was built on my position and my interpretations. I have called them 'Indians' and a family; I have said that they were watching the train. Everything may have been quite different for them. ... If we begin from the world as we actually experience it, it is at least possible to see that we are indeed located and that what we know of the other is conditional upon that location (Smith, 1990: 24-5).

In short, feminist sociologists more often write *through* the author than *about* her.

The role of power disparities in distorting knowledge has formed a recurrent preoccupation among sociologists during the last half-century, as well as – more inconclusively – equality as promoting it. None of these relationships is straightforward. Many participants in society are socially equal to others without understanding them in the slightest. Hence, the embarrassment felt by many authors because they belong to a different social class from their subjects, for instance, misses the point. The kind of equality which is centrally appropriate to authors is the hermeneutic equality of openness to what the other person is saying and doing, including the possibilities that one's own position is mistaken and the other's is correct (Gadamer, 1960: 297ff.), and that one's own conceptual and emotional structures may need radical revision in order to understand the other person. To the extent that class, gender or any other feature disturbs this openness, the manner in which it does so requires specific reflexive examination; merely naming a status inequality makes no impact on the process.

There are, it is clear, strong connections between ethos, as the author's self-presentation in writing, and ethics. But practices connected to ethos also form part of conventional methodology, even though they are seldom acknowledged or examined as such. Even unconsciously, writers attempt to convey a convincing ethos by using those markers which are treated within their knowledge community as conferring credibility. Since many such markers – references to prestigious universities attended or professorships conferred – have come to endorse conventional notions of power and prestige, this may give rise to tensions when aspects of that community are being criticised; but, in contrast, new social and political movements spread new conventions for displaying ethos. Today, ethos may be bestowed on figures (including women) who might not have acquired it half a century ago. Some writers use conventional ethos-related practices for unconventional ends; it is not necessarily embedded so inextricably into its setting that no communication between stances can be made. Gisela Kaplan's *Contemporary Western European Feminism* (1992), for instance, uses conventional markers to establish the force of her own intellectual status. She indicates how many languages she is able to speak, alluding to her rich and varied social experience. She quotes from de Beauvoir in the original French, but also uses an array of quantitative tables. All these markers assert proficiency in a wide palette of intellectual competences. Her chapter on women's status and employment uses the Washington Population Crisis Committee report to show that nowhere on the globe is there equality between women and men, and to explore the endemic nature of poverty, especially women's poverty. Far from confining her within an argumentative ghetto, Kaplan's feminist arguments are strengthened by her use of conventional forms of ethos and conventional data to argue against conventional conclusions.

Kaplan is not performing two operations here: first establishing fitness to argue, then arguing. Her presentation of quantitative tables establishes ethos *and* argues at the same time. She establishes trust *through* the arguments she conveys, and trust in the author is a legitimate component of the reader's mounting knowledge. This point can be made even more clearly in relation to Oakley's *Social Support and Motherhood* (1992). Like Kaplan, Oakley lays claim to familiarity with conventional statistical techniques in the first few pages of the text, just as she goes on to elucidate the history of social support research in health studies and the use of randomised controlled trials. At the same time, she emphasises that she is not confined by the conventional quantitative basis her data represent. She discusses post-modernism, Fritjof Capra and Dorothy Smith, underlining her sensitivity to the incomplete nature of our contemporary understanding of social knowledge as well as acknowledging its rootedness in the lived dilemmas of everyday existence. The subject-matter of her original research could hardly be more rooted: how to study and understand healthy childbirth and social interventions designed to support it. Again, Oakley's communication of her argument simultaneously conveys her ethos: her personal as well as her intellectual dedication to the subject she is treating. And, of course, she explicitly addresses the need for social science to acknowledge and adjust to emotional and experiential aspects of knowledge (Oakley, 1992: 17; 338ff.). Exploring her own attitude to these matters in the context of her work enables us to understand the author and enables us to understand her subject-matter: these are two sides of the same epistemological coin. Because it is the same coin, Oakley does not need to personalise her text with large amounts of specifically autobiographical data.

Stressing the sociality of knowledge, in this account, does not mean abandoning proper standards. It does mean paying more attention to what proper standards are, how they evolve, and what exactly their connection with knowledge and its communication should be held to be. If writing and expecting to be read means establishing suitability to argue, the question is what standards readers will respect as doing this. The lofty assumptions of objectivity adopted by the sociologists and anthropologists of the past did not derive only from their own preferences. The professional standards of the time required them to expunge their own presences from their texts, even though a number of them had, for example, engaged in quasi-marital relationships with women among their subjects which they were at pains to conceal. Had they not done so, their accounts of the Nuer and other cultures would have been dismissed by readers. Readers in the first half of the twentieth century prohibited admissions of emotional involvement from texts attempting to tell the truth. Now, diversity about the degree of involvement which readers accept as proper make decisions about their stances in their texts more complex for writers.

Many feminists try to record their research in terms of its pro-cessual development rather than as a set of results, and furthermore as a development in which real human beings were involved – showing how relationships with respondents were developed and refraining from pretending to the reader that smooth, successful, impersonal techniques alone were responsible for the 'results' of the study. Decisions about the degree of personhood to admit into the text thus relate directly to the way writers perceive their impact on the process of finding out. Is this a question of guaranteeing knowledge or underwriting the author's personal integrity? The two are bound up together. According to a neo-Aristotelian view, exploring the author's own part in her research possesses epistem-ological as well as ethical and emotional validity. It can enhance the authority of the researcher in a way she deserves: as readers we become virtual witnesses to the fact that the researcher has developed practices which give her insight into her subject. At the same time it allows the reader to form a highly elaborated appre-ciation of the situation of the author's respondents. This is not a matter of moral obligation by itself, let alone mere 'niceness' or feminist fashion, but a part of contributing to the truthfulness of what is written.

Contributions which depend on ethos, however, also involve several dimensions of activity by the reader. Since attempts to gain knowledge and reach decisions about social matters take place under circumstances which are prone to evolve, and since we now

live in a knowledge regime characterised by increasing specialis-
ation, trust in other arguers is more crucial than ever. It is far from
unreasonable that a strong safeguard to the reliability of what is
claimed to be knowledge should be located in the relationship
between a proponent of the knowledge and the people she is
addressing. But the sociality of this source is deepened by the fact
that its reliability depends on the mature judgement of the person
addressed; how much is she able to discern about the speaker and
what the speaker is claiming? The reader needs to be in, or to put
herself into, a position to assess how well-informed the writer is,
how morally competent and with what degree of intellectual integrity,
and whether she is anxious to maintain a genuine, constructive
relationship with her audience: one which emancipates rather than
deludes. In contrast, positivist accounts of the theory of science
unite with mainstream accounts of epistemology to dictate that the
person of the speaker should be ignored entirely when assessing
an argument. But in fact the person of the speaker makes an integral
contribution to the question of whether it is reasonable to trust her.
She does so, often, through her use of the practices required to
convey knowledge itself, through working together with the reader
rather than specifically by addressing her.

Pathos

The relations between writer and reader are dynamic rather than
static, as the writer tries both to move the reader and to do so in a
way which retains moral and theoretical integrity. The aspects of
this dynamic process which focus on the impact of arguments on
their recipients are referred to in the Aristotelian tradition as
phenomena making up 'pathos'. Pathos re-emphasises the implications of the fact that knowledge, or purported knowledge, is
conveyed *to* a person or persons with cognitive and emotional
dispositions, moral and political views, as well as contextual and
personal habits of thought and interaction. All these habits of mind
and dispositions can affect an audience's capacity to appreciate
information and argument, which is why the writer must adapt to
them. This is not just a matter of taking account of extraneous
emotional or political attitudes which may in principle be neutralised
just by admitting publicly what they are. It is a matter of adapting

to habits of mind in an audience which may exist on so deep a level that it is hard to describe them, but which are nonetheless capable of transforming perceptions of a text or blocking it out altogether – rendering the attempt to communicate null and void.

All this relates to methods of communication – often misunderstood in contemporary views of rhetoric – which emphasise its use to persuade, as if it were possible to refrain from persuading. It is often assumed that rhetoric is essentially a manipulative art, rather than an account of how human beings try to communicate reasonably with each other in order to reach the best conclusion in the circumstances. But, properly understood, pathos is not simply a tool for influencing other people's emotions. Although it is no doubt true that one's emotional position may influence one's judgement in relation to abortion, for example, that is not my main point here (Edmondson, 1984). Emotions can provide *motivations* to one standpoint or another, and perhaps it is sometimes possible to discern these motivations and remove oneself or others from being unduly influenced by them. But the major concerns of rhetoric in the neo-Aristotelian sense are different. According to this position, to be intelligible, any argument about human activities requires social, emotional and political components. Adapting these components to an audience is not a question of manipulation as much as it is a question of conveying *meaning*. Since these components help to establish meaning, naturally they cannot be removed. They are intrinsic to judgement itself. Pathos, therefore, is basically a set of means for adapting to the audience in order to establish meaning and convey knowledge. These means can sometimes be misused, clearly, and audiences can be swayed against their better judgements by strong emotion. Emotion itself, however, is not intrinsically misleading. Kaplan (1992), for instance, in the example given above, uses pathos by adapting to her audience's need for sober and academic detail; in this case, it is the approach to conviction which has the most impact.

It may be possible, then, to convey an argument effectively by using widely shared conventions about how good knowledge should be managed. Admittedly these conventions become contested over time, and vary according to different national, political or professional settings. (One of the tasks of the philosophy of the social sciences is to debate which conventions are appropriate, when and why.) In addition to this, social science writing generally follows practices which have not been made explicit (Edmondson, 1984), and whose purposes may not be adopted consciously by their authors. In many such cases we can detect uses of pathos in ways which illustrate their epistemological significance. To return to Ann Oakley's work, there are many instances in which the author attempts to impact on the mental and emotional state of a presumed reader – in order to convey her argument, not to manipulate agreement. Oakley's very emphasis on the fact that masculine domination of the natural and social sciences has been founded on 'profoundly gender-differentiated life experiences' in which masculinity and science each attempt to resist 'the enclosing structures of everyday domestic life' (Oakley, 1992: 19) may impact strongly on readers. It can shock them into a new view of knowledge, one in which feelings and experience have a strong and reasonable part to play in our understanding of the social world. And if the reader cannot grasp this view of knowledge, she is unlikely to follow the book's exploration of the role of sociality in health and motherhood. Her epistemological horizons will remain too narrow for her to appreciate the fact that feeling, partly through playing a constitutive role in knowledge, affects such empirical issues as the generation of health.

This does not imply forcing or cajoling the reader into agreement. It provides socio-emotional enabling devices so that an argument can be understood. At the same time, it expands our understanding of the place of emotion in the process of arguing. Uses of pathos properly attempt to put the reader in a socio-emotional position to *take in* the emphases and inferences involved, and to *join the author in making use of* particular conventions and practices for interpreting the world: author and reader are co-responsible for what the text effectively 'means' in any given case. Thus, only one of the reasons for which there can in reality be no neutral, invariant 'scientific attitude' to replace adaptation to a particular audience is that engagement on the reader's part is needed to make statements about human behaviour credible, to make them make sense. It is this connection with intelligibility which makes rhetorical aspects of communication, such as pathos and ethos, both an epistemological and a methodological question, not merely a pragmatic one. This makes politics and ethics intrinsic to the meaning of sociological writing; if authors do not strive to emancipate their readers and their subjects, they too easily do the opposite.

No piece of writing can be endorsed merely because it belongs to an emancipatory movement, or is directed towards certain groups of people (women). Tanesini (1999: 223; 239) is surely right to hold that questions about whether a claim is really correct cannot be replaced by referring to the social or personal characteristics of the person who made it, even though they can be augmented by them. Writing on behalf of specific groups in society does not automatically guarantee that writing. Pathos does direct us to pay attention to the social and/or personal situations of arguers, but it does not equip us with blanket guarantees for any group's particular worldview. Rhetorical elements of arguing direct us instead to the complexity of social communication. Shortcuts for assessing this complexity by analysing it in group terms are few. Helen Longino (1993), for example, also stressing the social nature of knowledge and knowledge production, argues that theories ought to be produced by communities which are able to facilitate transformative criticism. However, we need finer-scale criteria to determine whether and how such communities, if they really exist, affect research produced within them (see O'Neill in this volume). Perhaps we should endorse Bar On's rejection of the simple dichotomy between authority and its absence (1993). Rather than attaching epistemic authority to any particular social standpoint, we need to rework the detailed moral, emotional and political criteria which affect knowledge claims.

If we accept that knowing and communicating about human beings and their lives involves aspects which are not exclusively cognitive, communicating knowledge becomes intelligible as an *action*, carried out in circumstances which change and are affected by change. As Tanesini puts it (1999: 184), 'Knowing becomes a way of engaging with the world, and to understand it we must study the patterns created by interaction.' What is said or written about people and society does not exist statically in a personless vacuum. Aristotle draws attention to this at the start of the *Rhetoric* by stressing that the hearer is 'the speech's end and object'. What can be communicated as knowledge is determined not only by the speaker's or writer's view but also by that of the other person(s). If Oakley thinks her audience may overestimate the authoritativeness of national bodies overseeing sociological research, or of hospital 'ethics committees', she needs to (and does) stress the socio-political circumstances surrounding funding issues which influence what is eventually produced as knowledge, as well as the difficulties confronting attempts to secure acceptance for research which, because it is original, offends the expectations of ethics committees. She argues that conveying information is far from a simple matter of drawing up clear and distinct accounts. This complicates the matter of making comprehensible contact about any given state of affairs; it derives partly from what the author estimates that the reader needs to take in if the argument is to be intelligible (Edmondson, 1995). To write truly and comprehensibly, authors of sociological texts must respond to what they expect readers already think. How can this be distinguished from manipulation? Again, by criteria which are in part ethical, socio-economic and political; criteria which examine the author's commitment to what she writes, within the context in which she is writing it. We can see from this account that pathos does not function properly without ethos – including the writer's commitment to a constructive and emancipatory relationship with the audience – and that ethos entails attention to pathos which in turn gives the reader a real part to play in allowing the text to make sense.

Logos

All this tells us a good deal about the choices we make in composing sociological texts; and it allows us to read much of what texts contain in terms of the functions of ethos and pathos. This should not lead us to ignore the third element, logos, or 'the argument itself'. Logos blends cognition with ethos and pathos, but cognition itself is seldom 'pure'. Especially in relation to the social world, it is normal and appropriate for its make-up to include emotion – just as emotion includes reasoning (mothers in Russia becoming angry in reasoning that their sons are being used as cannon-fodder in Chechnya, for instance). This does not entail a relativist account of reason, however. For example, however much the social position of the Travelling population in Ireland results from certain forms of social construction, Travellers still suffer a higher proportion of infant mortality than other groups; more children actually die young among them than in other populations in the country. Though this state of affairs is clearly connected with social events and social perceptions, the truth of the claim that Traveller children die more often does not depend exclusively on someone uttering it. It is not the case that research objects only exist in terms of what people say about them. Both event and account are parts of reality, affecting each other. A rhetorical analysis tries both to chart and to regulate those effects. Since they cannot but involve judgements, for which the author should take responsibility (cf. Benhabib, 1995), we need practices guiding us in our attempts to avoid error. We depend in part on the vigilance of others to protect us from error, and others depend on us.

A rhetorical epistemology does not mean, then, that feminists must abandon any search for reliability in their writing. But criteria for reliability should move from an exclusive preoccupation with objects of discussion, and explore the sociopolitical, moral and interpersonal conditions which are conducive, in given circum-stances, to truthful communication. This exploration implies that producing texts is a practical as well as a theoretical question. Foucault (1971 and subsequently) is not the only writer to stress the ubiquitous involvement of power relations in practices claiming to lead to knowledge. If power relations always affect what seems to be knowledge, knowing is partly a political matter. Acquiring knowledge depends on resisting some forces and supporting others. Habermas (1968) suggests attempting to achieve situations of complete equality, devoid of personality and power, from which truthful discourse might be hoped to issue. This may be neither possible nor desirable (see for instance Edmondson and Nullmeier, 1997), and in the meantime we need to scrutinise particular cases of the effects of politics on the knowledge expressed in writing. Seeking logos means seeking to write the best possible accounts that, in dialogue with the reader, can emerge from the settings in which knowledge is being sought.

Conclusion

The conventional conception of social science texts is misguided to the extent that it fails to integrate successfully personal aspects of acquiring knowledge and communicating it into a new setting.

This fact accounts for many of the gulfs between what social science is meant to be in principle and what social scientists actually write (Edmondson, 1984). In the natural sciences, despite all disputes and deviations from official methods, there is much more consensus regarding how to go about research – what practical steps are really entailed by doing it and reporting on it – than in the humanities. We are still only beginning to understand what is really entailed for writing by recent developments in understanding how knowledge of the social world evolves. It is not surprising that Stanley and Wise (1979) complain that theoretical accounts of deduction, induction and the like fail to yield intelligible accounts of what researchers do, or should do (see also Nelson 1998 on the reasoning implicit in political science). Denzin (1995: 39) draws attention to the continuing problem of 'the representational crisis' which has resulted from assuming 'that much, if not all, social science and ethnographic writing is a narrative production', structured by a logic that 'separates writer, text, and subject matter'. Many sociologists think they are only describing, explaining and occasionally predicting, and this is a mistake. On the other hand, some of those who do not think this, err in the opposite direction – injecting personal and political elements into their work in a way which in the end obstructs the mediation process intended to help the reader understand.

This situation is partly a product of epistemological failure in the humanities. While most official accounts of methods remain derived from an excessively cognitivist understanding of what thinking is, and while this is clearly misguided, we need to use methods such as the rhetorical one, to understand in more detail what we need to do in order to optimise the mediation process. Writers do not, in practice, adhere to cognitivist expectations; they use all sorts of methods of communicating with their readers without being conscious of what they are doing. Much of what they write can, in the official version, only be categorised, and trivialised as colourful anecdotes or background material; thinking, arguing and writing are visualised as essentially cognitive; emotional, social, contextual aspects of thinking, arguing and writing are dismissed as irrational (Edmondson, 1984). Torn between obligation to this misleading canon and the need to communicate with and about real people, workers in the social sciences currently approach both research and writing haphazardly. If we return to the notion of writing as mediation, we can become more sensitive to the respective needs of each side in the equation.

The version of sociological writing explored here tries to go between the horns of the dilemma: to move between naïve objectivism and an excessively emotional relativism which would deprive us of ways of standing by any claims at all. It holds that we can take context into account without falling into contextual determinism, and it holds out the possibility that we can expand an understanding of thinking and reasoning about society which responds to the facts that they are done by people, in social settings, under conditions of pressure and uncertainty – but can reach conclusions which are, for the present time, acceptable. A compromise is thus offered between those who are anxious to connect knowledge with its setting, and those who insist – also rightly – that it is not so deeply embedded that it cannot be conveyed elsewhere. In this compromise, we need to acknowledge that conveying knowledge both uses and affects emotions, experiences and settings. It means attending to another side of the mediation process than the subjects' only: it means taking readers' beliefs, feelings and political stances into account and being prepared to change them – within bounds imposed by strict standards of integrity. Mediating between worlds is a more dangerous, but more responsible business than it is always easy to admit.

References

Aristotle, *Rhetorica*, trans. W. Rhys Roberts, Oxford: Oxford University Press, 1946.

Babbitt, Susan (1993), 'Feminism and objective interests: the role of transformational experiences in rational deliberation', in Linda Alcoff and Elizabeth Potter (eds), *Feminist Epistemologies*, New York: Routledge, Chapman and Hall.

Bar On, Bet Ami, 1993, 'Marginality and epistemic privilege', in Linda Alcoff and Elizabeth Potter (eds), *Feminist Epistemologies*, New York: Routledge, Chapman and Hall.

Benhabib, Seyla (1995), 'Feminism and postmodernism', in Linda Nicholson (ed.), *Feminist Contentions: a Philosophical Exchange*, London and New York: Routledge.

Bourdieu, Pierre (1980), *The Logic of Practice*, Cambridge: Polity Press.

Bourke, Angela (1999), *The Burning of Bridget Cleary*, London: Pimlico.

Brown, Richard (1977), *A Poetic for Sociology*, Cambridge: Cambridge University Press.

Denzin, Norman (1995), 'The poststructural crisis in the social sciences: learning from James Joyce', in Richard Harvey Brown (ed.), *Postmodern Representations: Truth, Power and Mimesis in the Human Sciences and Public Culture*, Urbana and Chicago: University of Illinois Press.

Edmondson, Ricca (1984), *Rhetoric in Sociology*, London: Macmillan.

Edmondson, Ricca (1995), 'Rhetoric and truthfulness: reporting in the social sciences', in Richard Harvey Brown (ed.), *Postmodern Representations: Truth, Power and Mimesis in the Human Sciences and Public Culture*, Urbana and Chicago: University of Illinois Press.

Edmondson, Ricca (1996), 'Uses of Empirical Data in the Sociology of Knowledge', International Sociological Association Research Committee for the History of Empirical Methods, Amsterdam.

Edmondson, Ricca (2000), 'Health promotion and the study of cultural practices', in Cecily Kelleher and Ricca Edmondson (eds), *Health Promotion: New Discipline or Multi-Discipline?*, Dublin: Irish Academic Press.

Edmondson, Ricca and Frank Nullmeier (1997), 'Knowledge, rhetoric and political action', in Ricca Edmondson (ed.), *The Political Context of Collective Action: Argumentation, Power and Democracy*, London: Routledge.

Fairhurst, Eileen (1990), 'Doing ethnography in a geriatric unit', in Sheila Peace (ed.), *Researching Social Gerontology*. London: Sage.

Finnegan, Frances (forthcoming), *Do Penance or Perish*.

Foucault, Michel (1971), *Madness and Civilisation: A History of Insanity in the Age of Reason*, London: Tavistock.

Gadamer, Hans-Georg (1960), *Truth and Method*, London: Sheed and Ward.

Geertz, Clifford (1972), *The Interpretation of Cultures*, New York: Basic Books.

Habermas, Jürgen (1972; German text 1968), *Knowledge and Human Interests*, London: Heinemann.

Kaplan, Gisela (1992), *Contemporary Western European Feminism*, London: Allen and Unwin.

Lewin, Ellen and Virginia Olesen (1981), 'Lateralness in women's work: new views on success', *Sex Roles* 6: 619-629.

Lloyd, Genevieve (1984), *The Man of Reason: 'Male' and 'Female' in Western Philosophy*, Minneapolis: University of Minnesota Press.

Lloyd, Genevieve (1993), 'Maleness, metaphor and the "crisis" of reason', in Louise M. Antony and Charlotte Witt (eds), *A Mind of One's Own:*

Feminist Essays on Reason and Objectivity, Boulder: Westview Press.

Longino, Helen (1993), 'Subjects, power and knowledge: description and prescription in feminist philosophies of science', in Linda Alcoff and Elizabeth Potter (eds), *Feminist Epistemologies*, New York: Routledge.

Nakano Glenn, E. (1990), 'The dialectics of wage work: Japanese-American women and domestic service, 1905-1940', in Ellen C. Du Bois and Vicky L. Ruiz (eds), *Unequal Sisters: A Multi-Cultural Reader in U.S. Women's History*. London: Routledge.

Nelson, John (1998), *Tropes of Politics: Science, Theory, Rhetoric, Action*, Madison: University of Wisconsin Press.

Nicholson, Linda (1990) (ed.), *Feminism/Postmodernism*, London and New York: Routledge.

Oakley, Ann (1992), *Social Support and Motherhood: the Natural History of a Research Project*, Oxford: Blackwell.

Olesen, Virginia (1994), 'Feminisms and models of qualitative research', in Norman Denzin and Yvanna Lincoln (eds), *Handbook of Qualitative Research,* London: Sage.

Popper, Karl (1959), *The Logic of Scientific Discovery*, London: Hutchinson.

Richardson, Laurel (1994), 'Writing as a Method of Inquiry', in Norman Denzin and Yvanna Lincoln (eds), *Handbook of Qualitative Research*, London: Sage.

Smith, Dorothy (1990), *The Conceptual Practices of Power*, Boston: Northeastern University Press.

Smith, Dorothy (1992), 'Sociology from women's experience: a reaffirmation', *Sociological Theory*, 10: 88-98.

Stanley, Liz and Wise, Sue (1979), 'Feminist research, feminist consciousness and experiences of sexism', *Women's Studies International Quarterly*, 2: 359-374.

Tanesini, Alessandra (1999), *An Introduction to Feminist Epistemologies*, Malden and Oxford: Blackwell.

Wörner, Markus (1990), *Das Ethische in der Rhetorik des Aristoteles*, Freiburg im Breisgau: Alber Verlag.

Young, Iris Marion (1995), 'Gender as seriality: thinking about women as a social collective', in Linda Nicholson and Steven Seidman (eds), *Social Postmodernism: Beyond Identity Politics*, Cambridge: Cambridge University Press.

Acknowledgements

For their interest I should like to thank Linda Nicholson and Markus Wörner, plus the participants at the Women's Network Conference in London in 1991, at which a forerunner of this paper was presented, as well as those at the conference on feminist research methodologies organised by Anne Byrne and Ronit Lentin in Dublin in 1999, and at the conference on rhetoric and politics organised by John Nelson at the American Political Science Association meeting in Atlanta in 1999.

8

Painting Women into the Picture

Romanie van Son

Claywork – Symbols

Introduction[1]

In the 1990s we benefit from an increasing body of research which underscores the mythologies securing capitalist society and which exposes oppressive assumptions about inclusion and exclusion, implicit in the public and private domain. In order to understand exclusion, by gender and class for example, we need to focus on barriers, prohibitions, constraints and realities from the viewpoint of the excluded.

The research project I describe in this chapter, using an innovative methodology, attempts to give a voice to the oppressive realities of women living in disadvantaged areas. It does so, while also recognising that in representing the world of the 'other', we must and should acknowledge the question of positionality.

I was aware that as a middle-class researcher, not being part of the (disadvantaged) community under observation, I was effectively an outsider, with little knowledge and experience of the realities of being born, and of living, in this community. I was mindful of the fact that in representing women living here, I could be unaware of, gloss over, misinterpret or misjudge certain aspects of their reality. Therefore, as a researcher I was seeking the most suitable way of enabling participants to explore and express their experiences.

As a trained arts worker involved with different interest groups and communities, I had an understanding of the benefits and value of working through art. Based on this insight and on previous experience as a researcher, I believed that research supported by art would be beneficial in enabling participants to tell their stories. Also, as I have been involved in arts related work for many years, I felt quite confident about using this method.

Women and research

Feminist analysis is most obviously about putting women in where they have been left out, about keeping women on the stage rather

---

[1] For the title of this chapter I am indebted to Eileen Evason who used the expression '... painting women into the picture...' first, in her contribution 'Women and poverty' in Ailbhe Smyth (ed.) (1993), *Women's Studies Reader*. I would like to acknowledge that the research on which this chapter is based would not have been possible without the input of the women who participated in the workshops.

than relegating them to the wings. But to do this suggests questions about the structures that have left women out; about the way academic disciplines work; about language, concepts, methods, approaches, and subject areas. Such a quest leads to profound rethinking (Pascall, 1997: 8).

Eileen Evason voices her concern that, from a feminist point of view, 'women have been largely invisible in an academic debate ...' (Evason, 1993: 163). This is particularly true of women who have been left out, who live in poverty, who are marginalised, and as a consequence possess very little social power. Bourdieu (1984) characterises 'social power' as the extent to which one's voice matters and is taken into account. Exclusion is a significant part of this debate, as 'the way in which we choose to "know" and measure poverty, has implications for how we deal with it' (Kabeer, 1995: 161). It is of essential importance to:

> paint women into the picture, so to speak, as failure to build women into the debates on definition, measurement and to a lesser extent, the causes of poverty, has meant hardship for women (Evason, 1993: 163).

Furthermore, it has led to policies which seem:

> incapable of grappling directly with the problems they are supposed to address, and a lack of fit between our concepts and methods on the one hand and the world that women and men recognise themselves as inhabiting, on the other (Evason, 1993: 164).

Research method

New developments in social research highlight increasingly the need to include 'subjects' in the research. This development has grown out of recognising the need to adopt a more empowering approach to the collection of 'knowledge', for 'persons as autonomous beings have a moral right to participate in decisions that claim to generate knowledge about them' (Heron, cited in Lather, 1981: 262). Besides, 'research that is reciprocal in nature leads to a research process where the richness of data can be greatly improved and insight in clearly defining situations is enhanced' (Heron, cited in Lather, 1981: 265).

Contemporary research is informed by the premise that 'no one discourse has a privileged place' (Richardson, 1991: 173). No single method can grasp the subtle variations in ongoing human experience. As a consequence qualitative researchers employ a range of interconnected interpretative methods, always seeking to know the worlds of experience of those they study. One such method is 'visual sociology' which is centred on the use of images (Berger and Mohr, 1989; Harper, 1994).

Visual sociologists have carried out research using visual imagery, such as photo documentaries, as a way of making visible cultures and concepts, which for many decades were difficult to grasp in traditional language-based research methods. Over time, visual sociology has moved on from a focus on the specific, which hid and muted the critiques of the system, to exposing social problems and injustices by inclusion of context and research subject in 'the picture'. In this context, Harper points out that:

> significantly the transition from images that created poverty and disorder to those that showed community and creative intelligence, was made only with the involvement of the subject (Harper, 1994: 403).

The use of images to facilitate respondents within the research process has changed and diversified over the past decade. Plays, puppets, painting and photographs taken by research participants themselves, are all elements incorporated in contemporary visual sociology. Images are resorted to, for example, in order to cut through some of the pretence, posing and self-editing that can dominate responses in a research situation, or when we do not want the question we ask to determine the answer we get. In the research described in this chapter, the 'images' are used as an alternative language, to support and enable participants to tell their stories.

Several studies acknowledge the role art can fulfil in the search for an alternative language, and in alliance with visual sociology (Bateson and Mead, 1942; Nisbet, 1981; Lippard, 1995; Swain et al, 1994). Art can provide a vehicle for perceiving and understanding different aspects of life, an alternative way of seeing and expressing reality, to create space for reflection, and to open up discussion. Working through art can create awareness of, for example, one's position in society which eventually could lead to a challenge of that position in society. A direct link between sociological enquiry and art can be found in the fact that both art and social science share a use of similar stimuli and creativity in their discovery process (Nisbet, 1981).

Bateson and Mead (1942), who used thousands of images as cultural evidence during their 'visual ethnographic research', emphasised the significance of the visual artist in social inquiry, and her/his ability to capture aspects of culture which science might not be able to record.

In the research presented in this chapter I aspired to facilitate women in exploring central issues within their daily lives which could lead to valuable insights, inform public debate, and ultimately lead to influencing policies. I intended to focus my enquiry on women least likely to be heard in general public discourse and debate, i.e. women marginalised by socio-economic and geo-graphical situations. In the process of carrying out this research, I employed an arts-based method to enable participants to best explore their realities. Working predominantly with art, and art forms, issues centring on women's exclusion were made visible. The research described in this chapter is a compilation of three different projects which took place during the years 1998-1999. For reasons of fluency and ease of reading, I describe the projects as one project. The groups consisted of ten to fifteen women, who by and large have similar socio-economic backgrounds, live in quite similar areas and share many central concerns and experiences. Therefore, synthesising the individual projects makes sense, as it is the method itself which I intend to concentrate on in this chapter. To protect the participants' privacy, I do not explicitly describe areas, venues or participants. I wish to acknowledge here the women who took part in the workshops and gave their 'voice', time, energy and expertise.

In the course of the research, one aspect that became evident was the 'invisibility' of the communities: their reality is seldom part of public knowledge and consequently is not part of public dis-course. Available information about these communities is often limited, biased, incomplete and sometimes even untrue. The obstacles to being part of, and partaking in, current political and policy-making debates concerning their own situation has much to do with specific, narrowly-based language and conventions, on which the body politic is based. Against this background I sought to research the lives and needs of women living in marginalised areas and to utilise methods and means which would be most effective in facilitating participants in telling 'their side of the story'.

Defining groups and location

In any culture it is those with power who define meanings and write the script and this power is tied up with language. It has come to be recognised that representation, knowledge and power are inextricably intertwined. Appadurai discusses 'the disenfranchisement of certain groups in society from participating in decisions about entitlements and hence about their distribution' (Appadurai, in Kabeer, 1995: 140). The place where a person lives, a 'socially ranked geographical space' (Bourdieu, 1984: 124), exerts a powerful influence on the options available to that person and concomitantly, on her/his choice-making.

Much of my research is concerned with constructing knowledge on the basis of women's voices, and by implication it is also concerned with 'having no voice' and with those people who have unequal access to language and speech in proclaiming their position and needs, whose voice is least likely to be heard or taken into consideration in public, official discourse. Reay argues that those most in need of having their case heard are those with the least resources and that:

> the experience of being listened to is much more novel for working-class women, than for example for middle-class women, who have already audiences to listen to what they have to say (Reay, 1995: 211).

Organisation

My first point of connection was typically through a resource centre, with an individual specifically concerned with the welfare of women. I explained my proposed project: to conduct an art-based enquiry with women and for women, focusing on experiences of their daily lives and exploring issues which they considered to be most relevant. It was envisaged that eventually the contributions of those involved would be documented in some form as a tangible record and that the images would not only be read but also exert influence.

The use of art materials and art forms was to be an integral and vital part of the project and would respond to 'the needs (of many) to find a voice to raise issues in a non-verbal way' (O'Donoghue, 1999: 9). Lynch and O'Neill draw attention to the fact that:

> the vulnerable and relatively powerless are the ones who are most often the subject of social scientific investigation as they lack the resources to protect themselves from scrutiny (Lynch and O'Neill 1994: 308).

I felt very strongly that the research project should be as much as possible of direct benefit to the participants. I hoped that conducting the research in the proposed way, and exchanging skills and enjoyment in the process, would make involvement worthwhile for the participants.

I left it to the discretion of the contact person to establish interest in participating in the project. Often the women already constituted a group, for example under a community development scheme, so finding a space to work in was rarely a problem. In most cases it was only feasible for the women to meet two hours weekly. The groups were made up of around twelve to fifteen women, ranging in age from early twenties to sixty plus. Most of the women had children (from babies to young adults), some had grandchildren, many had partners, others classified themselves as single, lone parent, or widow. Some participants came from outside the area and were in general better off. (The difference a few hundred yards can make!)

The project

For the project to succeed, it was vital to establish a good relationship and trust as:

> the development of trust and group bonding are conditions which fundamentally influence participation and the extent to which people are willing to explore issues through situations grounded in their experience (Treleaven, 1996: 153).

Establishing trust is a gradual process and I was conscious that it would require time and effort, getting used to each other and building up rapport. The initial meeting was predominantly introductory. I explained the aim, focus and nature of the project, emphasising that the women's own experiences, opinions and ideas were an essential part of the research and that their input as 'co-researchers' was valued. I clarified my role as facilitator and we explored how stories can be told in different ways, through talking, writing, singing, performing, dancing, drawing, or through symbols. The stories would concern the participants' own daily lives, their preoccupations, their family, their neighbourhood, their frustrations, their needs, their dreams. It was up to them which stories would be told. We discussed the possibility that all their work could be assembled in such a way that it could be seen and heard by other people, inform others about the issues they considered most relevant, and ultimately inform social, housing, or transport policies.

Art was to be used as a means, not as a receptacle or an end. Participants worked with materials of their choice, around certain themes or issues. Although in general the women liked the variety of art materials, some were apprehensive about working with them. Therefore, during the first weeks we just played around with the materials in order to become familiar with them. For example they tried out all the different colour combinations with paint, or any imaginable shape in clay. Allowing this space and freedom to play was very important, particularly to women who only began to get really involved once they realised they could do 'their own thing' and that 'perfect results' did not matter.

Activities concerning the 'self' were particularly significant in the initial workshops and our work was loosely centred around feelings, likes and dislikes, dreams and expectations through painting portraits and making collages or devising role plays. From there on we looked at women's place in the community, their support systems, and subsequently at other issues which impact on their lives.

The research method aimed at making 'real' the actual day-to-day reality of being marginalised. This can be illustrated by the following example which highlights the significance of access to transport for those who are marginalised. As part of one workshop we came to explore the environment of the participants, what they

Our environment: transport

think of it, how it looks, what it offers them. Later we followed this up with painting: collectively participants made a large painting of their place. Afterwards, during the ensuing talk, the image of a wagon in the frieze became the focal point for a discussion about transport facilities in the area. Few people possess a car in the area, so public transport is of vital importance. The bus service is quite good during the daytime, but only serves the area till mid-evening. This has all kinds of consequences, particularly as it is virtually impossible to get a taxi to come into the area after dark, because of its 'unsafe' reputation. The women had different stories about what this meant for them. One woman recalled how during the onset of labour of her first child, she 'had to hang in there', as she could not get a taxi to come out. In the early morning she managed to 'hobble' with her overnight bag and in great discomfort, to the nearest bus stop, to get the first bus to hospital.

On another occasion we engaged in activities centred around characters and qualities of people. Afterwards participants painted a portrait, portraying themselves as whoever they liked to be, a pop star, a politician. One of the women painted herself with great care, in the outfit she wore as a ten-year-old girl. It was an all-white leather outfit that her mother had bought her, because she liked it so much. She knew her mother could not really afford it and 'bills had to wait that week'. For her this outfit represented how her mother had looked after her and her siblings in spite of having very little money. This story sparked off other stories about how money had to be, and was, stretched over time.

Workshop structure

The workshops were all loosely structured in a similar way: an introductory activity would be followed by a discussion, after which we would engage in the 'main issue' and we would finish up with reflecting on the work done. This structure was flexible as, in accordance with findings in other studies (e.g. Finch, 1984), it soon became clear that there was a need among the women to just talk to each other, as they did not seem to have many other opportunities, if any, to collectively engage with other women in a supportive way. As a result we started each workshop with an informal chat session. The women would then participate in games or role plays.

'Me'

I hoped that in the process these games would clarify issues in a simple way, or provide different skills. In the initial stages of the project, activities concentrated on getting to know each other, building trust, feeling free to speak up. Later, activities were designed to include self-awareness and power relations. The women enjoyed these games as they were fun and they liked the fact that I joined in with them. As the women's energy levels were low at times, these activities helped to energise us.

One group, involved in a childcare scheme and working with children in an after-school-club, often talked about the fact that they 'ran out of things to do with them'. We discussed how they could adjust games to suit children and build up a repertoire to fall back on.

I had envisaged that every week, for possibly fifteen weeks, we would explore a different theme, such as 'health' or 'education'. However, themes never fitted neatly into the sessions. Issues often came up spontaneously, triggered off by recent events in the family, in the neighbourhood, or at work, or as a response to previous work done in the group. As a rule I would go with what was most pressing for the women and we would focus on themes or issues as they arose.

For example, one week President McAleese (the President of the Republic of Ireland) was about to visit the area and some of the participants were given the task of welcoming her. They were all very excited and talked about what they intended to say and do. We imagined the President having a magic wand and we discussed what they would ask the President if she could wave this magic wand and grant any wish. We talked about this for a while, and at the end we decided to make a graffiti wall and paint the wishes and concerns of the participants on a big piece of paper stuck on the wall instead of just making a little shopping list. The graffiti wall became a point of discussion and during subsequent workshops we referred back to it as a source for discussing certain topics, such as family.

On another occasion many participants appeared particularly despondent about their participation in an employment scheme, but they did not feel confident or capable enough to challenge particular issues. They said that 'they would not listen' and that 'nothing would change anyway'. We made a big, visual map with

Wish list

all the relevant issues drawn and/or written onto it. This clarified matters for them and it was easier to talk about the different issues. For example, they felt that there were not enough materials and games to keep the children entertained and they found some of the spaces not adequate for the type of groups they worked with. Subsequently we explored strategies to tackle their grievances through role-play. The women assumed different roles, the person in charge or the worker, and went through different scenarios. They also made up a plan chart and a needs chart. Afterwards they made their case to the relevant persons and felt great that they were listened to and were granted some of their requests.

Similarly, through the act of creating a response to some theme, using clay, paint or paper, different issues emerged, which were subsequently discussed. For example, in the process of making a collage, one participant came across an article about breast cancer which caught her interest. She herself had recently been 'through the wars' as a result of having had to deal with breast cancer. As a result, issues concerning powerlessness and the medical system became the topic of discussion. As facilitator, I encouraged the exploration of issues of powerlessness in general and in the medical domain specifically. On some occasions, an end product could become the start of a debate, often seemingly unrelated to our work: an image of a container signified for one participant the sense of 'feeling boxed in', and developed into a story about cramped housing conditions.

Clearly, images created during the workshops cannot be seen as standing alone; they have to be viewed in combination with commentary provided by the women themselves. The unreliability of a created image as a factual account is an important issue, as illustrated for example by Berger and Mohr (1989). Although different issues emerged within the individual groups, family and health related concerns were paramount in all the groups.

Methodological issues

• *The use of images*
The idea that early (mostly photographic) imagery in social enquiry carried documentary truth has long since been refuted. Instead, it has been argued that early image-based enquiry often said more

about the researcher than the researched (Harper, 1994; Berger and Mohr, 1989; MacDougall, 1994).

The use of images on their own with or without text as data sources raises important methodological issues: issues such as representation, ideology, and the degree to which the presence of the facilitator impacts on the image or the social situation of the people involved are all significant. Issues of privacy, confidentiality and anonymity take a completely new turn when visual media (such as still photographs and video) are used in data collection and reporting. Berger and Mohr (1989) highlight how images are open to a multitude of interpretations, emphasising that only occasionally are images self-sufficient. Gold (1989) points to the potential for harm in the absence of associated explanations when visual material is used, as images often tend to be seen as 'definitive'. The same holds true for images created *by* (not *of*) the people involved in the research process: they are the only ones who can account for the results. It is their personal language, not the language of the researcher, and it has to be kept in mind that the 'stories' attached to the images cannot be viewed as supplements, but form an integral part of the 'whole'. I was careful not to interpret the images produced by workshop participants, nor would I take an image on face value: the women themselves provided the explanations and that became the 'definitive version'.

• *The researcher as enabler*

To make it possible for the women to convey their stories and feelings effectively in their own words, a structured framework was required. This gave space to the participants, enabling them to explore their own experiences. Providing this space allowed for in-depth and rich contributions. As a facilitator I had extensive contact with the women and working through art and drama created opportunities both for me and for the women involved to see many different sides of each other. We got to know one another quite well in an open, easy, working atmosphere.

The position of being both facilitator and researcher could be difficult at times. I had to give as much leeway as possible, and at the same time keep things focused. In the process of exploring topics such as 'family' and 'health', participants might wander off to discuss different and seemingly unrelated issues. As enabler, I wished to allow space for that, but as researcher, I felt I needed to keep at least some focus, and not let proceedings get too unwieldy or unstructured. At times this became a real balancing act and sometimes frustrating. Particularly when things did not seem to go anywhere, it was hard not to jump in and force a direction or move things on. On other occasions the richness of the material compensated for the sometimes seemingly unstructured sessions.

• *Time frame*
Harper (1994: 412) emphasises that when researching in the field, we initially think and see only 'from our own cultural lens; thus we must learn to see through the lenses of the other'. Understanding the world of the other requires extensive contact. This has implications for the researcher-researched relationship.

  Working through the medium of art provided the women involved with an alternative language to express themselves and facilitated them in telling their life experiences in their own way. To this end, some fluency in the visual language had to be learned during the initial stages of the project. However, building up skills to enable the women to confidently and comfortably express themselves took time. Furthermore, this research is process-orientated: issues evolved during collective and individual explorations which were as much part of the enquiry as the final art product. Obviously, taking all the above into consideration, this type of enquiry entails a long process and can only be carried out within a generous time frame.

• *Side effects*
I was able to explore and clarify situations and issues in a clear, simplified way, together with the groups, creating awareness and insights which in turn could be equally helpful outside the workshops. It became evident that there was a positive spill-over from the research into other aspects of the participants' lives. This resulted for example in participants asserting certain needs and negotiating more space for particular projects they were involved in. One woman arrived to the second session in great form, great style, and positively beaming. She felt so good about being able to partake in activities on her own terms during the first session, that

afterwards 'she got her hair done and went with her sister to the cinema'. She had not done anything like that since her husband died years earlier. Another participant told us how she had decided to 'choose for herself and come to the workshop instead of doing the babysitting in her daughter's house'. On a different occasion a group had to miss a workshop because of a training day as part of the scheme they were involved in. At the next meeting they told us proudly how they 'did much better than other participating groups'. Much of the content of that day was familiar to them, as it was similar to what they had done in our workshops. They were even more pleased about the fact that they had been able to teach the facilitator some new activities.

• *Time-out*

Having fun was another positive aspect of the research process. When after one meeting I expressed some doubts, feeling that it 'did not go that well', the organiser remarked that she 'heard lots of laughter and laughter here is a sign of success'.

For the women the workshops were often a welcome break from harsh reality: 'Sssh, don't talk about that now. I am here and trying to forget about home.' A story-making session, using many different picture postcards, allowed the women to make fun of all kinds of situations and characters in the area: this exercise opened up opportunities for more serious reflections about power structures within the area, and the relationship with the police, for example.

• *Skills*

Besides providing enjoyment, the workshops also equipped participants with extra tools to express themselves, by acquiring new skills such as drama and art techniques. Continuously having to make do with limited resources undermines one's self-confidence. Furthermore, an elaborate interweaving of identifications with socially defined roles and expectations becomes part of our 'internal physic identities' (Meskimmon, 1996: 13). For people living in disadvantaged areas, projected and internalised qualities are more often than not feelings of being less adequate, less significant and less able.

An example of such internalised self-depreciative attitudes among the women surfaced during a discussion about an upcoming day trip in the new 'community bus'. An organised trip to Dublin was greeted with great enthusiasm, until participants discovered that the bus had the name of the area painted on its side. This was greeted by high indignity and hilarity: they would rather 'stay at home than go in that bus'; 'who could take this seriously?' All the shops would be closed anyway by the time they arrived, as the message that they were on their way would have reached the shopkeepers, who undoubtedly would take safety precautions and close up. In this case we explored, through 'status games', the position of the participants in society, and worked around the issue of self-image.

• *Practical issues*
The workshops took place once a week, not frequently enough to keep continuity going, or to discuss issues that had surfaced during the previous meeting. This became even more problematic at certain times, as the research was tied in with resource centres and with certain adult education schemes, and we had to observe school holidays, training days and outings. When the centre's crèche closed down because of training, several women could not come as they had no alternative childminding; very occasionally, participants would bring their children with them, and children would then happily paint or draw during the workshop. Overall, however, the process would have benefited from better continuity and focus.

Other groups also used our workshop spaces and as a result we had no space to leave our materials and 'creations'. This meant that materials and works had to be brought back and forth if we did not wish them to get lost or damaged. In one particular space, a church hall, the materials were almost crowded out by religious icons and pictures.

Operating in a context of having insufficient money to live on, 'drains a woman's emotional energy to the extent that it is difficult to do anything' (Reay, 1996: 582). Likewise, many women felt listless, tired, and without energy. They would regularly remark that they were 'just hanging in there', 'going through the motions', or 'dragging themselves around'. In many cases they also suffered from different kinds of ongoing ailments. Consequently, it was hard at times for some women to get enthusiastically involved. Sometimes they

Vying interests

admitted that they had only enough energy to talk. Their presence at the workshops was far from guaranteed and fluctuated from week to week. On the first Tuesday of the month, children's-allowance-day, attendance was often low. Child benefit, paid directly to mothers, is for many women the major source of independent income. For those struggling to make ends meet, child benefit can provide a vital mid-week stop-gap, tiding women over until their major source of income, in the form of earnings, income support or a housekeeping allowance, arrives. The women were quite frank about the fact that this was 'the only thing they got for free', and they wanted to get it as soon as possible, even if it meant they had to miss the workshop that day.

Conclusion

Richardson (1991) states that a new sensibility characterising qualitative research has as its core 'doubt that ... any method or theory has an universal and general claim to authoritative knowledge' (Richardson, 1991: 173). The researcher can, and has to, seek the most 'fitting' and suitable 'way of knowing'. Studies indicate that many women, and more particularly disadvantaged women, are excluded from mainstream and public discourse. One of the reasons why this is so has to do with language. Lippard expresses this strongly, when she observes, 'I am still struck by the psychological displacement of women who are alienated by and in language' (Lippard, 1995: 13).

The research described in this chapter attempted to deal with the issue of language in the enquiry process, through using visual language. I worked through art, allowing participants more input in shaping the direction and content of the research, with the result of the data being more personal, deeper and richer. I aspired to make involvement in the research a meaningful experience for the participating women.

I learned much from the project. It gave me an opportunity to learn about life in a disadvantaged area. I got a clearer sense of the difficulties, hardships, worries and frustrations generated by living in these communities. I also learned about humour, celebration, resilience, friendship and support. I realised that as a community, people living in disadvantaged areas are often left to fend for themselves in the face of many difficulties with very little help or understanding from 'outside', and that women often seemed to be resigned to the situation. I learned that these women did have a voice and were very clear about their situation but that their voices were often not heard or were ignored. The women who participated in the research project revealed much of their day-to-day life, their aspirations and needs, enriching me, and indeed, astonishing, challenging and uplifting me in the process. They themselves had an opportunity to tell their story, had fun and learned certain skills. This joint, co-operative sociological enquiry which included many individual voices contributes to a growing collectivity of voices of disadvantaged women in (re)defining their situation, and shaping their own present and future.

References

Bateson, G. and Margaret Mead (1942), *Balinese Character: A Photographic Analysis*, New York: New York Academy of Sciences.

Berger, John and Jean Mohr (1989), *Another Way of Telling*, Cambridge: Granta Books.

Bourdieu, Pierre (1984), *Distinction: A Social Critique of the Judgement of Taste*, Cambridge, Mass: Harvard University Press.

Evason, Eileen (1993), 'Women and poverty', in Ailbhe Smyth (ed.), *Women's Studies Reader*, Dublin: Attic Press.

Finch, Janet (1984), 'It's great to have someone to talk to: ethics and politics of interviewing women', in Colin Bell and Helen Roberts (eds), *Social Researching: Politics, Problems, Practice*, London: Routledge.

Gold, Steven (1989), 'Ethical issues in visual fieldwork', in G. Blank, J. McCarthy and E. Brent (eds), *New Technology in Sociology: Practical Applications in Research and Work*, New Brunswick, NJ: Transaction.

Harper, Douglas (1994) 'On the authority of the image: visual methods at the crossroads', in Norman Denzin and Yvonne Lincoln (eds), *Handbook of Qualitative Research*, London: Sage.

Heron, John in Patti Lather (1986), 'Research as praxis', *Harvard Educational Review*, vol. 56: 257-277.

Kabeer, Naila (1995), *Reversed Realities*, London, New York: Verso.

Lippard, Lucy, L. (1995), *The Pink Glass Swan: Selected Essays on Feminist Art*, New York: New Press.

Lynch, Kathleen and Cathleen O'Neill (1994), 'Colonisation of social class', *British Journal of Education*, vol. 15, no. 3: 307-324.

MacDougall, David (1994), 'Whose story is it?', in Lucien Taylor (ed.), *Visualizing Theory*, London: Routledge.

Meskimmon, Marsha (1996), *The Art of Reflection*, London: Scarlet Press.

Nisbet, Robert. A. (1981), 'Sociology as an art form', in Kenneth Thompson, and Jeremy Tunstall (eds), *Sociological Perspectives:* 477-481.

O'Donoghue, Helen (1999), *'......and to start to wear purple'*, Dublin: Irish Museum of Modern Art.

Pascall, Gillian (1997), *Social Policy: a New Feminist Analysis*, London, New York: Routledge.

Reay, Diane (1995), 'Feminist research: the fallacy of easy access', *Women's Studies International Forum*, vol.18, no. 2: 205-13.

Reay, Diane (1996), 'Contextualising choice: Social power and parental involvement', *British Educational Research Journal*, vol. 22 no. 5: 582.

Richardson, Laurel (1991), 'Postmodern social theory: representational practices', *Sociological Theory*, no. 9: 173.

Swain, John, Vic Finkelstein, Sally French and Mike Oliver (1994), *Disabling Barriers – Enabling Environments*, London: Sage.

Treleaven, L. (1996), in John Heron (ed.), *Co-operative Inquiry. Research into the Human Condition*, London: Sage.

9

Talking Back

Rosaleen McDonagh

Introduction

This chapter about Travellers talking back with regards to research methodology is an attempt to develop Anastasia Crickley's argument in her article entitled 'Feminism and ethnicity' (Crickley, 1992), where she points to the difficulties that Traveller women experience in the form of racism. The difficulty is in viewing Traveller women as being responsible for their own circumstances by refusing to assimilate into settled people's ideology and value system. This is very often sanctioned and validated by feminist academics. Although the context of Crickley's article is general with regards to the tensions between Travellers and feminism, I do believe that it initiated a discussion, part of which meant that settled women felt that racism among women could be challenged. As a Traveller feminist who has struggled in an academic environment for the past six years, I feel the need to talk back. Talking back for me means being strong about my Traveller identity.

To clear up any ambiguity, I believe that we as Traveller women can call ourselves feminist. Traveller women like Nan Joyce, Maureen Ward, Catherine Joyce, Missy Collins and Katleen Stokes are participating in political activism for Travellers' rights. There is a history of Traveller women being involved in political activism. However, our history is oral and our work for human rights is considered menial work, which is why it has not been documented as part of Irish women's history. If these women were settled their work would be valued in the overall struggle for human rights for women. But because they are advocating basic human rights for Travellers, their work is not valued enough to be considered part of the feminist movement in Ireland.

Over the years researchers have used me and other Travellers in ways that I know would not be tolerated by settled people. The abuse and intrusion is often done in isolation without the researchers being aware of their power base. Being exploited by researchers is something that we as Travellers have come to expect. The struggle in terms of social and political rights for Travellers is difficult enough without our having to be cautious about researchers who in a more equal setting could help us to challenge racism and do more useful work in the broader human rights arena.

This chapter deals with the researched, in this case Travellers, talking back. When a settled person decides to select an area of Traveller culture for research, suddenly there are no rules, there are no ethics, and our culture is viewed through a microscope of racism and stereotypes. Regardless of the topic of research, our culture and our ethnicity is objectified as traditional, patriarchal and 'useful' for researchers in terms of supplying paradigms of anthropology and sociology which bring all the cultural and social values of settled Western academics into play. Therefore the outcome of any piece of research, regardless of the area, continues to objectify and alienate us as Travellers from our own experience and thus devalues our sense of identity.

Academics usually belong to a dominant culture which does not value nomadic ethnic groups other than for their usefulness in particular areas of research. They often define us in the context of one particular area of discrimination. However, researchers do not believe that they perpetuate racism.

Using a feminist approach to research does not always guarantee anti-racist content or ideology; therefore this chapter works from the context of an anti-racist approach and then contextualises it in a feminist agenda in order to make room for many different Traveller voices. This approach proposes to place Traveller women at the centre of the research process and encourages researcher reflexivity when determining her outcome.

How to include an anti-racist ideology in a feminist approach

When I was younger I discovered feminism through the experience and dialogue of settled women. I did not think this was harmful. In fact, for a short period it was even useful. Because of this I trusted female researchers more than male researchers. I assumed they were working from a feminist agenda and this for me reduced the possibility of objectification or exploitation. As a non-academic and as someone who comes from an oral tradition, I felt in awe of the intellectual status of these researchers. I trusted the work they were doing. The title or the subject matter was usually presented to me. I had no role other than that of answering questions. This approach is still called 'participatory research' even if you, as informant, are there only in order to answer someone else's questions. I felt cheated or fooled, not so much about the researcher or the topic, but about feminism.

In the past, whenever I read about black or minority ethnic women, I found it difficult to introduce a Traveller experience into this dialogue because I had never read the experience of Traveller women in the context of feminist discussion. The low status attached to being a Traveller woman was such an intrinsic part of my experience of growing up and participating in research that I let questions around racism slip. No one ever told me that feminism, the kind of feminism that is aiming to empower and validate women's experience, and the feminist approach which is used in research, have the potential to perpetuate racism and exclusion.

In the early 1980s in Ireland the Black experience was presented to us in a form which undoubtedly set it up as being foreign, exotic and not part of the Irish experience. Colourism was the only way to define Irish racism. Traveller women were being talked about and talked at. We as Travellers were being used in order to provide information. That information was then interpreted and written in a way that excluded us from our own experience, and almost annihilated us. We were used in feminist discussions only as a tool for defining poverty and exclusion and an image was portrayed of us as being locked into a tradition that located women perpetually in a subordinate position in a patriarchal culture. The dominant culture was using us as an example of being victims of our own tradition by our refusing to assimilate or be settled. This voyeurism is still considered a norm among some feminist researchers.

It has been said of Traveller women that it is our fault and that our value system and loyalty to Traveller tradition and culture has left us outside feminist discussions. Elements of power and control often manifest themselves in the economic and ethnic differences among women. Our Traveller culture changes and adapts in that no two Traveller women will have the same response to racism other than knowing that the behaviour towards them is racist. As stated earlier, researchers are in a powerful position by the mere fact that they are settled and well educated. The main challenge to researchers is to employ 'qualitative, feminist and reflexive methodology' (Lentin, 1993: 119). Although Lentin's argument is used in a different context – the study of Israeli daughters of Holocaust survivors – this reflexive methodology could be useful in challenging racism towards Traveller women and its internalisation by Traveller women themselves. Lentin (1993: 124) cites Reinharz (1992: 240) who advocates the use of multiple research methodologies and disciplines in order to 'create social change while at the same time representing human diversity'.

Feminist dialogue, especially in Ireland, needs to constantly check itself in terms of anti-racist practice. Settled women in Ireland have changed in the past twenty-five years. In fact much of the economic and social developments that have taken place is a result of the fact that the majority of Irish women have thrown off the stereotype of 'my dark Rosaleen' in favour of making Irish women part of wider international feminist and human rights struggles. Changes have happened in the lives of Traveller women too. We have become politicised, both inside and outside the community, and some of us, like Catherine Joyce, for example, have made major contributions to both the Traveller women's movement and the overall struggle for women's human rights (Joyce, 1997). Sadly, due to the lack of appropriate accommodation, health care and legal status, our work is still very much concerned with practical change rather than theoretical discussions about reconstructing notions of womanhood.

Challenges to research

Research should acknowledge its potential in terms of positive and negative effects. But no researcher can ever be objective about her particular role in research and her particular subject. In order to take ownership and responsibility around research, there are some questions that need to be asked. The main concern is not so much the value or the importance of a particular area but how people are used in research and, more importantly, how research will be used as evidence to justify a particular new development. In

Traveller-related topics, it is important to illuminate how research is often the first mechanism used to perpetuate racism. Talking back is about responding to racism in its most insidious forms. Talking back is also about renegotiating power relations between researcher and researched. Racism is an ideology with an intellectual veneer which hides the implicit values of the researchers. It is like a cultural clash, but because the dominant settled culture has more status or recognition in terms of intellectual arguments, the difficulties that we as Travellers have about research and ethics are often overlooked. Researchers are usually connected to colleges and supervisors, who very often use Traveller culture as part of a research project to evaluate academic performance. It does not matter what sort of behaviour or methods the researcher uses; the fact of the matter is that university work is given higher status regardless of whether or not the topic is racist or is beneficial to Travellers.

In the past researchers have abused their power in so many ways in dealing with Travellers that one often wonders how a university can fund individuals who use tactics of voyeurism and bribery in order to acquire a degree or other university status. The bribery is often in the form of alcohol and money. I have been used by researchers and I have watched other Traveller women being used in a way which is totally humiliating and exploitative. Not only are we humiliated in relation to our ethnic identity but we are also humiliated by the mere fact of poverty and being trapped into corners by researchers who pose questions that create a cultural clash in ways that we as Travellers do not anticipate. Just as settled people do not notice the nuances of Traveller culture, I as a Traveller do not always understand or make sense of the nuances of settled people's way of communicating and formulating questions or ideas. This is often the way in which Travellers are exploited. Researchers want what they consider to be an 'authentic' Traveller voice. They want to work with Travellers who have not had the opportunity of being part of a Traveller organisation. Traveller organisations provide Travellers with skills on how to handle power relationships with researchers. Therefore, without organisational support, individual Travellers are in a vulnerable position. Researchers do not want Travellers who can talk back. They do not want Travellers who question how and why they are researching a particular topic. Very often researchers do not include in their bibliography works written about Traveller culture by Travellers or by Traveller organisations. They do not understand the nuances of Traveller culture. They think we are a homogeneous group of people and do not acknowledge differences between Travellers.

Researchers create stereotypes around Travellers and Traveller culture. Researchers can also use their interpretations from a settled perspective and then try to apply them to Traveller culture. This presents a completely different picture and context. An example of such a practice is found in the repeated references to the issue of domestic violence or begging, often presented as being inherent elements of Traveller cultural behaviour, although such behaviour patterns occur in the settled population as well. Violence against women is wrong whether it is happening to settled women, Traveller women, disabled women or refugee women. It is not a cultural norm. Researchers fail to put these sensitive subjects into the context of racism. This is where Lentin's proposition (1993: 124) of reflexive methodology could be useful for researchers in order not only to prevent them perpetuating stereotypes but also restrain them from projecting their particular points of view onto different cultural contexts.

Researchers explicitly or implicitly continue to blame Traveller women for their situation. They forget to put Traveller women's experience and the history of violence towards women in the Traveller community in a context of state violence, e.g. evictions, discrimination, and difficulties encountered when seeking support from statutory agencies and voluntary organisations. Meanwhile, the choice of reasonable accommodation is still a struggle for Travellers, although the 1998 Accommodation Act will challenge a structure which cannot come to grips with a nomadic lifestyle. These issues are very real for me as a Traveller: we live with them every day. This has created a system where racism is endemic. It affects every area of our lives. To some non-Travellers such issues are not very obvious, and racism is understood only on the basis of discrimination and a denial of cultural, social and political rights.

Some researchers have gone so far as to try to live on a halting site in order to have the 'true experience' of Traveller culture. I find this not only intrusive but also patronising, voyeuristic and completely unethical. Critical analysis implies a type of academic work which helps us to understand a human experience without actually living that experience. In order to understand a black woman's experience of racism, do I need to be black? This type of field research is a total abuse of power. Researchers ignore the ethnic element of our identity and the ingredients that go along with belonging to a different culture such as history, tradition and language.

In a recent discussion between a researcher and a group of Traveller women, a Traveller woman asked the settled anthropologist who boasted that she based her findings on having lived on a halting site, if she could pull her trailer into the anthropologist's back garden in order to understand the 'authentic settled experience'. I think the anthropologist got the point.

There are some really helpful research topics, particularly relating to health issues for Travellers, which have been based on a relationship of trust. The challenge for researchers who study Travellers is to question their own role in terms of being settled persons from the dominant culture. It is not enough to present self-confessions as a pretence form of solidarity which does not challenge racism. Researchers and academic institutions need to be aware that racism in academia is endemic.

Travellers talking back

Notions of empowerment and of cherishing women's personal narratives are the crux of a reflexive feminist approach to research. As stated earlier, research is important in the development of every culture. As a Traveller, the only way I can truly understand or analyse my ethnic identity is when I am in discussion about different elements of our way of life that are either good or bad. Research can be a good instrument for us to use in the area of health care and accommodation in discussions with politicians and policy makers. However, I believe that researching Travellers is not valuable unless Travellers or Traveller organisations are involved at every stage of the research process. The question of whether the researcher is settled should not be an issue.

In fact, suggesting that the research be conducted exclusively by a Traveller takes away the responsibility for all of us to challenge racism. It is too easy to suggest that a Traveller conducts the research in order to solve this problem. This has happened and will continue to happen, but it can become more frequent only when we are in a more equal position by way of educational standards. For the time being, research and researchers can use Travellers as their assistants and field workers to ensure solidarity and appropriate interpretation of the information collected.

Travellers and Traveller organisations need to challenge researchers and academic institutions by firstly outlining the areas of our lives and culture we want researched. As Travellers we have to select the topics that are of value and relevance to our culture. Secondly, we as Travellers need to be seen as equal partners in terms of how research projects are conducted. Thirdly, researchers need to develop their knowledge of Traveller culture and create a relationship with a Traveller organisation in order to ensure that they are not being racist or using unethical methods in conducting their research. As Travellers we have to own research by ensuring that personal narratives become the centre-piece of any research project. We cannot continue to allow settled researchers to portray us as being subservient to settled society or to present culturally inappropriate interpretations of Traveller culture and experience. As stated earlier, anti-racist paradigms do not develop of their own accord.

Will you answer my questions?

If we as Travellers talk back, will academics and researchers hear our questions? Talking back is about voicing our fear of being exploited, used and disempowered as Travellers. If they are to remain central to the research process, personal narratives have to be accepted as being authentic, individualistic and sometimes dangerous.

- *Authentic:* recognising that Traveller culture is fluid and changing all the time.
- *Individualistic:* recognising that ethnicity does not mean defining or restricting Traveller experience as mono-cultural; as Travellers, while celebrating our ethnicity, we need to be allowed to express opinions that may differ from each other, in the same way that settled people are allowed to have opinions that vary from each other.

– *Dangerous:* in our experience as Travellers we may have to challenge racism in every aspect of society and this includes academia and research methodologies. Even the very choice of a particular area of research, which may have been approved by well-respected academics, may not be appropriate where Travellers are concerned.

Power relationships are very real in the area of research. Travellers become nervous around academic structures. A particular piece of research may present Traveller culture as violent, misogynistic and patriarchal, and yet we as Travellers are not in a position to challenge that in an academic environment. Researchers and research agencies need to be open to challenges presented by Travellers, and the dialogue should not become less important because oralism is valued in Traveller culture just as much as literacy and academic formats are valued in settled culture. Oralism was, and to some extent still is, our only way of surviving as Travellers in an education system which has not reflected, and does not reflect, our culture or our experience.

Talking back is about Travellers demanding appropriate ethical approaches to racism in the area of research. No researcher is objective. No subject matter is easy. However, whether or not ethnocentric questions present themselves while researching Traveller issues, researchers can no longer be allowed to leave open-ended, questions around their approach to research concerning Traveller culture and identity. Moreover, they cannot be left unchallenged.

Conclusion

In conclusion, researching Travellers presents many difficulties. As a Traveller, I resent being exploited by researchers. Universities are given power over people's lives. Intellectual knowledge is seen as superior *vis-à-vis* experiential knowledge. My experience and my culture are often presented back to me in a way that I do not understand. I no longer trust researchers, regardless of their academic status, because ultimately, ethics is crucial in how one treats the narratives of participants. A code of conduct or a charter of principles is useless when Travellers are in the passive role. As the director of

Pavee Point, Ronnie Fay, points out, just because one comes from an oral tradition does not mean one is ignorant to the point that one does not know one is being exploited. In an article called 'Pavee Beoirs breaking the silence: racism and violence against women' (Fay, 1999), Fay, a settled community worker, identifies herself as a feminist, but more importantly, as an active member of the anti-racist movement. In doing this, Fay situates herself as an ally, not just around the safeguards of being a feminist, but also as being part of an anti-racist agenda. Her solidarity and her analysis is transparent because she does not see the feminist agenda as being sufficient to understand Traveller issues. This kind of solidarity is welcome. Research and ethics do not always engage with each other, but what I would like is to build on the feminist paradigm and include an anti-racist agenda. This has to be made explicit.

References

Crickley, Anastasia (1992), 'Feminism and ethnicity', in Dublin Travellers Education and Development Group, *DTEDG File: Irish Travellers – New Analysis and New Initiatives*, Dublin: Pavee Point.

Fay, Ronnie (1999), 'Pavee Beoirs breaking the silence: racism and violence against women', in Violence Against Women – An Issue for Community Work, *Community Workers Cooperative*.

Joyce, Catherine (1997), 'Political discrimination and persecution', in Niamh Reilly (ed.), *Women's Rights as Human Rights: Local and Global Perspectives. Strategies and Analyses*, the ICCL Conference on Women's Rights as Human Rights, Dublin, March 1997.

Lentin, Ronit (1993), 'Feminist research methodologies – a separate paradigm? Notes for a debate', *Irish Journal of Sociology*, vol. 3: 119-138.

Reinharz, Shulamit (1992), *Feminist Methods in Social Research*, New York: Oxford University Press.

10

Constructing the Self in Narrative:
Feminist Research as Auto/biography[1]

Ronit Lentin

Introduction

> When did the journey begin? ... You could have been a child from there, but they did all they could so you would be a child from here, a strong, earth-smelling sabra. ... Did they, secretly, think you wouldn't have survived had you been born there? (Lentin, 1989: 13).

> I didn't ask any more questions. Gaining a dead sister was enough for one day. I felt immobilised by the dead weight Mother had just burdened me with. But I realised now I had always carried that weight, always unknowingly struggled uphill, carrying my pain around my neck (Lentin, 1996: 31).

There are some research projects, born, as Liz Stanley (1996) would say, out of 'necessity,' which carry within them transformative possibilities for the researcher. If indeed feminist researchers carry out particular research because of the resonance between the topic or approach and the personal context of the research, and if indeed our 'intellectual auto/biography' (Stanley and Wise, 1993) can explicate the processes by which understandings are reached, then the myth of the detached scientific observer must be done away with. Instead we have an 'experiencing because knowing subject' whose 'ontologically based reasoning provides the claims to knowledge' (Stanley, 1996: 47).

In this chapter I posit this duality of knowing and experiencing,

---

[1] I would like to acknowledge my intellectual debt and my thanks to Liz Stanley, whose work opened my eyes to the possibility of using auto/biography as a feminist research strategy.

a duality, moreover, of double subjectivity. In my case this double subjectivity is that of an Israeli daughter to the 'first (Israeli-born) generation' schooled to despise the Jewish diaspora, and at the same time, that of a daughter not only of a diaspora family, but a family of Shoah[2] survivors. In the course of my research, these two very conflicting subjectivities became inter-twined, forming the kernel of my auto/biographical quest. My project was based on auto/ biographical personal narratives of Israeli daughters of Shoah survivors, who, like me, are also fiction writers. Like me, as I discovered in the course of conducting the research, they too grew up in families who were silent about their Shoah past and were in turn silenced by an uncomprehending society.

I begin this chapter by thinking aloud, as it were, about the contradictions involved in trying to research silence. How can you study silence about a topic such as the Shoah, about which clearly so much has been spoken, written, filmed? And how can you make sense of this silence and its consequences in a way which 'gives voice' to women's auto/biographies? I then theorise the strategy of auto/biographical personal narratives as a research method and as a writing strategy. I conclude by arguing that women's personal narratives, both our narrators' and researchers' own narratives, despite the crucial insights they offer us about women's lives and their place in society, are never linear, never open to conventional processes of verification and validation.

Very often stories, or personal narratives, more so than positivistic research methods, are the only way of closing the 'memory gap' (Grunfeld, 1995; Ringelheim, 1997) between traumatic experiences and the words available to us to tell them. My central argument is that auto/biographical narratives can be used to make sense of 'constructing,' rather than merely 're-constructing,' selves and lives, by 'making them, recording them differently from how they were first experienced' (Stanley, 1993: 211), thus representing the three components of auto/bio/graphy: self/life/writing.

Auto/biographical personal narratives, particularly narratives of

---

[2] I use the term 'Shoah' which means, in Hebrew, calamity or cataclysm, rather than the English term 'Holocaust' which derives from the Greek 'holocauston' meaning 'burnt offering', because of the latter's implication of the Jews being sacrificed.

trauma, because of their complex and often messy nature, are only 'as true as our lives'. However, auto/biography, if researchers are open to it, has endless performative, but also transformative possibilities, in terms of constructing the self, but often also of bringing about a transformation of society.

Researching silence

On the screen an old photograph of three young women, dressed in European pre-war style, short tailored jackets, flared knee-length skirts, and coifed hairdos, smiling at the camera.

There are subtitles, but we can hear no voice:

> I knew ...
> what camp ...
> Karola was in ...'

The picture changes to that of an elderly woman sitting at a kitchen table, writing in a school copybook.

The woman is speaking very softly: there still is no sound, yet the subtitles continue; the soundtrack is so soft that your hand moves to adjust the volume control of your video recorder, but nothing happens:

> So I ...
> begged ...
> begged him ...
> that German officer ...
> to send ...
> send me ...
> to Parsnitz ...
> in the Sudetenland ...
>
> When I met ...
> Karola ...
> when I met Karola ...
> Karola burst into tears.
> Karola asked me ...
> asked me:
> 'What?
> You're here too?
> sent here ...
> as a prisoner?'

This scene goes on for two minutes and fifteen seconds, a long time for a silent scene on film. Then the phone rings. The woman looks up. It rings again. She answers the phone and speaks to her sister, telling her how busy she is with her husband's illness, with making doctor's appointments for him, 'until I'm out of time … I've let myself go …'

The sisters go on to discuss their husbands' illnesses, their own illnesses, and their third sister who is in an old folks' home.

Three Sisters (Reibenbach, 1998a) is Israeli film director Tsipi Reibenbach's second film about her parents. Her first film, *Choice and Destiny* (1993), documented the everyday, banal existence of her Shoah survivor parents. As they shop, clean, prepare, serve and eat food, her father Yitzhak tells his Shoah story. He tells it factually, unemotionally, although the story itself is heartbreakingly horrific. All the while, her mother Fruma continues her domestic chores, a silent witness. Thirteen minutes before the end of the two-hour film, she speaks, for five whole minutes, about her unwillingness to remember, her inability to tell:

> What do you think? How can I tell everything? … I lie down at night and I can't fall asleep. … I lie there with my eyes open and I see it. … I lie down for hours and when nobody is at home, sometimes I walk around and I call out loud 'Sarahleh, Shimshele, where are you? Where are you? Where? I don't even have a tombstone for you. …' That's it. Tomorrow I can tell you a lot, a lot, a lot. I'll remember again. That's it.

Fruma's outburst is followed by a long silence as her husband and grandchildren look on. She then repeats again and again the names of her lost relatives.

Daughter-director allows her survivor parents to tell, but in the telling, her father seems to find it easier to speak while all her mother can do is mourn. Shoah survivor fathers have often found it easier than mothers to speak of their Shoah experiences. According to Zvi Dror (1984; 1992), who collected and documented scores of Shoah testimonies, Israeli male Shoah survivors tend to give general, factual testimonies in the spirit of Israeli hegemonic masculinity: 'the world of occupation is a world of men and it translated itself into the Israeli army, which is governed by a masculine set of rules, while women testify more emotionally' (personal communication, 1992).

Director-daughter keeps filming as her mother talks about the value of talking, after long years of refusal to talk, inability to remember:

> Heshik – he didn't live to tell. To get it off his chest. Maybe it would have been easier for him. Maybe he wouldn't have become so sick. … Maybe it'll be easier for me too. I'd be able to fall asleep at last. … (All those years) I didn't want to talk. I didn't want to. I have told you nothing … leave me alone, let me be. I don't want to remember. … (But) now, you see I'm talking, I could talk all day long. … So many events! So many! I never talked before and now maybe I'll feel better if I let everything out …

According to Reibenbach, as soon as the first film was completed, her mother began to talk. *Three Sisters* was supposed to be *her* story. Only that *Three Sisters* turned out to be a completely different project – the story of the minutiae of old age, of illness, of disintegration, spun very loosely but very carefully from the silent beginning of Fruma writing her story in that school copybook.

This is how Reibenbach describes the film:

> 'Life has passed and we have achieved nothing,' that's what Ester, the youngest (of the sisters) says. The eldest, Karola, keeps quiet. Fruma, who is also my mother, tries to write what she remembers. Three sisters in their seventies, Holocaust survivors. More than fifty years have passed and still they can't talk of their memories. This is a film about trauma. … Three sisters talk on the telephone occasionally but never meet. The film follows their daily life – three women who, in their old age devote most of their time to caring for their sick husbands. The camera follows them in the shower and during intimate medical examinations, exposes the wrinkles and varicose veins which will not go away and the taboo of the naked bodies of the elderly. They are forced to deal with the weakness, loneliness and anger of old age. The Nazis stole not only their youth but also their ability to grow old in serene fulfilment (Reibenbach, 1998b).

Reibenbach is one of a number of Israeli women writers and film makers who are daughters of Shoah survivors, who in recent years have begun writing or making films derived from their parents' Shoah experiences. While in most cases their work is not strictly auto/biographical, it is always informed by the experience of being a daughter of survivors in Israeli society.

Silence – silent Shoah families and the silencing of Shoah families in Israeli society – is central to the personal narratives of the nine Israeli daughters of survivors who are writers and film makers which I collected for a study of the gendered relations between Israel and the Shoah. Silence, despite the many words that are spoken about the Shoah and the imperative never to forget, is the central character in Reibenbach's films, the central feature in the lives of Shoah survivors, both those who are able to tell their stories and those who take their stories with them to their graves.

In my work, both fiction and academic (Lentin, 1989; 1996; 2000), I try to give voice to that silence. I ask, among many other questions, whether the daughter-writers' performative act of re-membering and 'memorising' the trauma that was the Shoah and its Israeli aftermath for the survivors can be termed a feminist project. This is particularly poignant because Israeli feminism often falls victim to discourses of 'national security' and 'no choice' war: 'the preoccupation with national construction and defence gave precedence to male actors and a "male" discourse' (Rappaport and El-Or, 1997: 575).

I began working on the gendered relationship between Israel and the Shoah on a hunch. I 'knew' – if 'knew' is the term for something known instinctively, but also experientially – that Shoah survivors were not considered on the same level as Israeli-born Jews or 'older' immigrants. A whole mythology developed around survivors allegedly going to their death passively, 'like lambs to the slaughter,' in stark contrast to the fictions Israelis were telling themselves about their own active resistance and heroic war against their Arab 'enemies'.

I also knew, and collected documentary evidence, that Israel was, and is, a masculine construction where, while women are active participants, society is built on axioms of a 'no-choice' ongoing military struggle. Necessarily, the ongoing wars privilege male soldiers who share in the dividends of military, social and political power to the detriment of women. Much has been written on both the discrimination against Shoah survivors upon their arrival (e.g. Segev, 1991; Yablonka, 1994) and the masculinisation of Israel (e.g. Hazelton, 1978; Shadmi, 1992; Boyarin, 1997). My instinct was to research daughters of survivors, who were the first members of the 'second generation' to put their experiences of being children of survivors into the public domain, in short stories, novels and films. My research goal was to link Israel as a masculine construction with the stigmatisation of Shoah survivors *via* 'reading between the lines' of the silences that enveloped Shoah survivors upon their arrival and that still envelop their children in contemporary Israel (although these silences are in the process of being gradually broken, thanks, in no small measure, to my narrators' works).

What I did not know before beginning the research process, which entailed extensive personal narrative interviews with nine such daughters, was how deeply implicated I was in all of this. When the narrators spoke of coming from 'silent families' where one 'knew and did not know' about the Shoah (Pines, 1993), I hadn't realised how much my own family was such a 'silent family'. Mother's insistence, until a very short time ago, that she never needed to speak of her past life in Bukovina, Northern Romania, a life she abandoned at the age of 19 to go to Palestine in 1941, was beginning to ring hollow. As I began transcribing the narratives, I realised, on the one hand, how much she *did* tell us about her Romanian childhood – when I visited Bukovina in 1984, her home town looked as I had imagined it, coming to life through her stories about 'there'. On the other hand, and somewhat contradictorily, I realised just how silent my own parents had been about the Shoah. This, despite having lost several members of their families, while other family members were exiled to the forgotten ghettos and camps of Transnistria[3] from which they arrived in Israel, broken people, in the 1950s. Because Mother and her family managed to escape on time, they never saw themselves as survivors – the mantle 'Shoah survivors' was not lightly assumed. Yet, according to a broader definition of survivorhood, we *were* a family of survivors, and I was a daughter of such a silent family.

As I was researching, the signs of that silence became more and more apparent. The whispered stories of Mother's relatives who congregated in grandmother's sitting room, whispers hushed when we, the Israeli-born children, were about. The compulsive attitude

---

[3] Transnistria, a series of ghettos and camps in southern Ukraine, where the Jews of northern Romania were expelled during the Second World War, and where some 700,000 Jews perished at the hands of the Romanians and the Nazis, has been the 'forgotten Shoah' until the late 1980s, when a number of books and films (Shachan, 1988) began to tell its story.

to food, feeding us too much, worrying when we did not eat enough. My parents' refusal to talk to us in German, their mother tongue, in which they talked to each other. The need to make constant contact, the fear of separation. As well as grandmother's grunting and weeping in her sleep, she had never quite forgiven herself for leaving her own mother behind when she journeyed to Palestine. The endless family trees I was obsessively drawing with grandfather when I was a young child. And the refusal to admit to my two Jewish-Yiddish middle names, given in memory of relatives from 'there', names shameful to a daughter of the 'new Hebrew', diaspora-negating first Israeli generation.

Auto/biography as a performative act

The realisation that I had always been engaged in 'researching' my split subjectivity – in my fiction writing (Lentin, 1989; 1996), but also in my obsessive interest in all Shoah accounts from a very young age – meant that in the course of conducting my research, the study became auto/biographical, in the sense of constructing my self and my life in narrative, through my identification with my narrators' narratives of their lived experiences.

But there was more. From the very early stages of research, I felt compelled to turn inwards. Like Ruth Linden, upon her return from the American Gathering of Holocaust Survivors, where she collected 200 life histories of survivors, I too kept feeling I was still 'in the field' long after I returned from field trips to Israel. I had never left the field, because I *was* the field. This was 'a liminal time when my social boundaries – the membranes between me and the rest of the world – were fragile and fluid' (Linden, 1993: 4-5).

During the research process, recalling my youthful contempt towards the survivors from 'there', I became conscious of another 'split'. I had a stake in a sense of belonging to a survivor family on the one hand, and in a profound Israeli guilt towards the survivors on the other. This duality is linked to what psychoanalyst Dinora Pines (1993) quotes Freud as describing as 'disavowal', or the 'blindness of the seeing eye in which one knows and does not know a thing at the same time' (Freud, 1925: 235). Writing about women survivors whom she saw in analysis, Pines confesses to her own 'survivor guilt':

I have engaged not only in the rediscovery of my patients' Holocaust history and its impact on their lives, but also … in the rediscovery of my own. Thus I too am deeply affected by the guilt of the survivor. The sense of psychic continuity that is important to us all was brutally broken in my patients' lives, but also to some degree in my own (Pines, 1993: 223).

Auto/biographical narratives as a research method

The study of narrative must struggle with the question of how much one needs to know about others to feel that one can understand something about them. Since 'life history subjects are … actively inscribed by means of narrative strategies' (Linden, 1993: 136), no matter how meaningful, researchers can never arrive at a 'complete' picture. Narrators are amply competent in organising and creating plots from disordered experiences and informants' stories do not mirror a world 'out there', but are constructed, creatively authored, rhetorical and interpretative.

Auto/biography is a social construct comprising both social reality and the subjects' experiential world, which is why they raise the question as to how to proceed from auto/biographical text to life itself (Rosenthal, 1993: 60). One answer to this dilemma is to consider life and story as part of the same fabric, in that life informs and is formed by stories. The meaning of life cannot be determined outside of the stories told about it; nor can the meaning of a story be determined without reference to human life as it is lived (Widdershoven, 1993: 2-20).

But traumatic events are often dealt with by banishing them from consciousness: survivors of trauma, political or personal, often silence themselves and are silenced by society. This is typical of Shoah survivors, many of whom remained silent for several decades. According to Funkenstein (1993: 22), the memory of Shoah survivors is fragmented. Although many camp survivors wanted to remember, they had been robbed of their identity by the Nazis. Israeli writer Aharon Apelfeld, who survived as a lone child in the ghetto and in the forests, writes this about the delicate balance between language and silence:

Speaking is hard for me, not surprisingly: during the war people did not speak. Every disaster states again: what is there to say?

> There is nothing to say. Anyone who was in the ghetto, in the
> camps and in the forests is familiar with silence, bodily. ...Only
> after the war did the words return ... (But) words cannot deal with
> catastrophes; they are poor, wretched vehicles, which soon become
> false ... (Apelfeld, 1999: 95-6).

Liz Stanley (1992; 1993) provides another clue to the relation
between the self (auto), life (bio) and text (graphy). Accounts of
the past which constitute the major part of our lives are structured
by means of referential assumptions, but they do so because people
are well aware that these are historiographical accounts, not history
itself. The process of 'accounting' that auto/biographies constitute
is an important means of making real and present what we all
know is actually memory and past. Stanley stresses that 'all writing
derives from, is the product of, helps to construct lives'. Experiential
claims are no less, but certainly no more, problematic than other
kinds of knowledge-claims, and both narrative and 'experience'
are suitable grounds for analytic investigation (Stanley, 1993: 206).
'Ultimately', she writes, 'whatever rhetorical means, the experiential
basis of knowledge is denied or silenced, nonetheless all knowledge
of the world is rooted in the knowledge-production processes,
engaged in by inquiring and experiencing therefore knowing
subjects' (Stanley, 1993: 214).

Women's lives have been outside the 'apparatus of ruling' of
which the academy has traditionally been part. Therefore women's
auto/biographical personal narratives are especially suitable
documents to illuminate the process of constructing the self and
exploring gendered self-identity (Personal Narratives Group, 1989:
5-6). Feminist research, theory and practice should start from
women's lived experience, but this does not suppose a common
viewpoint among women, since women's standpoint is grounded
in specific, multiple and often contradictory experiences (Harding,
1991: 285).

One way of illuminating women's multiple realities is to elicit
the narrative realities behind societal patterns. The personal
narratives of Israeli daughters of Shoah survivors are one way of
re-interpreting the dichotomy between 'masculine' Israel and the
'feminised' Shoah, and of breaking the silence about the
stigmatisation of the survivors in Israeli society.

Starting from a feminist perspective of a woman (who is a

daughter of a family of survivors, but also a sociologist and a fiction writer) researching other women (who are daughters of survivors, but also fiction writers or film makers) with whom she has much in common, my interview strategy was dialogic. Quite apart from reassuring narrators they were free to choose what to tell and what to omit, my strategy did not exclude self-disclosure. Interviews were more like conversations rather than conventional social science interviews where the researcher is limited to asking the questions and the researched to answering them (deemed a 'masculine paradigm' by Oakley, 1981). The resulting narratives are therefore the product of the interaction between the narrators and me, gendered situated subjects within the Israeli 'second generation' ontology.

Auto/biographical narratives as a writing strategy

When it comes to presenting auto/biographical narratives in our research texts we must consider three caveats. Firstly, the researcher's presentation of women's lives may not be recognised or agreed by the narrators and a balance between their visions and my understanding must be struck. Secondly, the narratives must be understood as products and reflections of the negotiation between narrators and researchers. Thirdly, contrary to the tendency to resolve, rather than contain ambiguities that arise in narratives, I agree with Luttrell (1994: 19) that 'studies are most successful when they preserve and highlight the multiplicity of views and voices that constitute the "circuits" of cultural production.'

Issues of consent, collaboration, voice, authority and authorship are never easily resolved, despite all the care we may take during the data collection stage, as argued in the introduction to this volume (see Stanley, 1985). Another issue is the difference between written and oral accounts, which, presenting dynamic narrator-researcher interactions as 'frozen texts' (Sparkes, 1994: 173), raise representational issues. Langer, who explored the unique way in which oral testimonies contribute to our understanding of the Shoah, argues that written and oral Shoah testimonies are completely different. Writing invites reflection, commentary, interpretation by the author as well as the reader, while oral testimony is distinguished by the lack of literary meditation. Oral testimony unfolds before our very eyes and ears: we are present at the invention of what, when we speak of written texts, we call 'style' (Langer, 1991: 57-8). This dichotomy between written and oral testimonies parallels the dichotomy between the dynamic interaction between narrator and researcher and the resulting 'frozen' text and will be recognised by most feminist researchers struggling to transform their narrators' words into texts. But there is another consideration. Research done from the narrator's point of view is an oxymoron, since the reflexive nature of fieldwork requires at least two situated, experiencing subjects. And this brings me to wonder whether, ultimately, all ethnographic writing is auto/biographical.

Because auto/biographical narratives, both ours and our narrators', are meaning-making structures, they must be preserved, rather than fractured, by researchers, who 'must respect respondents' ways of constructing meanings and analyse how it is accomplished' (Riessman, 1993: 4-5). But this is not as simple as it sounds and researchers are often tempted to conflate narrators' words with their own interpretations, by concealing the process of text production under a 'scientific' mantle.

Employing a dialogic approach as a text presentation strategy, I have opted to include verbatim quotations in order to allow readers some participation, though it was I, the researcher, who edited and selected these verbatim quotations. As a social scientist I have assumed a certain stance of authority, but there is also a degree of dialogue at work, since the full distinctiveness of narrators' voices can only emerge through their own words. Only through this dialogic strategy can all partners involved – writer, reader and informant – participate in the text. Ethnography is a text, but it is also a fiction, or as Liz Stanley (1992) would say, 'a fabrication', to the extent that it is produced by a social scientist who, in this instance, is also a fiction writer.

In order to do justice to the narrators' words, I have chosen three text presentation strategies. I present one narrative – writer Nava Semel's story – in its entirety as a separate chapter. Nava has seen the text and has commented on it, and her comments have been incorporated into the final text I used. Her story was a 'key story' to the interpretation of the other stories as it contained all the elements present in the nine narratives: silence, stigma, and breaking the conspiracy of silence by writing. In addition, her narrative presented a trajectory – from being a silenced child of Shoah survivors, stigmatised in the new state of Israel to being a woman, who, in her writing, is re-interpreting the puzzle of Shoah daughterhood – which resonated most with my own trajectory.

The second textual presentation strategy takes all nine narratives as a combined text, analyses them thematically, using lengthy excerpts from the narratives. The narratives are presented thematically, not sequentially, and support, albeit in a complex and multifaceted way, my evolving theories.

The third element of textual presentation is my own story, which threads through the whole text. My life story, my theoretical assumptions, my socio-historical situation as 'split' between being a daughter of a family of survivors and Israeli-born, voluntarily exiled from my homeland into the Europe of my parents' birth, as well as my gender, have all been factors in organising the narratives.

Conclusion: 'as true as our lives'

When speaking about their lives, people lie sometimes, forget a lot, exaggerate, become confused and get things wrong. Although they are revealing truths, these truths never reveal 'the past as it actually was'. They are not empirical findings in the positivist sense, nor are they open to corroboration or 'proof'. Yet personal narratives, if we allow ourselves 'to believe what we are told' (Schwartz and Jacob, 1979), are open to interpretation and, if we pay close attention to the context, may make us aware of our own place in the world.

Women's auto/biographical personal narratives are essential as primary documents for feminist research, yet the academy has often discouraged us from taking people's life stories seriously, demanding generalisations and elevation. But elevations and generalisations serve to control: control data, control irregularities of human experiences, and, ultimately, control what constitutes knowledge. Feminist theory seeks to disrupt the basic, safest ideas about truth, and asserts that 'if truth rests on generalisation, it must also take into account experience that has previously been ignored, forgotten, ridiculed and devalued' (Personal Narratives Group, 1989: 262-3).

The historical truth of an individual's account is not the primary issue, since 'facts' are products of an interactive and interpretative process and since it is always possible to narrate the same events in different ways. When we are dealing, as I am, with emotionally-laden topics, we can do worse than allow ourselves to be swept into the account and speak 'in our own voices' about research, which is 'necessary' because it is ultimately concerned with our own lives (Stanley, 1996: 48).

Narratives are laced with power relations, which are not constant over time. There is no reason why an individual's account should be consistent from one setting to another. In the case of severe trauma, survivors experience gaps in memory, and stories often change. Oral Shoah testimonies, for instance, are doomed to remain 'disrupted narratives', since they raise 'few expectations of renewal or hope for reconciliation' (Langer, 1991: xi). They do offer, however, an opportunity to make a 'reckoning' and, by telling and retelling, to begin to mourn the enormous loss that was the Shoah, providing, that is, that someone is listening.

But what about 'objectivity'? How can we justify the use of auto/biographical research methods in an increasingly positivist academy? Many feminist scholars shrug off the requirement to 'be objective' as impossible. Indeed, Stanley has argued that 'objectivity' and 'subjectivity' are false dichotomies, 'artefacts within the sexual political system' which need deconstructing by 'looking closely and analytically at the ... processes by which th(ey) are generated' (Stanley, 1990: 120). Through my split subjectivity, I have a high degree of identification with my narrators. This makes me part of what I am researching, but, having lived in Ireland since 1969, also distanced. As knower and known at once, I aimed to incorporate my reflexive observation of the written account at all stages of data collection and production. Whereas feminist researchers frequently present their research in their own voice, mainstream social sciences typically shun the first person singular. My use of the 'auto/biographical I' (Stanley, 1992) demonstrates how this project has become part of my life. Rather than being 'merely confessional', an accusation often levelled against auto/biographical sociological writing, the 'I' is one possible way of conducting research using my own intellectual and emotional auto/biography as an analytic framework and thus challenging scientism and positivism.

And what about validation, the process through which we claim the trustworthiness of our interpretation (not of the narratives)? Validation is, of course, crucial. But it is 'trustworthiness' rather than 'truth' we are after. Riessman (1993) offers several ways of approaching validation in narrative work. Firstly, she argues, you need to support theoretical claims by evidence from the narratives. Secondly, those who have been studied should recognise our interpretations as adequate, although the interpretation of researchers is rarely totally affirmed by the narrators. Thirdly, our research should become a basis for other people's work; this we can achieve by storing our transcripts and by publishing and engaging in debate.

Auto/biographical feminist research often initiates change, for the narrators and for the researcher-author. For my narrators, discovering their gendered 'collective story' may perhaps assist them in making a reckoning of their lives in new ways. However, I want to stress here the transformatory possibilities of auto/biographical feminist research for the researcher herself.

For me, as author, constructing and presenting the narrators' 'stories-within-stories' unsettled me. At the same time the research process enabled me to construct my own story and re-claim, for the first time, my membership in a survivor family. It also forced me to confront my 'survivor guilt' and begin mourning my personal losses by connecting to family members who had died in Transnistria during the Shoah, about whose lives I had written the novel *Night Train to Mother* (Lentin, 1989), from which I quoted at the beginning of this chapter.

Side by side with working on chapter drafts for my doctoral dissertation, I was editing another novel, *Songs on the Death of Children* (Lentin, 1996). The novel began life as something else but turned, during the early stages of research, into a book about an Irish-born Jewish journalist who, during a stay in Israel, comes face to face with being a daughter of (silent) Shoah survivors. Although not auto/biographical in the conventional sense – this is not 'my own story' and, in fact, the dissertation was far more 'auto/biographical' than the novel – it draws upon my re-claimed membership in a survivor family. There were days, when, working on one or the other, I spent hours weeping – for lost family members? For Jewish Shoah victims? For me?

During the research process I assumed the courage to be 'named' and as the narrators' stories became my own, I could hear myself, my mother, my grandmother, always measuring the ever-shifting distances between the narrators' narratives, their 'stories-about-stories' and my stories about their stories and about my own story. The research process transported me – in the sense of 'carried' but also in the sense of 'changed' – from the question 'where did the journey begin?' to the realisation that 'I had always carried the weight ... the pain around my neck' quoted at the start of the chapter.

Interpretative work has no canon, no recipes, no formulae, and different validation processes may be suited to different research problems. Auto/biographies cannot stand limited definitions of 'truth' that admit only one standard at a time for the perception and interpretation of a small segment of a complex reality. Instead, women's auto/biographies offer the plural truths of experience, history and perceptions, amongst other things, of the construction of a gendered self-identity. But women's auto/biographies are also a feminist political research instrument. In their fragmentation and refusal to fall within the clear-cut categorisations demanded by positivist social science, they can be a resistance strategy that subverts conventional social science research methodologies. Ultimately, women's auto/biographies and the knowledge they impart are 'as true as our lives' (Personal Narratives Group, 1989: 262-3): messy, complex, and often quite incredible.

References

Appelfeld, Aharon (1999), *The Story of a Life,* Jerusalem: Keter (Hebrew).

Boyarin, Daniel (1997), *Unheroic Conduct: The Rise of Heterosexuality and the Invention of the Jewish Man,* Berkeley: University of California Press.

Dror, Zvi (1992), *They Were There: With the Remnant of the Deliverance,* Tel Aviv: Hakibbutz Hameuchad (Hebrew).

Dror, Zvi (ed.) (1984), *Testimonies of Survival: 96 Personal Interviews from Members of Kibbutz Lochamei Hagetaot,* Kibbutz Lochamei Hagetaot: Bei Lochamei Hagetaot, Hakibbuts Hameuchad (Hebrew).

Freud, Sigmund (1925), 'Narration', in James Strachey (ed.), *The Standard Edition of the Complete Psychological Works of Sigmund Freud, Vol. 19.* London: Hogarth, 1953-1973.

Funkenstein, Amos (1993), 'The incomprehensible catastrophe: memory and narrative', in Ruth Josselsohn and Amia Lieblich (eds), *The Narrative Study of Lives, Vol. 1,* Newbury Park: Sage.

Grunfeld, Uriel (1995), 'Holocaust, movies and remembrance: the pedagogical challenge', Unpublished paper, Pennsylvannia State University.

Harding, Sandra (1991), 'Who knows? Identities and feminist epistemology', in Joan A. Hartman and Ellen Masser-Davidow (eds), *(En)gendering Knowledge: Feminists in Academe,* Knoxville: University of Tennessee Press.

Hazelton, Lesley (1978), *Israeli Women: The Reality Behind the Myths,* Jerusalem: Idanim (Hebrew).

Langer, Lawrence (1991), *Holocaust Testimonies: The Ruins of Memory,* New Haven: Yale University Press.

Lentin, Ronit (1989), *Night Train to Mother,* Dublin: Attic Press.

Lentin, Ronit (1996), *Songs on the Death of Children,* Dublin: Poolbeg Press.

Lentin, Ronit (2000), *Israel and the Daughters of the Shoah: Re-occupying the Territories of Silence,* Oxford and New York: Berghahn Books.

Linden, Ruth (1993), *Making Stories, Making Selves: Feminist Reflections on the Holocaust,* Columbus: Ohio State University Press.

Luttrell, Wendy (1994), '"Becoming somebody": aspirations, opportunities and womanhood', in Gay Young and Bette J. Dickerson (eds), *Color, Class and Country: Experiences of Gender,* London: Zed Books.

Oakley, Anne (1981), 'Interviewing women: a contradiction in terms', in Helen Roberts (ed.), *Doing Feminist Research,* London: Routledge.

Personal Narratives Group (1989), *Interpreting Women's Lives: Feminist Theory and Personal Narratives,* Bloomington, Indiana: Indiana University Press.

Pines, Dinora (1993), *A Woman's Unconscious Use of Her Body,* London: Virago.

Rappaport, Tamar and Tamar El-Or (1997), 'Cultures of womanhood in Israel: social agencies and gender production,' *Women's Studies International Forum,* vol. 20, no. 5-6: 573-580.

Reibenbach, Tsipi (1993), *Choice and Destiny,* Documentary film.

Reibenbach, Tsipi (1998a), *Three Sisters,* Documentary film.

Reibenbach, Tsipi (1998b), *Three Sisters,* Film notes.

Riessman, Catherine (1993), *Narrative Analysis,* Newbury Park: Sage.

Ringelheim, Joan M. (1997), 'Gender and genocide: a split memory', in Ronit Lentin (ed.), *Gender and Catastrophe,* London: Zed Books.

Rosenthal, Gabrielle (1993), 'Reconstruction of life stories: principles of selection in generating stories for narrative biographical interviews', in Ruth Josselsohn and Amia Lieblich (eds), *The Narrative Study of Lives, Vol. 1,* Newbury Park: Sage.

Schwartz, Harry and Jacobs, Gerry (1979), *Qualitative Sociology: A Method to the Madness,* New York: Free Press.

Segev, Tom (1991), *The Seventh Million: The Israelis and the Holocaust,* Jerusalem: Keter (Hebrew).

Shadmi, Erella (1992), 'Women, Palestinians, Zionism: a personal view', *News from Within,* vol 8, no. 10-11: 13-16.

Sparkes, Andrew (1994), 'Life histories and the issue of voice: reflections on an emerging relationship', *Qualitative Studies in Education,* vol. 7, no. 2: 165-183.

Stanley, Liz (1985), 'Our mothers' voices', Paper presented at the Third International Interdisciplinary Congress on Women, Dublin.

Stanley, Liz (1990), '"A referral was made": behind the scenes during the creation of a Social Services Department "elderly" statistic', in Liz Stanley (ed.), *Feminist Praxis: Research, Theory and Epistemology in Feminist Research,* London: Routledge.

Stanley, Liz (1992) *The Auto/biographical I: Theory and Practice in Feminist Auto/biography,* Manchester: Manchester University Press.

Stanley, Liz (1993) 'The knowing, because experiencing subject: narratives, lives and autobiography', *Women's Studies International Forum,* vol. 16, no. 3: 205-215.

Stanley, Liz (1996), 'The mother of invention: necessity, writing and representation,' *Feminism and Psychology,* vol. 6, no. 1: 45-51.

Stanley, Liz and Wise, Sue (1993), *Breaking Out Again: Feminist Ontology and Epistemology,* London: Routledge.

Widdershoven, Guy (1993), 'The story of life: hermeneutic perspectives on the relationship between narrative and life history', in Ruth Josselsohn and Amia Lieblich (eds), *The Narrative Study of Lives,* Newbury Park: Sage.

Yablonka, Hanna (1994), *Foreign Brethren: Holocaust Survivors in the State of Israel 1945-1952,* Jerusalem: Yad Yitzhak Ben Zvi Press and Ben Gurion University Press (Hebrew).